Y0-AQM-881

DISTINGUISHED MEN AND WOMEN OF SCIENCE, MEDICINE AND THE ARTS

AN OVERVIEW OF BIOMEDICAL SCIENTISTS AND THEIR DISCOVERIES

DISTINGUISHED MEN AND WOMEN OF SCIENCE, MEDICINE AND THE ARTS

Additional books and e-books in this series can be found on Nova's website under the Series tab.

DISTINGUISHED MEN AND WOMEN OF SCIENCE, MEDICINE AND THE ARTS

AN OVERVIEW OF BIOMEDICAL SCIENTISTS AND THEIR DISCOVERIES

MANUEL F. VARELA
AND
MICHAEL F. SHAUGHNESSY

Copyright © 2020 by Nova Science Publishers, Inc.

All rights reserved. No part of this book may be reproduced, stored in a retrieval system or transmitted in any form or by any means: electronic, electrostatic, magnetic, tape, mechanical photocopying, recording or otherwise without the written permission of the Publisher.

We have partnered with Copyright Clearance Center to make it easy for you to obtain permissions to reuse content from this publication. Simply navigate to this publication's page on Nova's website and locate the "Get Permission" button below the title description. This button is linked directly to the title's permission page on copyright.com. Alternatively, you can visit copyright.com and search by title, ISBN, or ISSN.

For further questions about using the service on copyright.com, please contact:
Copyright Clearance Center
Phone: +1-(978) 750-8400 Fax: +1-(978) 750-4470 E-mail: info@copyright.com.

NOTICE TO THE READER

The Publisher has taken reasonable care in the preparation of this book, but makes no expressed or implied warranty of any kind and assumes no responsibility for any errors or omissions. No liability is assumed for incidental or consequential damages in connection with or arising out of information contained in this book. The Publisher shall not be liable for any special, consequential, or exemplary damages resulting, in whole or in part, from the readers' use of, or reliance upon, this material. Any parts of this book based on government reports are so indicated and copyright is claimed for those parts to the extent applicable to compilations of such works.

Independent verification should be sought for any data, advice or recommendations contained in this book. In addition, no responsibility is assumed by the publisher for any injury and/or damage to persons or property arising from any methods, products, instructions, ideas or otherwise contained in this publication.

This publication is designed to provide accurate and authoritative information with regard to the subject matter covered herein. It is sold with the clear understanding that the Publisher is not engaged in rendering legal or any other professional services. If legal or any other expert assistance is required, the services of a competent person should be sought. FROM A DECLARATION OF PARTICIPANTS JOINTLY ADOPTED BY A COMMITTEE OF THE AMERICAN BAR ASSOCIATION AND A COMMITTEE OF PUBLISHERS.

Additional color graphics may be available in the e-book version of this book.

Library of Congress Cataloging-in-Publication Data

ISBN: 978-1-53617-420-5
Library of Congress Control Number: 2020931182

Published by Nova Science Publishers, Inc. † New York

This book is dedicated to my loving wife, Ann Varela, who tirelessly helped me with all aspects of the writing and to my two children Timothy and Edward, both of whom affectionately put up with their father.

—Manuel F. Varela

I join in dedicating this text to my darling wife who has the patience of a saint to allow me to continue teaching and writing and responding to e-mails while at the same time taking care of our two dogs.

—Michael F. Shaughnessy

CONTENTS

INTRODUCTION

The intersection of biology and medicine- is one that has challenged, perplexed, exasperated, and excited scientists, and physicians for many centuries. The physical and the medical interact in ways in which we often do not understand comprehend or grasp. This book attempts to shine light on the parts of the human body that are relevant, salient and germane to the healing process and the causal factors in terms of disease.

Cancer—a word that strikes fear into people, physicians, and related personnel alike. It is a complicated, confusing, combination of perhaps environment, perhaps genetics, perhaps food, perhaps carcinogenic elements, perhaps an infection and perhaps a virus. This book will feature chapters relevant to cancer and causality. There are certain scientists that bear particular mention in this realm. The work of Francis Rous, David Baltimore, and Renato Dulbecco deserve extraordinary mention. All of the scientists in this book, in a sense, deserve not just recognition- and while many may have won the Nobel Prize others have been nominated, and some are even currently being considered.

Cholesterol—another word that seems to permeate our consciousness today. We hear about LDL, HDL, and the impact on the human body. Yet how did we begin to even understand its beginnings and importance? Alfred Alberts, Konrad Bloch, and Joseph Goldstein all deserve recognition for their work on cholesterol, the precursor, and contributing factors to heart disease. It is not known how many lives were saved of prolonged by the work of these individuals.

Nerves—The human body is permeated by nerves, and their importance is pervasive- Nerve impulses and the growth of nerves and the connections between nerves-all of these things have challenged scientists and empiricists and investigators for years. Some of the individuals that bear mention not only contributed to this realm- but multiple domains. Their lives and work transcend recognition beyond the "nerve." Julius Axelrod, Andrew Huxley (of the famous Huxley family), and Santiago Ramon y Cajal (a name probably introduced in almost every high school in America) and of course, Rita Levi-Montalcini. Obviously, we have tried to recognize all scientists from all parts of the world and acknowledge their endeavors.

Blood—Perhaps the single most crucial element in the human body as it transports oxygen to all parts of the body and brain, yet it was only recently that Karl Landsteiner was able to "type" blood into various "types"- (A, B, AB and O) and specify Rh Factors that are relevant to survival. Blood typing is almost routine nowadays, and blood transfusions are prevalent and life-saving. Yet how much does the general practitioner or nurse know about blood and how it was investigated and typed. Gerald Edelman also deserves much recognition for his investigations and explorations into the fascinating world of antibodies in the blood.

Cells—The cell, often thought of as the basic building block of growth and the cell cycle (Tim Hunt) are available to us now to examine, explain and understand due to the work of many different scientists and their discoveries.

Genes—All too often, we find that there is some type of gene malfunction or distortion or a specific gene that is specifically relevant to a particular disease, for example, Huntington Disease. Leroy Hood and Michael Smith are the shoulders that many scientists stand on in terms of investigating genes and their role in disease and related realms.

All in all, this book is intended to support all those who attempt to a) understand diseases, and the disease process (both at the molecular and cellular level), to prevent disease and cancer and delay death, and lastly to treat and help in the recovery process via a comprehensive understanding of the mechanisms of disease and the disease process.

Viruses—Those pesky viruses that cause so much damage and chaos to the human body are explored and examined here. The realm of human virology owes much to the leaders in this field covered in this book.

The Immune System—Only recently have scientists delved into the system of the human body, if you will, that of the immune system. As we all know, there are many "systems" to the human body, and hopefully, they all work in unison to protect the human body from germs, disease, bacteria, viruses, etc.

This book not only delves into these domains but also allows us to reflect on the trials and tribulations that many of these scientists had to endure. As one peruses these pages, they will reflect on anti-Semitism that occurred in the past. They will learn about discrimination against people of color, outright racism, and how many women went on to achieve in spite of their sex and their backgrounds. Some of the scientists in this book have achieved and gone on to win the Nobel Prize in spite of not having a medical degree.

Thanks must be given to Ann Varela for her extensive assistance with some of the illustrations and pictures and to Dr. Matthew Barlow for his clarifications and validations along the progress of the book.

Further, we acknowledge Jimmy Kilpatrick as many of these interviews were first posted online at www.educationViews.org, a website that also acknowledges Martin Haberman (now deceased). We are indebted to both of these individuals.

Manuel F. Varela
Michael F. Shaughnessy
Eastern New Mexico University
Portales, New Mexico, US

Chapter 1

ALFRED ALBERTS – CHOLESTEROL DRUG LOVASTATIN

1. *Alfred Alberts is most known for his discovery of a cholesterol-lowering drug called lovastatin. Where was this "unsung hero" educated, and where did he initially work?*

Professor Shaughnessy, the "unsung hero" whom you speak of, Alfred William Alberts, noted for having discovered the famous cholesterol-reducing drug called lovastatin, was an American scientist born in Manhattan, New York, on the 16th day of the month of May, in the year

1931. During Alfred's childhood years, the Alberts family moved to Brooklyn, where Alberts later attended a high school called Erasmus Hall. Alberts then enrolled in Brooklyn College, taking his degree in the field of zoology.

A short while later, in 1953, Alberts married Helene Cuba, nicknamed Sandy, his high school sweetheart, whom Alfred had met a few years earlier on a blind date. Shortly after this, Alberts signed up for the Army, working 2 years in a military laboratory while serving duty. After an honorable military discharge and using the GI bill as a source of funding for his education, Alberts entered graduate school, joining the Ph.D. program at the University of Kansas, in Lawrence, Kansas, focusing his interests in the field of cell biology, a fledging area of the biomedical sciences.

Before finishing his graduate degree, however, young Mrs. Alberts apparently had a strong dislike of living in isolation at Lawerence as a "laboratory widow," a seemingly common occurrence amongst spouses of scientific investigators. The young married couple consequently moved to the less isolated University of Maryland at College Park, MD, where Alberts continued his graduate studies.

While enrolled in the Ph.D. program at Maryland, Alberts had progressed as far as completing his graduate courses and, importantly, completing his experiments for the dissertation project, which was also a requirement for the doctorate degree. Unfortunately, however, the GI bill funding for graduate school was slated to terminate, and Alberts had yet to write up his dissertation even though his experimental work for the doctorate had been primarily finished. His status, frequently a common one encountered by students in graduate school, was considered ABD, that is, "all but the dissertation," a situation characterized by having essentially all necessary data collected but the final write-up coalesced into a dissertation or a thesis not yet completed and approved by a graduate committee. Alberts had yet to finish writing the dissertation. Thus, the doctorate remained elusive.

At about this time, in 1959, with funding a critical issue for Alberts, a biochemistry professor by the name of Dr. Earl Stadtman, had casually announced one day in lecture about a job opening at the National Institutes of Health (NIH), a nearby research-intensive institution, in Bethesda, MA, where Dr. Stadtman had been working as a research scientist. Alberts realized this was an excellent opportunity to acquire funding in order to support his growing family. He consequently quit the doctoral program, abandoning his dissertation project without finishing his graduate degree at the University of Maryland in order to work as a laboratory technician at the prestigious NIH. For Alberts, it was a fateful move that would change his life forever. The end result was that he never again would have the chance to earn the coveted doctorate.

At the NIH, Alberts met and eventually began working under the direction of Dr. Pindaros Roy Vagelos, also known as P. Roy Vagelos or simply Roy Vagelos, a physician-scientist working initially as a postdoctoral fellow in the NIH laboratory of Dr. Stadtman and later as an independent investigator, still at NIH. Dr. Vagelos taught biochemistry to Alberts, who partook in studies pertaining to the discovery of an acyl-carrier protein, known merely as ACP. It is at this point in the career of Alberts in which he made another fateful decision.

In 1966, Alberts chose to accompany Dr. Vagelos to the Washington University, where they had a School of Medicine in St. Louis, Missouri. Dr. Vagelos was appointed chair of their biochemistry department, and Alberts was appointed an instructor of biochemistry. While at Washington University, Alberts had been promoted to an assistant professor of biochemistry and later to associate professor with tenure.

In 1975, Alberts made another fateful decision. Leaving a tenured position as an academic faculty at a prestigious research institution, Alberts followed Dr. Vagelos to Merck Research Laboratories in Rahway, New Jersey, where Dr. Vagelos later became their CEO, and Alberts later became director of Merck's department of biochemical regulation.

The move to Merck by Alberts had been undertaken despite the advice not to do so by Dr. Vagelos, who had encouraged Alberts to stay on at Washington University, where he had an established research program. It is, however, at Merck, later in 1979, where Alberts would make his world-changing discovery, namely, that of mevinolin, a fungal metabolite that later became known as lovastatin. This discovery by Alberts not only changed the course of history for countless millions of patients suffering from coronary artery disease, but it was also a discovery that Dr. Vagelos attributes solely to Alfred Alberts, who never got a doctorate.

2. *It seems that like many others– collaboration was a significant part of his work. Who did he work with, and where, and what were some of their discoveries?*

Indeed, one of the first vital papers to be published regarding the lovastatin discovery had 20 authors. Alfred Alberts collaborated with several key individuals, all devoted to the same task, testing the hypothesis that cholesterol had a role in conferring cardiovascular disease. Working towards testing this idea with Alberts was Julie S. Chen. Alberts and Chen set out to find inhibitors of the critical enzyme that was committed to the biosynthesis of cholesterol.

The critical enzyme of interest was called HMG-CoA reductase. The acronym HMG-CoA stands for 3-hydroxy-3-methylglutaryl coenzyme A, an essential substrate for the metabolic enzyme. The letter A of coenzyme A (CoA) stands for "activation of acetate," a biochemical phenomenon discovered (and name coined by) the great Dr. Fritz Lipmann, in 1946. In any case, the idea considered by Alberts and colleagues was that if indeed cholesterol build-up was associated with (or, indeed, a cause of) cardiovascular disease, then inhibition of cholesterol biosynthesis would then alleviate the detrimental effects of the disease.

An important task to perform was the screening of microbes, such as, in this case, the fungus called *Aspergillus terreus*, as sources for potential inhibitors of the HMG-CoA reductase. The microbial screening process was developed for Chen and Alberts by another Merck colleague, Dr. Art Patchett, who had taken his Ph.D. from Harvard and had just completed a postdoctoral fellowship at NIH before moving to Merck. This fungal screening technique permitted Alberts and Chen to conduct a high throughput experimental method for testing large numbers of samples from the screened fungi for rapid measurement of enzyme inhibition.

Although the method was capable of analyzing thousands of potential enzyme inhibitors in a short amount of time, the team found a promising candidate after testing fungal compound number 18! The correct chemical name for this compound was 1,2,6,7,8,8a-hexahydro-β,δ-dihydroxy-2,6-dimethyl-8-(2-methyl-1-oxobutoxy)-1-naphthaleneheptanoic acid δ-lactone. The shortened named for this fungal-derived agent was mevinolin, and later the metabolite's name was changed to lovastatin.

Interestingly, the lovastatin breakthrough by Alberts and colleagues was not the first of the statins to be discovered. That credit goes to another biomedical investigator by the name of Dr. Akira Endo, who screened over 6,000 distinct fungal samples of *Penicillium citrinum* in the mid-1970s at Sankyo drug company, searching for the elusive HMG-CoA reductase inhibitor, a compound which he later called compactin, known in 1976 as ML-236B.

The compactin discovery almost destroyed the progress with lovastatin, not because compactin was first to be discovered, but rather because a rumor had emerged that the compactin caused cancer. It did cause lymphoma in experimental dogs, but only if given at 200 times the proper dosage. It did not cause cancer at regular doses, but the damage had been done—it killed all further progress for compactin development. Furthermore, the rumor almost threw a permanent wrench in the works for lovastatin, except that it was provided to patients only at healthy physiological and therapeutic doses, not in the excessive amounts like those given with the compactin fiasco.

3. *Why is the discovery of this "lovastatin" important?*

Lovastatin and other "statins" lower the production of cholesterol, which is widely believed to combine with the so-called fatty acid protein called low-density lipoprotein (LDL). The buildup of the LDL-cholesterol occurs in the form of plaques that materialize within the interiors of coronary arteries, which oxygenate the heart, resulting in the blockage of these arteries. This coronary artery blockage of the oxygen-containing blood supply to the heart is called atherosclerosis. This cholesterol-LDL complex, the so-called "bad cholesterol," is, thus, associated with the formation of atherosclerotic plaques.

These arterial plaques contain the LDL-cholesterol complexes plus cellular debris, fibrous-like proteins, and deposits of calcium. Together, these accumulated arterial fatty cholesterol deposits will narrow down the insides of the coronary arteries that provide oxygenated blood to the heart. The occluded coronary arteries are less able to supply the heart with its required oxygen, leading to cardiovascular disease. As with all or most living tissues in mammals, oxygen is necessary for the heart muscle to function correctly. Without oxygen, the cardiac muscle will be damaged and die in the process. The risk of stroke and heart attack is enhanced. In developed countries, coronary heart disease is the number one cause of human death.

The development of lovastatin was a significant discovery that, for the first time in history, permitted the lowering of blood cholesterol on a massive scale. It allowed clinicians to confront the detrimental effects of coronary artery disease directly. Lovastatin was shown in extensive clinical studies to lower the incidence numbers of strokes and heart attacks, both of which were hypothesized to be due to high blood levels of the bad cholesterol. Thus, lovastatin changed the course of medical history.

4. *As I understand it, today there are a number of "statin" drugs– that seem to all reduce cholesterol– but how do they really work? What exactly do they do?*

In short, the statins function to reduce blood cholesterol by directly binding to the HMG-CoA reductase enzyme, thereby preventing the enzyme from eventually making cholesterol. This enzyme usually works by converting the substrate called β-hydroxy-β-methylglutaryl coenzyme A (HMG-CoA) to the product called mevalonate. The molecular structures of the statin family display a close resemblance to the structure of the mevalonate. As a result, the statin binds to the HMG-CoA reductase enzyme in such a fashion that it (statin) competes with the HMG-CoA substrate and the mevalonate binding for the active site of the enzyme.

The active site of an enzyme is the location where the catalytic chemistry takes place, converting the substrate to the product in a biochemical reaction. Interference of an enzyme's active site by, in this case, competitive inhibition, prevents the enzymatic biochemical activity and thus prevents the catalytic formation of the product. This phenomenon is frequently referred to as competitive inhibition. In our case here, the complex between a given statin (competitive inhibitor) and the enzyme prevents the formation of the mevalonate. This then results in the lowering of the cholesterol levels later on down the biochemical biosynthetic pathway.

Typically, the biosynthesis of cholesterol starts with a critical metabolite called acetyl-CoA, which is then converted to HMG-CoA in multiple biochemical steps. From the mevalonate production, the biosynthesis pathway proceeds through another series of biochemical reactions making intermediate metabolites along the way and eventually producing the cholesterol at the end of the pathway. The statins serve to inhibit this cholesterol-making pathway by inhibiting the principal metabolic enzyme, the HMG-CoA reductase. The statin-mediated lowering in the cholesterol manufacture process thus lowers the atherosclerotic plaque production which in turn prevents coronary artery occlusion and, therefore, permits the heart to acquire its needed oxygen.

While lovastatin is a naturally produced compound, made from a fungus, other members of the statin family are made artificially, such as in the case with atorvastatin (commonly known as Lipitor) or with rosuvastatin (known as Crestor).

The statins play essential functions in improving the flow of blood through an individual's arteries. These statin molecules also help to stabilize the plaques that may already be in the patient's coronary arteries, preventing them from becoming larger or from breaking off into pieces, which might cause a stroke otherwise. Lastly, the statins are known to reduce vascular inflammation, another morbid process that can be associated with heart disease.

The statins, however, may not be perfect. In patients, the statins have been documented to cause a rather lengthy list of albeit rare but adverse side effects. Some of these otherwise rare side effects can be serious, such as in the case where patients may suffer from debilitating muscle weakness and pain, as a result of taking statins.

5. *Some individuals do not seem to respond to statin drugs (or maybe they are eating all the wrong stuff on the sly), but is there a genetic component to cholesterol? Are there some individuals who seem to be genetically predisposed to cholesterol– and in your mind– why is cholesterol essential? Other than it seems to block arteries, veins, capillaries, etc.*

While a diet that is low in saturated fats and cholesterol can undoubtedly play a prominent role in reducing blood levels of the so-called bad cholesterol, the LDL-cholesterol, there are specific individuals who are nonetheless genetically pre-disposed to very high cholesterol concentrations. In rare cases, dieting may not always help such patients. Such individuals may have, for instance, a genetic-based disease, such as the one called familial hypercholesterolemia. These individuals exhibit quite elevated levels of blood cholesterol. It is these very types of patients for which the statins play an essential role in alleviating such cholesterol levels in their blood sera. The statins have been shown in clinical studies to reduce blood serum levels in familial hypercholesterolemia patients significantly.

Regarding your question about the importance of cholesterol, it is perhaps not so well known that there are various advantageous aspects to this seemingly pathological molecule. For example, cholesterol is the starting point for the biosynthesis of steroid hormones, such as the glucocorticoid called cortisol, which functions in regulating metabolism and the immune response.

Cholesterol is also a metabolic starting point for the mineralocorticoid called corticosterone and aldosterone, which function in kidney absorption of critical electrolytes, like sodium, chloride, or bicarbonate. Cholesterol is also a precursor for the production of the sex hormones testosterone and estradiol.

Cholesterol resides in the membranes of our cells. In the plasma membrane, cholesterol controls the fluid nature of such membranes. In this sense, cholesterol is having a positive biological effect. Often dietary cholesterol will go the membranes of our cells, and when these cellular membranes become saturated from consuming an overabundance of fats and cholesterol, the cholesterol will be shunted to the LDL-cholesterol pathway and form the basis of the patient's atherosclerosis.

There is, for instance, the so-called "good cholesterol," which is in the form of a complex with high-density lipoprotein (HDL). The HDL-cholesterol is readily transported to the liver, where it is degraded into another form like bile salts, which are then stored in the gall bladder. Ultimately these bile salt end products are excreted into the gastrointestinal tract when an individual consumes a meal. The bile salts may be taken back to the liver and cycle back to the gall bladder.

Another positive aspect of cholesterol is that a variant of it can be converted to the necessary vitamin D with the help of sunlight. Suitable exposure of the skin to sunlight will facilitate the conversion. Vitamin D, in turn, then plays a role in regulating phosphorus and calcium metabolism.

6. I understand he recently died– did he ever receive the acknowledgment that he so truly deserves?

It is estimated that over a dozen Nobel prizes have been awarded for studies pertaining to cholesterol, a molecule that two of these Laureates, Joseph Goldstein and Michael Brown, have described as the "most celebrated molecule" ever. It seems rather odd, therefore, that the Nobel did not ever go to Alberts for his contribution to the statin discovery and the lowering of blood cholesterol for countless millions of suffering patients. As your chapter title aptly states, this may be a primary reason why Alberts was referred to as an "unsung hero" of cholesterol reduction efforts.

Despite the inability of Alberts to obtain his sought-after Ph.D., the University of Maryland nevertheless bestowed an honorary doctorate upon him in later years, in 1994. Back in 1959, however, Alberts had had to abandon his Ph.D. dissertation research at this same institution in order to acquire a paying position (at NIH) to support his family. He was never able to go back to his doctorate project to finish it.

Interestingly, the so-called Alfred Alberts Biochemistry award was established and given to outstanding biochemistry, biology, or chemistry students at the City University of New York (CUNY) in Brooklyn.

7. *What have I neglected to ask about Alfred Alberts?*

The statin story actually starts first with Dr. Nikolay Nikolaevich Anichkov, an experimental pathologist who was housed in St. Petersburg, Russia, in 1913. Dr. Anichkov treated laboratory animals, namely rabbits, with high dietary cholesterol and observed the atherosclerosis pathology in the experimental animals. The findings later became known as the lipid hypothesis, characterized as an association between blood serum levels of cholesterol and the production of the atherosclerotic plaques. While the work took a fair amount of time for widespread acceptance, verging on decades, Dr. Anichkov's work nonetheless turned out to be backed up by many reports of supporting experimental evidence.

For a number of decades, a controversy had been in the works with the cholesterol connection to cardiovascular disease. The main sticking point was the alleged neglect for other associated risk factors such as diet, smoking, exercise, genetics, etc. all factors of which are also known to be important in the development of cardiovascular disease.

Sadly, Alfred Alberts died of coronary artery disease. Though he had been living in New Jersey, he became ill while visiting his son Eli in Colorado. While still in CO, Alberts had suffered a heart attack, and he underwent an emergency coronary artery bypass surgery. Unfortunately, neither the surgical nor the statin treatments were to be useful for Alberts.

He passed away in Fort Collins, Colorado, at the age of 87 years on the 16th day of June, in the year 2018. Alberts left behind his adoring wife, Sandy, their three children, Heather, Mitchell, and Eli, plus two grandchildren, Jacob and Nellie.

For additional information about this scientist go to:
https://www.youtube.com/watch?v=QxJxZbT1mxA

Chapter 2

JULIUS AXELROD – NEUROTRANSMITTER CATECHOLAMINE

1. *Julius Axelrod– a pharmacologist, Nobel Prize winner, and investigator– has researched more chemicals than anyone I can personally think of. Where was he born, and where did he get his foundational education?*

Dr. Julius Axelrod, an American biomedical scientist, and Nobel Laureate was born on the 30th day of May in the year 1912 in New York

City, New York, in the U.S. His parents were Polish immigrants of Jewish origin who had met after each of their respective arrivals to the U.S. His father Isadore and mother Molly lived in tenement housing, on East Houston Street, in the lower East Side district of Manhattan. The Axelrod family lived in near poverty. Isadore Axelrod was a grocer and basket-maker who sold groceries from a horse-drawn wagon in the streets of Manhattan.

Young Julius ("Julie") attended a public elementary school called PS22 (public school number 22), in Manhattan. It was an old school that had been established prior to the onset of the Civil War and for which another student of prestige had been a pupil, namely, renowned physicist Dr. Isidor Isaac Rabi, a 1944 Nobel Laureate who helped build the first atomic bomb.

His high school, called Seward Park, located in New York City, had been his second choice because his family could not afford the more prestigious Stuyvesant high school. While Seward Park High was a less than desirable educational institution, it had certain other famous alumni, such as Tony Curtis, and Walter Matthau nonetheless. Dr. Axelrod was later to remark that his real education during his high school years was on account of having spent a great deal of time reading books voraciously on his own at the Hamilton Fish Park Library, which had been located nearby to his tenement home. He graduated from high school, in 1929, at the start of the Great Depression.

It had been during this time period that Axelrod had decided to become a physician.

Thus, after his high school graduation from Seward, Axelrod entered college at New York University in 1929, focusing his studies on pre-medicine courses. However, his funding for university had been depleted after only one year of course study. Consequently, in 1930, he moved to City College of New York, where there had been no charges incurred to students for their tuition costs. Nevertheless, he still had to work as a laboratory assistant in the Bacteriology Department at the New York University Medical School while also a student attending university, in order to have spending money for living expenses.

While in attendance at CCNY, Julius Axelrod focused his major studies primarily on pre-medicine related disciplines, such as Chemistry and

Biology. His top academic performances, however, had been in other courses, such as history, philosophy, and literature. This particular institution was located relatively further from his home, and it required that he commute back and forth by subway. The daily commute, a two-hour round trip, provided an opportunity for him to study his course materials on a moving subway during the transits. He later pointed out that this studying experience, in noisy city trains, had solidified his proficiencies for pure concentration during the learning process. He took his undergraduate degree, his Bachelors of Science, a B.S., in 1933, from City College. In addition to Dr. Axelrod, the institution, CCNY, is known for having graduated remarkable alumni, such luminaries as Nobel Laureates Drs. Robert Hofstadter (1961) and Leon Lederman (1988).

As a new university graduate, he had applied to a small number of medical schools, and every single one of them had rejected him outright. It had been apparent that these rejections had much to do with anti-Semitism that had been a conspicuous characteristic of the U.S. during that era, especially during the midst of the Great Depression years. Thus, Axelrod took on employment in a laboratory setting until, that is, the sources of funding had been exhausted, in 1935. Thus, he took on another job as a laboratory assistant at the New York Health Department, working as a chemist in their Laboratory of Industrial Hygiene, where he stayed until 1946. His duties were to assess the various methods for the measurements of vitamins contained within food and drink samples.

While working in the day at the New York laboratory during the Great Depression and World War II, Julius Axelrod had also enrolled in night school, taking graduate courses, in the master's program, at New York University.

His M.S. thesis project at the University was based on work in the biochemical field of enzymology (esterases) and in the biology of tumors. It was during this time that an unfortunate laboratory accident resulted in the loss of his left eye, and he had to wear a patch over it for the rest of his life. In 1942, he took his M.S. graduate degree.

The route to the Ph.D. for Axelrod took more than an additional 10 years. In the meantime, he was employed as a research associate at the

Goldwater Memorial Hospital until 1949. Then, he worked as a chemist and later senior chemist at the National Heart Institute until 1953. Next, he moved to the Department of Health, where he became section chief of the Pharmacology division, until 1955. During this time, he had been continually encouraged by many of his colleagues to pursue a doctoral degree.

It had been at the National Heart Institute where he had learned that without a Ph.D. in hand, he could not proceed beyond his then-current rank, and it was at that time that he decided to pursue the doctorate. Thus, he enrolled in graduate school at George Washington University in Washington, D.C., working under Dr. Paul K. Smith, who became his graduate thesis advisor. Axelrod's thesis project dealt with his previous work involved with the metabolism of so-called sympathomimetic amine compounds like ephedrine and amphetamines. For this, he had studied rabbit liver slices and delineated the various factors needed to metabolize the drugs. He had determined that the metabolic pathways encompassed various biochemical steps, like conjugation, deamination, demethylation, and hydroxylation.

Axelrod also was to locate the cellular location of the amphetamine-metabolizing enzymes, a preparation known as microsomes, now known to consist of parts of endoplasmic reticulum material laced with bound ribosomes, which are protein-making machinery. Later, investigators were to confirm Axelrod's work, referring to these metabolic drug systems as cytochrome-P450 monooxygenases. Submitting these publications to the graduate school and taking an additional year of graduate-level university courses, was all that were necessary for 42-year old Julius Axelrod to take his Ph.D. degree, from George Washington University, in 1955.

2. Let's talk glands first– tell us about his work on the pineal gland.

The pineal gland is an organ that is well-stocked with nerves of the so-called sympathetic nervous system. Dr. Axelrod's interest in the pineal gland was first stoked, in 1958, by a scientific paper he read that had been written by Dr. Aaron Lerner regarding his isolation of a compound called 5-methoxy-*N*-acetyltryptamine, known now as melatonin, from the pineal glands of cows. Dr. Axelrod's interest in the pineal gland work stemmed from the fact that the melatonin structure was said to contain a serotonin platform with a methoxy group attached to it. The serotonin molecule was thought to be involved in generating psychosis in humans because of its structural similarity to lysergic acid diethylamide (LSD). The methoxy group was reminiscent of the metabolic work he had performed with the catecholamines called epinephrine and norepinephrine. Thus, Dr. Axelrod started work with the pineal gland in an effort to work out the metabolism of melatonin.

Another project dealing with the study of the pineal gland was centered around assessing the effects of light on the biochemical activities of the organ. Thus, Dr. Axelrod and a medical student, Richard Wurtman, housed laboratory rats either in total darkness or in total light, instead of cycling the dark-light cycles in a conventional manner. The rats living in total darkness showed changes in the levels of certain enzymes that make melatonin—the melatonin-making enzymes were elevated, compared to the rats living in total light.

When specific nerves, called the superior cervical ganglia, which are connected to the pineal gland and innervate it, were surgically removed by Axelrod, the result was stunning. Cutting off the pineal gland's electrical connection had abolished the effects of total darkness and the enzyme levels! It turned out to be a major breakthrough as the experiment demonstrated that the melatonin enzymes and its connection to light in the pineal gland were under the neuro-control of the sympathetic nervous system, as the phenomenon involved the superior cervical ganglia.

Another investigative focus by Dr. Axelrod upon the pineal gland was placed on the neurotransmitter called serotonin because it had served as a starting point for the biosynthesis of the melatonin. Dr. Axelrod and one of his postdoctoral fellows, Dr. Solomon Snyder, who would later become a world-renowned neuroscientist in his own right, examined the relationship between light exposure and the levels of serotonin and melatonin. They discovered that in rats exposed to total darkness for a prolonged period of time, the up and down rhythm of serotonin levels was unaffected, strongly suggesting an internal clock mechanism was responsible.

However, when Drs. Snyder and Axelrod housed the laboratory rats in total light for long periods, the circadian rhythm of serotonin (i.e., its alternating high and low levels) was gone! The biological clock was stopped in its tracks with continuous light exposure!

A follow-up experiment conducted by Drs. Wurtman and Axelrod involved the surgical removal of the ganglia that innervated the pineal gland, a so-called ganglionectomy, and it resulted in the abolishment of the newly discovered serotonin circadian rhythm. When the control of the superior cervical ganglia was removed from the pineal gland, the cycling serotonin levels were observed to be lost. Thus, the work strongly suggested that the biological clock and the effects upon it by light exposure was located somewhere within the brain that was innervating the pineal gland. Based on this work, Dr. Axelrod concluded that the pineal gland played a role as a sort of neuroendocrine transducer, where light signals were transformed into regulatory mechanisms that controlled levels of hormones. Furthermore, he concluded that the brain, via its noradrenergic neurons, was permitting the transducer functions.

3. *Often some evenings, I take some melatonin to help me sleep. How was Axelrod involved in this?*

In the early 1960s, Dr. Axelrod started work that was devoted to learning how melatonin was made in the pineal gland. In 1961, Dr. Axelrod's melatonin work revolved around studying the effects of the compound on pineal gland activities. For instance, he and Wurtman discovered that the weights of rat ovaries were decreased by exposure to melatonin. Next, Dr. Axelrod working with Wurtman and collaborator Dr. Harvey Shein, from McLean Hospital, tested the hypothesis that the pineal gland tissue that was cultured from rats could convert the amino acid tryptophan into the melatonin. The data strongly favored the hypothesis that tryptophan was a precursor for the biosynthesis of melatonin.

Next, they showed that the neurotransmitter called norepinephrine somehow regulated this conversion of tryptophan into melatonin in the pineal gland — additional work by Drs. Wurtman and Shein demonstrated that the so-called β-adrenergic receptor was the conduit for its activation by noradrenaline.

Dr. Axelrod started working with Dr. Herbert Weissbach, and the collaborators set out to delineate the biosynthetic pathway for melatonin. They injected cow pineal gland extracts with a radioactively labeled precursor called SAM, for *S*-adenosyl-l-methionine, which was a suitable starting molecule that could introduce methyl groups into the biosynthetic pathway, plus a metabolite of serotonin called N-acetylserotonin. They found that the pineal gland extract produced the desired melatonin.

In another investigative push, they set out to purify the enzymes that were responsible for making the melatonin in their pineal gland extracts. In so doing, they discovered an enzyme they named as hydroxyindole-*O*-methyltransferase (HIOMT), now called acetyl-serotonin-*O*-methyltransferase (ASMT) which then converts *N*-acetyl-serotonin to melatonin. They also discovered and purified the enzyme called serotonin-*N*-acetyltransferase (AANAT), which converts serotonin to *N*-acetyl-serotonin. Lastly, they proposed the entire melatonin biosynthetic pathway of biochemicals, starting with the amino acid tryptophan. To this day, the pathway is presented in textbooks of neuroscience and biochemistry.

The works of Shein and Wurtman with the β-adrenergic receptor system sparked further interest by Dr. Axelrod into examining the relationship between the receptor regulation and its hormone. In 1970, Dr. Axelrod studied levels of the serotonin *N*-acetyltransferase enzyme using agents that blocked the β-adrenergic system. Such blocking agents included reserpine, protein synthesis inhibitors, and surgical removal of the ganglia—the so-called ganglionectomy. The result was that the β-adrenergic blockers also blocked the increase in the enzyme typically observed after exposure to a continuous dark environment. These results suggested that the noradrenaline, which was secreted by elements of the sympathetic nervous system, actually activated the β-adrenergic receptor, thus causing the production of the enzymes that are involved in the synthesis of the melatonin.

4. *We often joke about Thanksgiving– and sleeping after eating turkey, which contains tryptophan. How do these things relate to each other and the pineal gland?*

Humans cannot make tryptophan on their own. We need this molecule in order to make our own proteins. We lack, however, the underlying biochemical machinery for its synthesis. Therefore, we must intake tryptophan in our necessary diet. There are other potential effects of tryptophan.

The basic idea is that because the amino acid tryptophan is a biochemical precursor to the synthesis of melatonin, a compound that is associated with the sleep and wake cycles, then dietary intake of tryptophan during meals should make an effective sleep-aid for insomniacs. The melatonin is produced by the pineal gland, and it uses tryptophan as a starting point to make it. The tryptophan is one of 20 amino acids that are found in protein, and meats like turkey, beef, and pork all have a high protein content. Thus, the content of tryptophan would be correspondingly higher as one increases the intake of relatively high protein diets.

The tryptophan-sleep connotation is problematic, however, because a heavy meal, such as that accomplished with enjoying a Thanksgiving dinner, turkey with all of the trimmings, can also direct enhanced blood flow to the gut in order to handle the heavy meal, for digestion purposes. It is believed that the altered blood flow can make a person sleepy, as well. Another putative problem with tryptophan is that in addition to being a metabolite, it is also a neurotransmitter precursor, serving as a foundation point for the synthesis of serotonin. So, large doses of tryptophan may result in unintended side effects after it partakes in downstream biochemical and neurological processes.

5. Catecholamines – what exactly are they, and how was Axelrod involved?

The catecholamines are a group of hormones called neurotransmitters. The three most-studied of the catecholamines include epinephrine (used to be called adrenaline), norepinephrine (was noradrenaline) and dopamine. The primary source of catecholamines is the amino acid called tyrosine. In the catecholamine biosynthetic process, tyrosine is converted to L-DOPA, which is then converted to dopamine, which then goes to norepinephrine and then to epinephrine as the endpoint of the pathway. All three neurotransmitters act on the α- and β-adrenergic receptors to various extents.

While the body of work dealing with catecholamine studies by this investigator is extensive, Dr. Axelrod's prime involvement with these biochemicals has to do with their disappearing acts after they are released by neurons and perform their various neuronal functions. Dr. Axelrod discovered that rather than their degradation, they were merely taken back by the neurons, a process now known as neurotransmitter reuptake. It was to become his major Nobel Prize-winning work.

Epinephrine has also been colloquially referred to as the "flight or fight" hormone. This is due to the fact that during times of acute stress, epinephrine is secreted by one of the body's organs, such as the adrenal medulla. The secreted epinephrine mediates a series of physiological consequences, such as a faster than average rate of heart beating and the mobilization of the body's energy storage forms in order to generate the increased need for energy during the stress by breaking down the body's stores of glycogen and lipids.

Norepinephrine works on the body's noradrenergic system. This neurotransmitter is secreted from the so-called postganglionic synapses of the sympathetic portion of the overall autonomic nervous system. Norepinephrine serves a suppression type of role in the sympathetic system, resulting in a corresponding suppression in the activities of the gut and in the reduced flow of blood.

Dopamine is a rather potent neurotransmitter that regulates various functions of the brain. This neurotransmitter is produced by so-called dopaminergic neurons that reside in the inside of the brain. The absence of dopamine in patients with Parkinson disease results in severely debilitating neurological consequences. Film actor Michael J. Fox has the aliment and has been a longtime advocate for investigative studies. While there is no effective cure for Parkinson disease, specific treatments can alleviate the symptoms. One such treatment includes L-DOPA, which is a precursor along the synthetic pathway for norepinephrine and epinephrine. The motion picture film *Awakenings* features the accidental discovery by Dr. Oliver Sacks, portrayed by actor Robin Williams as the fictional character Dr. Malcom Sayer, of the benefits of L-DOPA, for the treatment a catatonic disease called encephalitis lethargica, sometimes called "sleeping illness" or "sleepy sickness."

6. *Some of his work led to what we abbreviate as SSRI- Selective Serotonin Reuptake Inhibitors (most notably Prozac), which apparently stops the reuptake of the neurotransmitter serotonin. (Great book for future reading– "Listening to Prozac"- a medication still used today).*

Dr. Axelrod's Nobel Prize-winning work involved discovering the reuptake mechanism of neurotransmitters, such as serotonin. This molecule is a precursor to the synthesis of melatonin in the pineal gland. Dr. Axelrod's earlier work in the area started with elucidating the synthesis pathway for melatonin, starting with serotonin as a precursor metabolite. His laboratory also learned that in the pineal gland, the serotonin concentrations varied depending on the light/dark cycle, observing elevated serotonin concentrations during the daytime and lowered concentrations during the nighttime. The work was profound as it pointed to the presence of an internal cellular, molecular clock system, a so-called circadian rhythm for alternating the levels of serotonin!

Serotonin has also been known in scientific circles as 5-hydroxytryptamine (5-HT), and it has long been thought to be involved in certain aspects of depression and schizophrenia. There are two main hypotheses for the involvement of serotonin with depression. The first one states that low serotonin concentrations lead to depression, and the other hypothesis maintains at this point that depression itself leads to lowered serotonin concentrations.

Similarly, there are two seemingly different hypotheses for serotonin's involvement in schizophrenia. The first hypothesis holds that, in post-mortem studies, patients with schizophrenia exhibit higher than average concentrations of specific integral membrane proteins called 5-HT_{1A} receptors that bind to the serotonin in the frontal cortex of the brain. The other hypothesis states that in patients with schizophrenia, the serotonin binds less well to their 5-HT_{1A} receptors that reside in another portion of the brain called the amygdala.

Regardless of the cellular mechanism for the role that serotonin plays in depression or schizophrenia, the reuptake system for the re-use of serotonin appears to be a prime target for anti-depression and antipsychotic drugs. Hence, the SSRI drugs that you mentioned are of great importance. Let's briefly discuss the serotonin reuptake system.

First, tryptophan is metabolized to synthesize serotonin. The newly synthesized serotonin is stored in vesicles, in presynaptic neurons, waiting for their release into the synapse, the space between adjoining neurons. The newly released serotonin in the synapse then binds to the post-synaptic receptor and mediates its common electrophysiological effect, depending on the receptor's location in the brain. After serotonin performs its post-synaptic function, it is taken back into the pre-synaptic neuron that had released it in the first place. The serotonin uptake (re-uptake) is performed by a dedicated serotonin transporter protein that resides in the membrane of the pre-synaptic neuron. The re-acquired serotonin can then be stored in presynaptic vesicles until they are needed again.

The SSRIs interfere with this serotonin reuptake system, often at the level of the presynaptic serotonin transporter, blocking the transporter, and thus leading to relatively higher concentrations of serotonin within the synapse, the so-called synaptic cleft between two given associated neurons. The increased serotonin levels now permit its function to go ahead. The SSRIs, such as Prozac (chemical name fluoxetine) and others, are increasingly used by clinicians to treat a variety of conditions, such as depression, psychosis, and other disorders, like anxiety.

7. *Epinephrine and norepinephrine (Also known as adrenaline and noradrenaline) are really very foundational drugs/chemicals) (and epi-pens are widely used today. Can you explain his work in these areas?*

As I mentioned earlier, Dr. Axelrod was awarded the Nobel Prize for his work in determining that catecholamine neurotransmitters like epinephrine and norepinephrine are taken back ("re-acquired") by neurons after participating in conducting electrical nerve transmission. These neurotransmitters that are regained back by neurons are then saved as inactive forms within these nerve cells while residing inside tiny intracellular packets called vesicles. The re-captured neurotransmitters can then be re-used for the next nerve conduction process.

His first experiment in this area involved the metabolism of epinephrine. Dr. Axelrod had been interested in this biochemical because of its purported involvement in schizophrenia. Two prominent psychiatrists had hypothesized that epinephrine was broken down into another compound called adrenochrome, which then produced specific schizophrenia-like behavioral and hallucinogenic effects, after exposure to the adrenochrome.

Thus, Dr. Axelrod was interested in understanding the events that occurred after epinephrine performed its nerve transmission duties. He wanted to know whether epinephrine was degraded. Its effects, after all, were known to disappear almost as quickly as it appeared, after conducting its neuronal transmission. We now know he discovered that epinephrine was retaken back by the pre-synaptic neuron, a Nobel-worthy finding, but Dr. Axelrod first considered whether and how it was degraded metabolically.

Thus, Dr. Axelrod first examined whether epinephrine was deaminated, a process in which an amino chemical group is removed from (in this case) an epinephrine structure. So, he measured epinephrine's effects in the presence of inhibitors of enzymes known to deaminate compounds, such as the monoamine oxidases, a family of related enzymes. He and his laboratory colleagues found that the epinephrine still disappeared even in the presence of monoamine oxidase inhibitors. It was a significant scientific finding.

Dr. Axelrod considered next whether other oxidative enzymes metabolized epinephrine to make it disappear after mediating its neuronal effects. These enzymes did not, either, and it was deemed another disappointing dead end. Next, he and co-workers examined whether epinephrine was methylated. Exploring this methylation avenue further, they failed to find how epinephrine was inactivated but did manage to elucidate new enzymes that metabolized it, calling one of these enzymes catechol-*O*-methyltransferase. After publishing these works, in 1957, Dr. Axelrod considered himself a *bona fide* connoisseur of neurochemistry, making contributions to the biochemistry of catecholamine catabolism.

He next turned to the question of epinephrine's deactivation, rather than its metabolic degradation. Some of his findings pointed to an inactivation mechanism for epinephrine because inhibitors of catabolism did not produce the desired increase in its effects. The inactivation proceeded even in the presence of degradation inhibitors. These next efforts led to the Nobel.

At about this time, he was fortunate enough to get his hands on newly radioactively-labeled epinephrine! Using epinephrine labeled with tritium (a radioactive form of the hydrogen atom, referred to commonly as ^{3}H), Dr. Axelrod could find out what happened to it once it finished its neuro-electrical duties. A short time later, he was able to get ahold of tritium-labeled norepinephrine, as well. He examined various tissues in cats to learn the fates of the catecholamines ^{3}H-epinephrine and ^{3}H-norepinephrine.

To his shock, Dr. Axelrod found that after injecting cats with the ^{3}H-epinephrine and ^{3}H-norepinephrine, the labeled catecholamines remained stable within their tissues long after the catecholamines conducted their neurophysiological effects! Interestingly, Dr. Axelrod and his laboratory personnel noticed that the tritium-labeled epinephrine was exceptionally stable in cat tissues, which were innervated by nerves belonging to the sympathetic nervous system. Next, they formulated their hypothesis: catecholamines could be re-taken back up by presynaptic neurons and then stored there. They referred to this catecholamine fate as uptake and retention of epinephrine and norepinephrine by neurons. Then, they tested their Nobel Prize hypothesis.

The critical Nobel Prize experiment involved cat surgeries. Dr. Axelrod and co-workers surgically removed specific nerves called superior cervical ganglia from one side of the cat-eye muscles and of the saliva-producing gland, leaving the other side intact, complete with their innervations uncut. Then, they injected the tritium-labeled catecholamine, the ^{3}H-norepinephrine, into the surgically-treated cats, and the results were dramatic!

The norepinephrine appeared to be re-absorbed and stored only on the uncut (intact) innervated sides of the eye muscles and salivary glands. However, the norepinephrine seemed to be almost entirely missing from the denervated side, with its nerve supply having been surgically removed! These data were interpreted to mean that sympathetic neurons selectively took up and kept catecholamines, rather than degraded and re-made them biochemically, a process of which would use up so much energy to perform repeatedly.

In a follow-up experiment, Dr. Axelrod found that when the intact nerves were stimulated to conduct an electrical pulse, the labeled catecholamine ^{3}H-norepinephrine was taken up by neurons and secreted into the synapse when turned on. These data were then interpreted to mean that after working at the post-synaptic neuron, with its function complete, the neurotransmitter was then quickly inactivated by being re-absorbed back into the pre-synaptic sympathetic neuron, rather than destroyed and re-made later on. It was a fundamental breakthrough in the functioning of neurotransmitters and led directly to the Nobel.

8. Codeine, morphine, and methamphetamine (all end with the "ine" ending). But what are their uses, and how are they alike, yet different? And how was Axelrod involved?

Codeine, also known by its chemical name 3-methoxymorphine, is an opiate chemical that is used for the medical treatment of pain. Morphine is another member of the opiate chemicals (known in modern times colloquially as opioids) that's been frequently used for pain on a historical basis. Codeine and morphine have similar chemical structures, differing primarily by only a few atoms, with codeine harboring a methoxide (CH_3–O–) substituent at one location on the basic structure while morphine harbors only a pure hydroxide (OH–) moiety at the same position. Methamphetamine, also known as N-methylamphetamine, is structurally dissimilar to either codeine or morphine, but is on its own is a potent neurological stimulant of the central nervous system and an illicit drug to which many people are highly addicted.

Each of these drugs seem to have various levels of addictive qualities. In 1956, Dr. Axelrod provided an early indication of why this seemed to be the case. After having discovered, in 1953, how these drugs were metabolized biochemically (see below), he made an astute observation. He found that repeated exposure of these narcotic drugs, such as morphine, to laboratory animals, resulted in a certain level of tolerance to the agents and, importantly, to a decreased ability to be degraded, as well. That is, after repeated administration to these drugs, they worked less well (needing more drugs to do the same work) and showed less metabolic degradation each time. Furthermore, opiate antagonists prevented tolerance induction but also seemed to inhibit the degradative enzymes.

Dr. Axelrod astutely provided an explanation. He hypothesized that the enzymes had morphine binding sites that were similar in structure to the morphine receptor sites. Thus, with morphine continually binding to both enzymes and receptors, it resulted in the inactivation of both proteins. That is, the degrading enzymes and morphine receptors became inactive, requiring more of the drug to mediate the same level of effects as before.

Dr. Axelrod's first foray into studying these compounds, however, started with his interest, in 1953, in certain so-called sympathomimetic amines, such as ephedrine and amphetamine, which had been previously shown to stimulate neurons belonging to the sympathetic nervous system. He then carefully examined their various metabolic pathways. For instance, Dr. Axelrod provided some evidence that ephedrine could be degraded metabolically by two distinctive pathways, one by demethylation (removal of methyl groups) and the other by hydroxylation (addition of hydroxyl groups). He then demonstrated that different species of laboratory animals had favored one or the other of these two pathways.

Next, Dr. Axelrod carefully studied methylamphetamine and amphetamine. He demonstrated their various metabolic fates when acted upon by the body's liver enzymes. Biochemically, Dr. Axelrod showed that these two agents possessed an assortment of metabolic fates, depending on whether the drugs were deaminated (amine removal), demethylated, hydroxylated, or conjugated together. In much the same way as before, Dr. Axelrod then showed that various animal species treated these compounds differently, depending on the types of metabolic enzymes present in the animals. He exposed laboratory rabbits to amphetamine. What he found surprised him. The drug simply disappeared with nary a trace.

Not being a biochemist who knew about enzymes at the time, in the early 1950s, Dr. Axelrod nevertheless became interested in how the amphetamine was degraded. He inquired of his colleagues who were biochemists, such as Dr. Gordon Tomkins, who told Dr. Axelrod that all he needed to study amphetamine breakdown was a laboratory technique for the detection of the drug, some liver from a laboratory animal, and a razor blade!

So, Dr. Axelrod took rabbit livers out of the animals, sliced the extracted livers with his razor blade, incubated the liver slices in buffers, added the drug, and measured levels of the amphetamine in order to determine its fate. He then saw the amphetamine simply disappear!

Next, he blended the animal livers, making a so-called rabbit liver homogenate and repeated his amphetamine addition to the newly blended animal organ. This time the drug failed to disappear! In order to make the liver homogenate degrade the amphetamine, Dr. Axelrod needed to add back certain biochemicals, such as enzymatic co-factors like ATP, NAD^+, and NADP. Quickly becoming a competent biochemist, Dr. Axelrod decided to find out what cellular component was responsible for making the amphetamine disappear. Thus he then broke up the liver into certain cellular parts, like the nuclei, ribosomes attached to membranes of the endoplasmic reticulum (called microsomes), mitochondria, and the cytoplasm (called cytosol). Disappointingly, he found that none of the cellular parts acted upon the amphetamine, even if he added back all of the various enzymatic co-factors. However, if Dr. Axelrod combined each of the previously separated microsomes with the purified cytosol and added the necessary co-factors, the amphetamine readily conducted its disappearing act.

Follow-up experiments by Dr. Axelrod and colleagues showed that amphetamine's vanishing act involved a biochemical deamination step, making phenylacetone and ammonia end-products in its wake. At about this same time, he discovered that ephedrine was demethylated to make norephedrine, plus formaldehyde! Since the enzymes responsible for these biochemical degradations were localized to the endoplasmic reticulum-ribosome mixture, the microsomal fraction of liver cells, many other investigators entered the burgeoning field started by Dr. Axelrod. The liver microsome enzymes are nowadays referred to as the cytochrome-P450 monooxygenases. This particular liver biochemical system is essential for metabolizing a great variety of chemical and biochemical agents, some of which may be potentially toxic to humans, and to this day, the system still represents a critical biochemical field in the biomedical sciences.

9. *Certain mornings, I stop at McDonald's to chat with my good friends and colleagues in the Biology department– but Axelrod also looked at the mechanisms and effects of caffeine. Tough question– but can you tell us about caffeine, its impact, addictive qualities, stimulant qualities, and Axelrod's work in this realm?*

I fondly recall your frequent visits with us scientists during our morning coffee breaks! I believe our visits over a cup of coffee ultimately led to our collaborations on these wonderfully delightful books. It has been great fun working together on these projects, and it was our shared interest in consuming caffeine that started it all!

Caffeine is a fantastically popular substance, being consumed since ancient times in staggeringly large amounts worldwide in the form of coffee, cocoa, and certain teas. It is a powerful stimulant of the central nervous system. Its historical popularity is evident in playing essential roles in commerce, economics, human migration, politics, and even in cultural and societal norms. In modern times, many of us enjoy occasional visits to bookstores with their adjacent coffee houses.

While caffeine, an alkaloid biochemical agent, is derived from over several dozen different species of plants, the most common source seems to be the beans of cocoa trees from the *Coffea* genus, such as *Coffea arabica* and *Coffea canephora*.

Biochemically speaking, the structural nature of caffeine, a member of the methylxanthine group of chemicals, is similar to those of theobromine (found in cocoa), theophylline (found in teas) and adenosine (found in DNA). The adenosine molecule, a nitrogenous base, is also a neuromodulator, serving to reduce the numbers of spontaneous neuronal firings and thus to decrease the release of other neurotransmitters. The overall effect of adenosine is to permit us to sleep.

Caffeine, on the other hand, is said to counteract the sleepy effect of adenosine. Thus, instead of waking us up, caffeine actually hinders the regular sleep-inducing role of the adenosine. The mechanism of this anti-sleep effect by caffeine is by way of its binding to the adenosine receptor, occupying the adenosine-binding site and preventing the adenosine from binding it to its dedicated receptor. The caffeine prevents adenosine from binding to its receptor. The physiological effects of adenosine receptor blocking by the occupying caffeine molecules are to induce the so-called "caffeine buzz." Among these effects include increased heart rate, increased blood vessel constriction, and in permitting muscles to flex more readily.

For medical purposes, caffeine has been used traditionally to treat migraine headaches, asthma, and low blood pressure. It has also been used as a diuretic. Many scientific studies attest to its relatively safe effects and, in some instances, being a generally good substance.

However, caffeine can be toxic if consumed in staggeringly large concentrations. For instance, in a regular cup of coffee, on average, the amount of caffeine can range between 80 and 200 milligrams per cup, depending on how the coffee is brewed. A lethal dose of caffeine, however, is about 10 grams. Thus, in order for a human being to consume a lethal dose of caffeine by drinking cups of regular coffee, over 50 cups of the strong coffee (or over 120 cups of weaker coffee) must be consumed in one sitting! That's obviously a tremendously impossible number of coffee cups that need consuming in order to be deadly!

The biochemical effects of caffeine are extensive. In addition to serving an essential role in antagonizing the adenosine receptor, caffeine also has the ability to regulate the cellular mobilization of calcium stores inside muscles. The result of this is to lower the number of signals needed to induce muscle contraction and to prolong these muscular contractions. Caffeine also inhibits the degradative activities of so-called cyclic nucleotide phosphodiesterase enzymes, resulting in increases in the concentrations of cAMP (adenosine 3',5'-cyclic monophosphate) and in permitting increased effects of the catecholamines.

Relatively high concentrations of caffeine are reported to affect the concentrations of certain neurotransmitters. For instance, caffeine increases the biosynthesis and breakdown of both noradrenaline and acetylcholine. However, caffeine is known to increase the cellular concentrations of dopamine and serotonin in the brain. Caffeine can also induce the amounts of glutamine, an amino acid with an inhibitory neurotransmitter role.

Like other neuromodulatory agents, caffeine addiction involves specific withdrawal symptoms, such as headache, tiredness, and drowsiness. In cases where an individual has consumed an excessive amount of caffeine, additional withdrawal symptoms may include nausea and vomiting. Caffeine that is consumed continually or chronically is said to increase the numbers of the adenosine receptors and decreases in the numbers of both cholinergic- and β-adrenergic receptors in the brain. While caffeine is also reported to bind to so-called benzodiazepine receptors, its effects on this system are less clear with respect to caffeine tolerance and addiction (dependence).

Dr. Axelrod's work with caffeine involved his interest in the physiological and biochemical dispositions of the agent within human beings. First, he and co-workers developed a technique for measuring caffeine levels in blood plasma. With this method at hand, they then determined the tissue distribution of caffeine, publishing the results in 1953. The work led to his interest in studying amine-containing compounds.

10. We hear it all the time – Tylenol and acetaminophen – how was Axelrod involved, and what are the issues here?

Dr. Axelrod's efforts in studying acetaminophen (the active principle in Tylenol) were sparked after his discussions on the topic with his good friend and collaborator Dr. Bernard Brodie, known affectionately as "Steve" by Dr. Axelrod. The topic was relevant in the sense that it was Dr. Axelrod's first significant experience in conducting research after having earned his M.S. degree. He writes in his memoir that it was this topic that enhanced his interest in biomedical research as a career.

The exciting topic involved the question about why or how the analgesics called acetanilide and phenacetin produced a severe consequence in patients in which they exhibited met-hemoglobinemia. It was a condition characterized by the production of an abnormal concentration of a hemoglobin metabolite called met-hemoglobin, hence the name met-hemoglobinemia. They set out to determine whether and how acetanilide might result in the abnormal condition.

Their first hypothesis to explain the severe side effect of the met-hemoglobinemia caused by the two analgesics was that acetanilide made aniline, an agent known to produce the abnormal condition. Their study showed that as the blood concentration of aniline increased, so did the production of the met-hemoglobinemia! Dr. Axelrod was hooked—on biomedicine-based research, that is.

A follow-up experiment examined what happened to the acetanilide in the body. Drs. Axelrod and Brodie found that the acetanilide was missing from the urine, suggesting that it was metabolized to other forms. So, they searched for possible metabolites that may have resulted from the degradation of the acetanilide. One of these metabolic candidates was identified as *N*-acetyl-*p*-aminophenol, which was produced from hydroxylation of acetanilide and is also known as acetaminophen!

Another follow-up experiment by Drs. Brodie and Axelrod delineated the direct conversion of the acetanilide into the acetaminophen. Furthermore, they showed acetaminophen itself was, surprisingly, *more* potent as an analgesic, compared to the more notorious acetanilide, and as an added benefit, the acetaminophen failed to produce the confounding met-hemoglobinemia! They had solved both a mystery *and* a problem at the same time! The first project was published in 1948. It was Dr. Axelrod's first scientific paper. A second publication followed in 1949.

11. Apparently, Axelrod was also interested in vitamin supplements (such as Linus Pauling was interested in Vitamin C). What were his contributions?

Dr. Axelrod's involvement with vitamin C started with one of his first jobs after graduation from university in 1933. At the New York Health Department, he was tasked with evaluating the vitamin supplement content in foods and drinks. The list of vitamins to be tested by Axelrod included, in addition to vitamin C, vitamins A, B, B_2, and D. The purpose of these studies was to ensure the accuracies of the vitamins in randomly selected food and milk samples, as the importance of vitamins was just beginning to be recognized in human food and drink production circles.

The discovery of vitamin C, also known as ascorbic acid, by Dr. Albert Szent-Györgyi was of significant importance. Because vitamins, by definition, cannot be biosynthesized by a living being, it becomes crucial that such individuals are supplied with the necessary substances by dietary means in order to ensure that their biological effects are conducted. Thus, the field was so crucial that Szent-Györgyi was bestowed the Nobel Prize, in 1937, for having performed such an important discovery for the proper metabolism of living beings. Thus, a significant push was on to include vitamin C and other vitamins in foods and drinks that were provided to humans. In later years, Dr. Pauling was to make vitamin C even more relevant as a putative health substance and potential preventer of cancer.

Dr. Axelrod's duties as an examiner of vitamin content in foods and milk involved learning new methods. This laboratory approach necessitated that he acquire the expertise of sorts in disparate fields, such as chemistry, biology, and microbiology, in order to conduct the various assays for vitamin compositions in foods and drink. It also necessitated that he delves into the scientific literature in order to make sense of the new methods. Following the published literature permitted him to modify any given method when necessary. It also provided a particular self-confidence in the laboratory setting. Furthermore, the experience of testing vitamins in foods taught him how to approach the scientific method of conducting biomedical research in later years.

12. Those who knew him and knew about him – were aware of the eye patch he wore – what is the story about the loss of one of his eyes?

The incident with his eye occurred during the time just prior to the start of World War II, when Axelrod was a graduate student in a master's program at New York University. A laboratory accident involving an exploding bottle of ammonia caused Axelrod to lose one of his eyes.

He was forever to wear a patch on the affected left eye, sometimes wearing glasses with one of the glass lenses darkened. The permanent eye injury had prevented his participation in the military during the Second World War.

In later years, in 1986, two years after retirement, he studied cow eyes, examining the outer rod segments. With interest in molecules called phospholipase A_2, which could turn on GTP-binding proteins, also known as G-proteins or transducin, he and colleagues found that these molecules consisted of sub-units called alpha, beta and gamma. Furthermore, he learned that they could combine into various dimers, such as beta-gamma, and that these dimers could turn on the phospholipase A_2 molecules. The dimer could then form a trimer, alpha-beta-gamma, to turn off the receptor. The work was submitted to *Nature* and rejected, but not before having first undergone a rather prolonged review period. Thus, their work was sent to the *Proceedings of the National Academy of Sciences* (PNAS) and duly published. Afterward, many other investigators repeated the work, not only confirming Dr. Axelrod's findings but also extending them. Dr. Axelrod had firmly established a new biomedical field.

13. *What kind of summary can we provide? Perhaps all those medical schools that rejected him – did us, and the field, a service? What do you think?*

Given his rather astonishing array of biomedically-based discoveries, having been performed both without and later with a Ph.D., I can understand your inquisitiveness about Dr. Axelrod having been largely rejected from medical schools. His rejections, however dreadful for Julius Axelrod, have been tremendously beneficial to humankind.

Indeed, Dr. Axelrod's scientific excursion into a vast array of scientific biomedical fields is astonishing. His scientific body of work extends into many aspects of our own everyday lives.

Many human beings take vitamins on a daily basis as a matter of routine. Many foods are fortified with them, and many others supplement their diets with vitamins. Vitamins are, after all, vital. We need them as proper co-factors for many of our enzymes. We may also need them for better health, maybe even to circumvent cancer, as has been touted by certain proponents, like the famous Dr. Linus Pauling has proposed with the vitamin C.

Countless millions of people take analgesics for pain; the extent of this practice for pain treatment is monumental. It is a daily practice for physicians to prescribe analgesics to their patients, and over-the-counter equivalents are extensive on a vast scale.

The neurotransmitter reuptake mechanisms discovered by Dr. Axelrod has had an enormous contribution to our understanding of nervous system functioning, both on a purely fundamental basis and on a practically applied basis. This Nobel Prize-winning work is a prime topic in any basic neuroscience course, taught to any undergraduate with interest and to medical students as a matter of course.

The work involving the handling of certain chemicals by liver enzymes of the cytochrome-P450 monooxygenases is a major mechanism for controlling the levels of toxicity for potentially dangerous metabolites. This work has contributed significantly to our understanding of basic metabolism and cancer biochemistry. Biomedical science has been made an essential field of study because of this discovery. It is surprising to me that Dr. Axelrod did not receive a second Nobel Prize for this work, as well.

The work with the effects of narcotic drugs by Dr. Axelrod continues to be an important topic, even to the present day, with the problem of addiction to opiates. Scientifically, the issues are apparent. Sociologically, politically, and economically, however, drug tolerance and dependence (addiction) is a seemingly intractable problem.

Caffeine seems to be a universally enjoyed substance, providing many a grateful coffee drinker with great joy! The health benefits of pure caffeine (without confounding cream and sugar) can be profound, helping both the heart and the mind. This one substance has had and will continue to have a profound influence on the daily lives of its followers, many of whom are its most influential advocates.

The discovery of the serotonin circadian clock and its light/dark cycle has relevance to every sleeper; Dr. Axelrod's studies of synthetic melatonin pathway has relevance to every insomniac. These biomedical findings have universal relevance.

Although it was not mentioned above, Dr. Axelrod also studied a series of compounds called glucuronides, discovering that morphine could be converted into glucuronide conjugates using rat liver enzymes. It was thought that these enzymes could play a role in reducing bilirubin. The work had a direct role in the importance of bilirubin, which is pronounced in its levels in patients with individual genetic disease patients, premature babies, and neonates with jaundice. The high bilirubin levels inherent in the jaundice condition could perhaps be reduced by glucuronide-specific enzymes.

Dr. Axelrod's enduring catecholamine research will no doubt be of great importance in the biomedical sciences for a great many years to come. His work is a permanent contribution to our understanding of neurotransmitter metabolism, nerve conduction, and synapse functioning. Along these lines, the pineal gland work with neurotransmitter metabolism will forever remain a major component to our understanding of the brain within the neuroscience field of biomedical sciences.

After retirement at the age of 72 years, he was to make more important scientific contributions. Working with his postdoctoral fellows, he studied several neurotransmitter receptors, namely, the so-called bradykinin receptor and three new muscarinic receptors. He also studied the cytokine called interleukin-1 in which he found that it activated phospholipase A_2 and that it released the second messenger molecule called arachidonic acid by working through one of several G-proteins. The G-protein activation had effects in terms of regulating the activities of other molecules such as adenylate cyclase, phospholipases A_2 and C, and in the functioning of ion channels.

For future study go to:

https://www.youtube.com/watch?v=UxYTGMiSvq0
https://www.youtube.com/watch?v=FHbdykwW6u4

Chapter 3

DAVID BALTIMORE – TUMOR VIRUSES

1. *Professor Varela, we have heard the term "Renaissance Man" many times, but I daresay that David Baltimore seems to be the closest thing to a Renaissance man living today. Let's start at the beginning– where was he born and where did he go to school?*

Dr. David Baltimore was born in the city of Manhattan, New York, U.S., on the 7th day in the month of March, in the year 1938, to parents Richard and Gertrude Lipschitz Baltimore. His father, a manufacturer, was Orthodox Jewish and raised David to practice the faith. Young David and his brother, Bob, were strongly encouraged by their mother to become physicians. She was a degreed psychologist and professor housed at Sarah Lawrence College, a private liberal arts institution located in Bronxville, Yonkers, New York. She is described as being a mother who was devoted to the education of her two progeny. In later years, Dr. Baltimore attributed his love of biology to his mother, who was among the first people to introduce the topic to him as a child.

The family lived in various suburbs of Queens, such as Rego Park and Forest Hills. David was enrolled in elementary and high schools in Great Neck, NY, where he performed quite well in the topics of mathematics and science. In his junior year at high school, Baltimore enrolled in a summer research program at the Jackson Laboratory, in Bar Harbor, Maine, in the U.S. It is in this unique program, in 1955, that David met a university senior named Howard Temin who was to serve as a peer advisor to the younger high school students and who would also become a co-Nobel Laureate with Baltimore in later years.

Temin's influence upon Baltimore was profound. Because Temin had been a senior student at Swarthmore College, it was one of the key factors in Baltimore's decision to enroll in the same institution upon his subsequent graduation from high school. Another key factor was Baltimore's mother, who was also keen on his decision to give Swarthmore a college try, as she had had longtime friends who were on the faculty, and they had provided a positive assessment of the college.

Thus, after high school graduation, Baltimore enrolled at Swarthmore, located in Philadelphia, Pennsylvania, in 1956, focusing his studies on the field of Biology and then later in Chemistry, so that he could perform a senior research thesis project. He graduated from Swarthmore College in 1960, having taken his undergraduate degree in Chemistry as his major while minoring in Biology, with the institution's highest honors. While Baltimore derided his science education as second-rate, he nevertheless valued the liberal arts experience, developing a lifelong appreciation of music, art, literature, politics, and photography.

Upon gaining his undergraduate degree from Swarthmore, in 1960, Baltimore attended the Massachusetts Institute of Technology (M.I.T.) but later moved to Rockefeller in order to study more closely animal viruses. The graduate work at Rockefeller was quite productive, dealing with viral replication, and Baltimore took his Ph.D. in 1964.

2. *For college, he went to Swarthmore, graduating with high honors in 1960. While some may not know it, Swarthmore is an exceptionally fine school, graduating many top-notch scholars and researchers. Whom did he study under while there and who mentored him?*

To put it succinctly, Baltimore's undergraduate experience at Swarthmore was, in a word, adventurous. Baltimore had participated in several civil rights protests, as the college had had a low percentage of enrolled minority students at the time, and Baltimore and his fellow student protesters were demanding more progress on the integration process.

One of his adventures included the routine hiding of a forbidden car. Swarthmore College students were not allowed to have cars on campus. One of Baltimore's college dorm buddies owned the contraband car, which was often concealed by being parked in neighboring streets and alleyways. The car-hiding system permitted them to travel to Philadelphia's pubs and Jazz clubs during weekends. The ruse worked for a while before the clandestine car was eventually discovered and banished.

Living in the Swarthmore dormitory, in Mary Lyons hall, Baltimore met new people about his age, many of whom became lifelong friends, such as Detmar Finke (the secret car owner), Lannie Rubin, Gil Harman, and Peter Temin, who was Howard Temin's younger sibling. You'll recall it was Howard Temin's influence that inspired the younger Baltimore to attend Swarthmore. The gifted and talented Howard Temin had already enjoyed a reputation as being of genius status while a college student. The college environment of Swarthmore during the time of Temin and of Baltimore has been described as relaxed and not terribly rigorous, academically-speaking. Thus it provided extra time for the pursuit of one's intellectual interests.

During Baltimore's first summer break from Swarthmore, after his freshman year, he had been invited to participate in a research laboratory at Mt. Sinai Hospital, where he studied under Bob Ledeen examining sea cucumbers. The purpose of the work had been to extract specific anti-tumor agents from the sea cucumbers. While his particular summer work was never published in a journal, the experience provided useful laboratory techniques that he would use in later years.

Enrolling in Biology courses, Baltimore found them lacking in their treatments of experimental and molecular biology. He had learned about these new fields as a member and later as president of the Swarthmore Biology Club. Worse, he found that no textbooks on the topic of molecular biology had been available at the time. This is likely due to the fact that molecular biology was a fledgling field. Nevertheless, Baltimore went to the scientific journals, attempting to read original papers on the topic, but found them teeming with unclear jargon. Therefore, Baltimore spent his spare time poring over review articles, which he found more understandable than the first papers. The problem with this approach, however, was that the Swarthmore library contained few of the molecular biology-based journals. Thus, he spent lots of his time at the Bryn Mawr and Haverford college libraries, reading review articles on molecular biology, his primary interest.

He read about the works of famous scientists of the time, such as Drs. Joshua Lederberg, George Beadle, Edward Tatum, Frederick Griffith, Salvador Luria, Max Delbrück, Martha Chase, Alfred Hershey, Oswald Avery, James Watson, and Francis Crick, all early pioneers of molecular biology. Molecular biology became a lifelong passion for Baltimore.

One of Baltimore's favorite courses was a Microbiology seminar, where papers dealing with molecular biology were sifted through. During these discussions, Baltimore learned that he could get his hands on bacteriophages! The place to go was the Cold Spring Harbor Laboratory in New York. Thus, while back home on Easter vacation during his junior year of college, Baltimore borrowed his parent's car and drove to Cold Spring Harbor Laboratory. There he became acquainted with investigators Drs. Helen Gay and George Streisinger. Impressed with Baltimore's interest, Dr. Streisinger was glad to teach him the techniques used in working with bacteriophages, such as culturing *Escherichia coli* bacteria, the hosts of the widely used T4 phages, and the famous plaque assay, for culturing the phages.

Upon Dr. Streisinger's suggestion, Baltimore, in 1959, took a summer research course later that same year in a program known as URPP (Undergraduate Research Participation Program), at Cold Spring Harbor Laboratory, and he was mentored by Streisinger himself. The URPP had been funded by the National Science Foundation. Not only did Baltimore benefit from the newfound technical knowledge of phage biology, but he also had the opportunity to meet the authors of the review articles he had voraciously read: Drs. Watson, Delbrück, Luria, Hershey, etc. Additionally, Baltimore had the chance to attend the latest research seminars of many young and established investigators of molecular biology. These connections permitted Baltimore to be recruited to attend M.I.T. as a graduate student after graduation from Swarthmore.

During his last year at Swarthmore, working under the tutelage of Dr. Philip George, professor of chemistry, Baltimore conducted his senior research thesis project, which entailed studying ATP chemistry and protein purification. While the work was not published, it nevertheless provided Baltimore with a biochemistry methods toolkit, which he would later put to good use on the road to the Nobel.

3. *Apparently, he entered MIT and was known as somewhat of an innovative, brash, but brilliant student who perhaps approached the study of biology quite energetically and enthusiastically. What do we know about his early interests in phage genetics? (Then animal viruses.)*

Indeed, Baltimore, a newly minted graduate student at M.I.T., quickly acquired his brash but brilliant and innovative reputation. In 1960, Baltimore moved to Cambridge, Massachusetts, to enter graduate school at the prestigious Massachusetts Institute of Technology (M.I.T.), focusing his studies on the topic of Biology. Having met Dr. Cyrus Levinthal, from M.I.T., while participating as an undergraduate in a summer program at Cold Spring Harbor Laboratory, in New York, Baltimore chose to work in Levinthal's research laboratory. At first, he studied phage genetics, joining a project devoted to assessing whether an individual phage had one or more chromosomes and examining the amount of genetic information contained within the phage genome.

For his Ph.D. thesis project, Baltimore had instead decided to focus on animal viruses, that is, viruses that infect higher organisms. A major problem at the time, however, was that no faculty at M.I.T. had expertise in the field of animal virology. Thus, Baltimore spent a summer at the Albert Einstein School of Medicine, studying the animal virology field in the laboratory of Dr. Philip Marcus and in a summer course at the Cold Spring Harbor Laboratory. Having been seemingly rejected by a brand new faculty member, Jim Darnell, at M.I.T. to study animal viruses, Baltimore thus transferred to Rockefeller University and entered the research laboratory of Dr. Richard Franklin, who had a laboratory devoted to the study of viruses that infect animals at the institution.

4. *He moved to Rockefeller Institute in New York City–another quiet place of study, but one that produced many great discoveries and soaring staggering intellects. What did he study there? What is an RNA replicase, and what did he do his Ph.D. on?*

At Rockefeller, Baltimore concentrated on viruses that contained RNA as their genomes, such as influenza virus, Newcastle virus, and in particular, the mengovirus, which infects mice. The synthesis of RNA had been detected in the cytoplasm of mice cells in culture but was lacking in the nuclei of the cell; it had been an observation made in the laboratory by a student intern, Jon Rosner. Following up on this observation, Baltimore reasoned that the viral RNA was synthesized by machinery that functioned in the cytoplasm, circumventing standard RNA synthesis machinery contained within the cell's nucleus.

In late 1962, Baltimore decided the best approach was to purify the viral RNA polymerase, also called RNA replicase. It had been laborious, painstaking work. It was work that was also fraught with microbial or chemical contamination, either of which could easily confound any one of the many steps involved in the protein purification process.

During the course of his Ph.D. thesis work at Rockefeller, Baltimore managed, however, to make a startling discovery. He accumulated evidence for an RNA polymerase that needed RNA as a starting substrate, strongly implicating the presence of a protein that was an RNA-dependent RNA polymerase! Typically, according to the central dogma, RNA synthesis depended on DNA as a starting substrate. Baltimore was proposing that RNA could be made with RNA as a starting substrate. The notion, in a sense, had violated the central dogma! Nevertheless, Baltimore and Dr. Franklin published the work together in 1962. In the end, however, he was not successful in completely purifying the elusive RNA replicase.

Satisfied with having discovered the presence of the mengovirus RNA replicase activity, although the purification of the actual protein would not happen for another 15 years, Baltimore nevertheless, moved on to another project while a Ph.D. student at Rockefeller. He turned his attention to another RNA-based virus, namely that of poliovirus, the causative agent of the potentially harmful poliomyelitis in humans. At the time, polio, as it was colloquially referred to, was wreaking havoc worldwide, causing severe outbreaks, with devastating consequences. Very quickly, Baltimore was able to discover another RNA replicase enzyme activity in the poliovirus.

Following up on his poliovirus RNA replicase discovery, Rockefeller graduate student Baltimore and postdoctoral colleagues Drs. Igor Tamm and H.J. Eggers, next examined the effect of the poliovirus on the host cells, in this case, the famous HeLa cells, with respect to the protein synthesis machinery. They found that poliovirus shut down HeLa cell translation and replaced it with a completely different poliovirus-directed mode of translation. The trio of investigators published three articles in scientific journals. It was a ground-breaking work.

At about this time, an event occurred that was to change the direction of Baltimore's education.

His graduate advisor, Dr. Franklin, had decided to leave Rockefeller, heading for a new post at Colorado. This constituted a unique and unprecedented problem for Baltimore. The choice was to either follow Dr. Franklin to his new location or graduate somehow with his Ph.D. thesis as it stood. Because of Baltimore's work ethic, he had already accumulated 4 papers worth of data, certainly enough for a Ph.D. The problem, however, was that Baltimore had been at Rockefeller for only 18 months, which was considered by the university insufficient time for a proper Ph.D.

Rather than choosing to "write slowly" his thesis for a few additional years and bide his time, he simply left Rockefeller, in 1963, and headed for a postdoctoral position at M.I.T. to work under Dr. Jim Darnell. It is recorded that Dr. Baltimore was granted the Ph.D. from Rockefeller in 1964, which was a couple of years *after* he had already left the institution for postdoctoral training.

5. *He later studied with Jerard Hurwitz at the Albert Einstein College of Medicine– delving into virus replication and studied enzymology– for the uninitiated, could you first tell us exactly what enzymology is?*

Briefly, enzymology is the study of enzymes, which are proteins that catalyze biochemical reactions in living beings. Enzymes work by binding to a dedicated substrate to conduct a chemical reaction upon the substrate, producing a product at the end of the biochemical process. The enzymes will conduct their particular biochemical reactions repeatedly, performing the same reaction over and over, a result of their catalytic activities. Thus, the enzymes can function efficiently over time, producing a high concentration of product from their substrates.

The enzymes in biological systems also permit chemical reactions to proceed without the requirement for the extremely high temperatures that are typically needed for conventional chemical reactions in a scientific laboratory. The enzymes can function at relatively lower temperatures, like 37°C, average body temperatures, such as those seen in humans and other animals. Thus, the enzyme activities allow living beings to conduct their needed biochemistry reactions without being also burnt to death in the process!

In 1964, at the Albert Einstein College of Medicine, in the Bronx neighborhood of New York City, Dr. Baltimore took on a postdoctoral position working under the supervision of Prof. Jerard (Jerry) Hurwitz. Interestingly, it was at about this time that Baltimore's Ph.D. degree arrived in the mail, after having been a postdoctoral fellow for several years at M.I.T. in Cambridge, MA. Dr. Baltimore's interest in learning enzymology had been based on his earlier work with the RNA replicase enzyme, which he had not yet purified. He had nevertheless already determined the conditions for RNA synthesis, in Dr. Darnell's M.I.T. laboratory.

At the Einstein College of Medicine, Dr. Baltimore, in particular, had had an interest in the enzyme responsible for making DNA, a protein called DNA polymerase. After several months of work, his efforts to determine for the first time in history the necessary conditions for the initiation of DNA synthesis had failed. In an effort to make the starting conditions known, Dr. Baltimore played with various temperatures, with various concentrations of substrates, the nucleotides that were supposed to come together to make DNA, with various pH levels, etc. He could not get his experiments to start making DNA. All of these laboratory efforts had led nowhere.

During these difficult times, Dr. Baltimore had taken sanctuary in Dr. Darnell's laboratory, now housed at the Albert Einstein College of Medicine, having moved there from M.I.T., studying the poliovirus, an effort that ultimately led to the publishing of a small number of papers in journals. Thus, Dr. Baltimore was able to establish a certain level of productivity even in uncertain times with his other failed DNA experiments.

Thus, Dr. Baltimore turned his attention to the synthesis of RNA, likewise focusing on the initiation of the synthetic process. Dr. Baltimore was able to add some purified RNA polymerase enzyme that he had borrowed from one of his colleagues in his boss's laboratory, plus some borrowed substrates, which consisted of radioactively labeled ribonucleotides. The new effort proved successful. With a short row about who deserved the most credit for the discovery occurring between the three investigators, they agreed to share authorship of the publication.

Though Dr. Baltimore had failed to learn the secret to initiating DNA synthesis, the mystery was indeed solved in later years by others. The problem had been that during the reaction mixture, Dr. Baltimore had been unaware (as had every other scientist up to that time) of the reaction's requirement for RNA! During DNA synthesis, RNA was found to be needed as a primer. RNA was another requirement, and, in fact, the term is now referred to as an RNA primer. RNA as a primer was needed in order to make DNA. It was, perhaps, evolution's way of maintaining the biological relevance for RNA once the ancient RNA world gave way to the new DNA world of life.

Interestingly, it was at about this time that Dr. Baltimore learned of a new opportunity to work with the great scientist Dr. Renato Dulbecco, who was soon to move to the newly constructed Salk Institute, housed in the city of La Jolla, in California. The new institute was established in honor of the famous Jonas Salk, who had developed the beneficial polio vaccine.

Thus, in 1965, Dr. Baltimore cut short his enzymatic misadventures at Albert Einstein College of Medicine and moved to southern California, taking his brand new wife, Sandra Woodward, with him. Unfortunately, the marriage to Woodward was short-lived.

6. *Another career move followed to the Salk Institute for Biological Sciences in La Jolla California – what happened there?*

Dr. Baltimore and his wife Sandra moved to La Jolla, CA, in order to pursue a research associate position under Prof. Renato Dulbecco, who, in 10 years' time, would win the Nobel along with Drs. Baltimore and Temin. The new post would provide some freedom for the first time to pursue his own independent line of biomedical research.

Dr. Marc Girard, whom Dr. Baltimore had recruited as his very first postdoctoral fellow to come to the Salk Institute, had studied the process involved in the synthesis of RNA in the poliovirus. Soon Dr. Baltimore hired his first graduate student, Michael Jacobson, to advise directly while starting out at the Salk Institute. Dr. Baltimore hired another postdoctoral fellow, Dr. Alice Huang, originally from China, but fresh from earning her doctorate at the prestigious Johns Hopkins University, having studied the vesicular stomatitis virus. Jacobson was charged with examining the synthesis of protein in poliovirus, and Dr. Huang was charged with studying the interplay between the poliovirus itself and its host cells.

In 1965, an exciting episode occurred at the Salk. It had to do with the overabundant production of live poliovirus necessary to study its protein synthesis and cellular infection. Other investigators at the Salk grew nervous at the thought of live and potentially infectious poliovirus being produced in vast quantities in the Baltimore lab. Even though all of the personnel at the Salk Institute had been dutifully vaccinated against the dreaded polio, many at the Salk nevertheless personally knew of someone who had previously contracted the severe paralytic form of the disease, and they were somewhat jittery of the poliovirus work coming out of the Baltimore lab. Furthermore, they regularly made their concerns known. To make matters worse, these concerns were present in light of an outbreak that had occurred in 1962, involving a poorly produced batch of the polio vaccine. Dr. Baltimore had lamented that his Salk colleagues, most of whom studied phage biology and who knew little of animal virus biology, were unnecessarily nervous.

The studies conducted in the Baltimore lab nevertheless were fruitful. First, they discovered that during protein synthesis in poliovirus-infected cells, the viral protein was produced as one giant polypeptide, with all of the inherent viral proteins attached to each other in tandem. The giant polypeptide, once it was complete, would then be broken up into various smaller pieces, each piece constituting a functional viral protein, making as many as 10 new fully functional poliovirus proteins. It had been a fantastic discovery of quite a remarkable mechanism for protein synthesis. No one else in the world had ever seen such a similar ground-breaking discovery.

With Dr. Baltimore's scientific life producing beautiful results with a terrible virus, his personal life was becoming a shambles. He had become involved in more political and anti-Vietnam War protests, and his wife's art show had been unceremoniously shut down due to an offensive display involving the U.S. flag; his marriage to Woodward was at an end. To make matters worse, a job interview at Harvard had been a disaster, having failed to get along with the departmental chair, and as a consequence, no professorship offer would be forthcoming from Harvard.

In despair, Dr. Baltimore made a phone call to his longtime friend Dr. Salvador Luria, who then made arrangements for Dr. Irwin Sizer from M.I.T. to readily make a job offer to Dr. Baltimore. In 1968, Dr. Baltimore moved to M.I.T. to become a new associate professor of Microbiology.

7. *Way above my head – he studied proteolytic processing in the synthesis of eukaryotic proteins – why is this important to understand?*

The process you speak of is of tremendous interest to protein biochemists, molecular biologists, and virologists alike. The so-called proteolytic processing during eukaryotic protein synthesis has to do with the discovery that Dr. Baltimore made while he had been at the Salk Institute. It involved a newly discovered protein synthesis mechanism that no other scientist in the world had ever known about.

In short, the process involves the making of one large protein, called a polypeptide, which is made during the translation of poliovirus. The large protein is then cleaved into pieces, i.e., proteolytically processed. It is called as such because various other proteins are involved in breaking down the large protein into several smaller proteins, each of which in turn can function.

As you may have deduced, the poliovirus harbors an RNA-based genome. But what may not be known is that the RNA genome is covered by a large protein called a protein coat or a capsid. The viral capsid is a macromolecule, and it is made up of a large number of small proteins. The poliovirus virion (i.e., intact mature virus) is also made up of a number of other proteins in its viral structure, and it has other functional proteins that are needed for other purposes, such as infection of host cells, especially cells that constitute brain neurons.

The virus has solved the problem of having to make one massively huge protein supra-molecule to cover its RNA genome, which, by the way, is way too small to accommodate a giant-sized gene that would be needed encode such a supra-protein anyhow. The solution to the problem (not enough genomic RNA from which to make a supra-sized capsid molecule), was invented by the poliovirus, and was discovered by Dr. Baltimore, is to make as large a protein as it can simply, and then cut it into smaller proteins. The smaller proteins can be used inside the host neuron to assemble into the larger viral capsid, like stacking small bricks to construct a massive wall—only the protein wall covers an RNA genome in the poliovirus. Other smaller proteins can help perform other needed duties for the complete virion to manifest itself in large numbers.

The process invented by the poliovirus and discovered by Dr. Baltimore and colleagues is as follows. Viral RNA is used as a template from which to produce the giant protein using host neuronal eukaryotic translation machinery. The result is the production of an unprecedentedly large macro-sized protein, called a polyprotein precursor, consisting of three domains called P1, P2, and P3. Then, proteolytic processing takes place. This involves the cutting of the polyprotein precursor by protease enzymes into two smaller pieces, called P1 and P2-P3, the latter of which has the two domains, P2 and P3 still attached, but with the P1 piece becoming a separate entity. The breaking up of the large proteins into smaller sections is referred to as proteolytic processing.

Next, P1 peptide is, in turn, broken down by protease enzymes into three smaller pieces called VP0 (for viral protein 0), VP1, and VP3. Then VP0 is further cut into pieces called VP2 and VP4.

Then, the still connected P2-P3 domain polypeptide is cut up by protease enzymes. The P2 domain is broken down into smaller portions called 2A, 2B, and 2C. On the other hand, the P3 domain is cut into two smaller parts, called 3AB and $3CD^{pro}$. The 3AB protein is also called VPg, and it binds to the front end of the RNA genome, possibly serving a role in the initiation of RNA synthesis. The $3CD^{pro}$ is further cut into $3C^{pro}$ and $3D^{pol}$.

Each of these small end-point proteins harbors specialized functional viral proteins that help poliovirus infect a brain cell. For instance, the VP1, VP2, and VP3 proteins assemble together like toy Legos to make the capsid outer covering to protect the poliovirus RNA genome on the inside. Interestingly, some of the proteases that cut up the viral proteins into their smaller fragments are themselves a part of these protein pieces. These latter proteases are $2A^{pro}$ and $3C^{pro}$. This amazing viral process for infection is regularly included in textbooks of molecular biology and virology.

8. *His wife Alice S. Huang worked with him at MIT and a grad student at the time, Martha Stampfer uncovered that VSV involved an RNA polymerase in the virus. Why is this important, and what is it all about?*

Dr. Baltimore's second wife, Dr. Alice Huang, was the second postdoctoral fellow to be hired to work in the Baltimore laboratory at the Salk Institute. She was born in Nanchang in Kiangshi, China. For her graduate work at Johns Hopkins, Dr. Huang had studied the mode of cellular infection by the so-called vesicular stomatitis virus (VSV). The VSV was a causative agent of a notorious disease in cattle. When Dr. Baltimore accepted a new post at the M.I.T., in 1968, Dr. Huang accompanied him. As a newly minted associate professor at M.I.T., Dr. Baltimore hired his first graduate student, Ms. Martha Stampfer, in 1969. Together, the Baltimore-Huang-Stampfer research team decided to examine a so-called "interesting property" of the VSV, an endeavor that would ultimately lead to the Nobel Prize.

The property of interest was that the VSV microbe had an RNA genome that was negative- or anti-sense. That is, the RNA strand that made up the VSV genome was of the complementary sense to a normal positive- or sense-strand that was typical of the poliovirus genome or of the RNA found in humans and other animals. It posed a problem if one was interested in knowing how the VSV genome replicated itself when infecting host cells.

One could argue that the RNA polymerases found in human and animal cells are all of the so-called DNA-dependent kind, that is, that they needed a DNA template as a starting substrate. Thus, the VSV obviously required an RNA-dependent RNA polymerase in order to produce a positive-sense RNA product from the negative-sense RNA template strand. It then stood to reason that the VSV virion must harbor just such a bizarre enzyme. That is to say, the VSV must carry inside its capsid a so-called RNA replicase, which could make a positive-stranded RNA product by reading the negative-stranded RNA viral genome. This notion made sense because no animal cell known to mankind had hitherto (or since) been found with an RNA-based RNA replicase. Thus, the virus itself must carry it!

The trio of investigators had heard about a new theory that had been proposed by Dr. Howard Temin, Dr. Baltimore's good friend from the Cold Spring Harbor days. He had proposed that such viruses, with their positive-sense RNA genomes, integrated into the DNA-based genomes of their hosts, thus, implicating a DNA intermediate nature for viral RNA genomic replication, thus contributing to the host cancer-causing result. In order to make this hypothesis tenable, Dr. Temin had thus proposed the idea of a so-called RNA-dependent DNA polymerase, which was believed to require RNA as a starting point for the production of viral DNA. He was proposing the reverse of transcription, i.e., RNA being converted to DNA! He even had provided some preliminary experimental evidence to support the idea.

The implications were enormous; it suggested that in making more RNA, the RNA viruses would go first through a DNA intermediate, strongly implicating the notion that there must also be a reverse of transcription, i.e., a reverse transcriptase! Needless to say, Dr. Temin's idea was widely and quite vigorously criticized, especially if reverse transcription by viruses somehow also involved carcinogenesis.

The idea for viral genomic integration into host genomic DNA was not entirely farfetched. Dr. Allan Campbell had hypothesized just such a phenomenon for a bacteriophage called lambda (λ) and its viral genomic DNA insertion into the genome of its dedicated host, *Escherichia coli*. In fact, Dr. Renato Dulbecco, future co-Nobel Laureate, was eventually to provide evidence demonstrating the integration of oncogenic viral DNA into host genomic DNA.

Nevertheless, Dr. Baltimore decided to test the idea that had been hypothesized by the brilliant Dr. Temin. The Baltimore laboratory at M.I.T. examined the insides of the VSV and of the Rous sarcoma virus (RSV), another RNA-based virus with an RNA genome, and they found a DNA polymerase enzyme in both viruses! They quickly wrote a manuscript describing the historical discovery and sent it to *Nature*. Next, Dr. Baltimore called Dr. Temin on the phone and told him of the shocking news: a tumor-causing RNA virus harbors a DNA polymerase inside of it! What Dr. Baltimore didn't know at the time of the phone call was that Dr. Temin had already discovered the same sort of thing, telling all who would listen at a scientific conference only days prior to the call—he had yet to write the paper on his discovery. Another phone call was made, this time to the editor of *Nature*, so that each of the investigators could publish their own respective works in the same issue of the journal.

They would share the discovery of the famous reverse transcriptase! It was a discovery that altered the course of history for all concerned molecular biologists.

9. Please tell us about the Rous sarcoma virus – and its importance and his involvement with this.

The Rous sarcoma virus has its scientific roots embedded in 1911 the studies of Dr. Peyton Rous, who had provided evidence that the virus was associated with causing solid tumors of the cancerous type within laboratory chickens. This finding, viral causation for cancer, led to an ultimate understanding of the cellular and molecular bases of cancer in modern times. The biology of cancer is now a large, complex, ongoing field of contemporary study. Dr. Baltimore's contributions to this field consist of three fundamental principles.

First, he discovered a DNA polymerase enzyme packaged inside of the intact virion of the Rous sarcoma virus, which had an RNA genome. Second, his virology work led to the development of a virus classification scheme based on their modes of transcription and genomic nucleic acid replication. In fact, the scheme is called the Baltimore classification of viruses, and it is gathering widespread acceptance amongst the virologists.

Third, Dr. Baltimore's studies led to the use of the Rous sarcoma virus as a molecular tool for other studies. One prime example of this type of study involved the so-called insertional activation mechanism for generating new tumors. In this system, the Rous sarcoma virus was used to insert its genome into the genomes of host cells, thus breaking the genes encoding cellular "off-switches" for cell growing functions. The Rous sarcoma virus genome would insert itself into the middle of these checkpoint genes, keeping them from preventing cell growth when they were supposed to and, thus, allowing unchecked cellular growth, i.e., tumorigenesis. Such an insertional activation mechanism has been thought to have played a role in an unwanted induction of leukemia after gene therapy had been used to treat a particular genetic disease. It had been a terribly unfortunate incident, and it set back the progress towards genetic disease treatment. The incident meant that biomedical scientists and clinicians had to go back to the drawing board and learn more immunology and virology.

The Rous sarcoma virus was used to test the notion that during the tumorigenic transformation of healthy cells into potential cancer cells that such tumors and cancers lose an essential property called contact inhibition. That is, when healthy cells grow, they then later stop growing when they have made physical contact with neighboring cells in culture. On the other hand, cells that are transformed by Rous sarcoma virus continue growing despite making contact with their cellular neighbors. Such tumors simply pile up into large masses of clumped cells, having lost their contact inhibition property.

Later studies by 1989 Nobel Laureates Drs. Harold Varmus and J. Michael Bishop showed that the loss of contact inhibition is due to a Rous sarcoma virus gene called *src*, which is a rather famous gene amongst molecular biologists, virologists, biochemists, cancer biologists, and biomedical scientists. The name "src" was derived from the sarcoma name of the virus. The *src* gene is known to encode a protein tyrosine kinase enzyme, which in healthy cells is referred to as *c-src*. It was also a good proto-oncogene in the sense that its gene product, a protein called c-Src, dependably halted cell growth, when it was supposed to. The "c" in the *c-src* gene and the c-Src protein stands for normal cellular functions. The growth of healthy cells was regulated by the c-Src protein. On the other hand, the oncogenic version of the *src* gene, a mutated variant, called *v-src,* did not regulate cell growth. The "v" in *v-src* and v-Src stand for virus, having been discovered residing within the genome of the famous Rous sarcoma virus.

10. What was the big idea or central dogma of genetic theory that Baltimore overturned?

The central dogma, the big idea, known now in modern times as the flow of genetic information, refers to the direction of the genetic information stored in genomes of all organisms. The central dogma term is a historical expression meant to denote the fact that early molecular biologists brazenly believed in its basic tenets despite a noticeable lack of evidence to support the notion, i.e., a dogma. The expression "central" takes its meaning from the idea that the genome made up of DNA is central to life, the blueprint for conferring life and in maintaining it through the generations.

In the central dogma scheme, the genetic information is stored in DNA, and it is replicated into another DNA copy, which is then sent to the next generation of individuals. Furthermore, the genetic information in DNA is also transcribed into an RNA form, making RNA as an intermediate. The genetic information now in the form of RNA is then translated into protein, which in turn directs the cellular and molecular functions of living beings. In this scheme, the direction of information flow was clear: DNA → RNA. This was the very basis of transcription, RNA synthesis.

Drs. Temin and Baltimore were now asserting that genetic information was flowing in the opposite direction, i.e., RNA → DNA! It was the REVERSE of transcription! Their very notion of a reverse transcription had violated the direction of information flow inherent within the central dogma itself. It deeply upset all of the molecular and cellular biologists virtually. Drs. Temin and Baltimore had committed a scientific heresy of sorts.

In the end, we know now, of course, that the experimental evidence in favor of reverse transcription is overwhelming. But at the time, when it was published in 1970, it was heresy. Converts emerged, albeit slowly. The universal acceptance of reverse transcription was complete with the 1975 Nobel award to Profs. Baltimore, Temin, and Renato Dulbecco.

11. Baltimore's Nobel Prize (with Howard Temin and Renato Dulbecco) was for, and I quote, "for their discoveries concerning the interaction between tumor viruses and the genetic material of the cell." Why is this important?

The implications are enormous. On the face of it, the connection between viruses, especially those causing tumors, and the biological elements of a regular cell, speak to their tremendous potential effects on all living beings on Earth. In this case, the Nobel is most certainly warranted. The discoveries by Drs. Baltimore, Temin, and Dulbecco have ramifications across all living beings.

First, the interactions between tumorigenic viruses and host cell genomes speak to the fundamental processes that occur in living systems. It speaks to life itself. The viral-host interaction is at the forefront of life and non-life. Many scientists are actually uncertain whether viruses can be considered living microbes or non-living aggregates of complex molecules consisting mainly of nucleic acids and proteins. In any case, viruses are at the cusp of what constitutes life. A fundamental question that has moved many generations of scientists is, "what is life?" In a sense, many biomedical scientists are just as fundamentally affected by such curiosities.

Second, viruses can cause cancers. Therefore, we need to know how they do so. Importantly, we must know how to stop these viruses and to prevent them from causing cancers in the first place. Such interests lead to serious effort in conducting biomedical investigations by scientists, trying to find anti-cancer treatments, such as chemotherapy, or immunology and vaccines, in an attempt to thwart the oncogenic onset before they take hold of an individual.

Another ramification involves the use of the molecular biological information gleaned from studies involving the effects of viruses upon host cells. For example, the reverse transcription phenomenon now widely accepted by biomedical scientists, is actually routinely used in scientific laboratories worldwide as a fundamental molecular-based method. The reverse transcription is used to discern new genes that perform desired cellular functions, such as making products we need, e.g., medicines, vitamins, gasoline, plastics, bioremediation, etc.

The procedure of using reverse transcription, i.e., making DNA from RNA, to find new genes that conduct useful processes can be invoked as follows. First, cells that are performing a useful process, e.g., insulin-making, can be grown, and their RNA harvested. Presumably, the cellular RNA represents the transcribed genes from DNA that encode the useful process, e.g., insulin-making. Next, reverse transcriptase is used to convert the cellular RNA into a double-stranded version of DNA. The newly made DNA is often called copy DNA (cDNA). The cDNA is then cloned, sequenced, expressed into proteins, and the gene products purified. The products are then studied biochemically and examined functionally. The proteins can be tweaked by mutagenesis to perform the processes more efficiently. However, the method is used, the new products can be produced readily and used clinically (insulin), or industrially, or biotechnologically, etc. The possibilities can be endless.

12. *Along the way, Baltimore held a host of other administrative positions, leaving one to wonder how the heck he could have accomplished as much as he did–your final thoughts?*

That is a most interesting question. I think that if we all knew the answer to your inquiry, biomedical scientists, and scientists all over the world, would be invoking these solutions straight away, attempting to make great discoveries and perhaps even garnering a Nobel for themselves. It is widely considered amongst scientists in general that a Nobel cannot be planned from the outset. As a college student, Baltimore and his fellow classmates, living in the Mary Lyons dormitory, at Swarthmore, spent many an evening and night discussing this very possibility. They reckoned that a Nobel could be garnered if one played their cards correctly. They played their cards, and it worked for Baltimore.

The young Swarthmore students deduced that if one were to win the Nobel, it would require creativity that was spent at a very early stage in their research careers. This particular avenue was so important, in Baltimore's mind, that during one of his premiere autobiographical reviews, he specifically mentioned how. He wrote that when he received the Nobel, he was only 37 years of age. He had already been conducting research for approximately 14 years at the time. He was already a full professor, and he received his first NIH grant when he was only 28 years old. Today Dr. Baltimore has lamented that many of these hallmarks in a scientist's career come along many years later during one's lifetime. The average first-time recipient of a grant from the NIH is approximately 42 years of age. Many principal investigators do not garner a tenure-track assistant professorship until they are well into their thirties. Dr. Baltimore explicitly states that if more independence were given to biomedical scientists and at a much younger age, they might, too, benefit from their own creativeness and make great discoveries, just as well.

Another notion, noticed by Baltimore, was that he paid attention to the literature published by pioneers of molecular biology, for instance, he read review articles about great discoveries by their actual discoverers. He also met many of these early pioneers in person, and he learned a great deal about the art of conducting science from their examples.

There is another issue that is inherent in your question, namely, that of how, with all the associated administrative duties, was Baltimore able to make so many distinctive and vital discoveries. This is, not surprisingly, a more difficult question. Dr. Baltimore seemed to make it look easy. In many of Dr. Baltimore's scientific investigations, however, he conducted more than one at any given time. Furthermore, he relied on back-up projects, many of which he conducted in laboratories of his friends and colleagues. He also relied upon many of the techniques, practices, and strategies that he acquired early on in his career.

Many Nobel laureates explicitly state that luck played a major role in their discoveries. One has to be leery of such seemingly awkward attempts to be humble. The fact of the matter is hard work, insight, creativity, time management, being in the right place at the right time, learning from the examples of pioneers and other great scientists, funding opportunities, and, yes, a certain degree of luck, all certainly come into play when making great scientific discoveries happen. Such strategies that are geared towards the garnering of scientific success, and of a Nobel in particular, are tremendously challenging to plan ahead of time.

For more information go to:

https://www.youtube.com/watch?v=X-woQ6fgD4I
https://www.youtube.com/watch?v=skC7XgkpAD8
https://www.youtube.com/watch?v=2o-t3vugqTc

Chapter 4

FREDERICK BANTING – INSULIN

1. *Professor Varela– we have heard those terrifying words– often misunderstood by non-medical personnel– and those words are DIABETES. First of all, I know there are different types– but could you elaborate on these different types (Type 1, Type 2)?*

Professor Shaughnessy, a medical disease called diabetes, has been a scourge for centuries. In many developed countries, it's considered a significant health problem, affecting approximately 5 percent of the world's human population. Diabetes can be defined in patients as having an excess of the sugar called glucose in the blood. The technical name for the illness is diabetes mellitus, in which the term diabetes itself refers to the excessive urination exhibited by patients, whereas the term Mellitus refers to the Latin phrase "sweetened with honey," as diabetic patients can have detectable sugar in their urine.

Diabetes is a complicated clinical disease involving many aspects pertaining to the function and behavior of the human body. These aspects include diet, obesity, metabolism, biochemistry, autoimmunity, chronic inflammation, genetics, infection, and medicine.

As you mentioned in your question above, there are, in general, two types of diabetes, type 1 and type 2. Type 1 diabetes is generally known as insulin-dependent diabetes mellitus (IDDM). Type 2 diabetes is also known as non-insulin-dependent diabetes mellitus (NIDDM) and insulin-resistant diabetes. Both clinical conditions of diabetes are characterized by abnormal glucose metabolism in which the blood levels of this sugar are elevated above normal concentrations.

Type 1 diabetes typically arises in patients early on in their lifetimes. It affects approximately 0.2 percent of children in the U.S., an incidence rate that has actually doubled in the 20 years between 1999 and 2019. Type 1 diabetes is an autoimmune based disease. The body seeks out its own pancreas and destroys the insulin-making islet cells. Thus, type 1 diabetics cannot produce insulin, and it is, thus, required as a daily treatment.

The type 2 diabetes often manifests itself in the latter stages of a patient's life. The so-called adult onset of type 2 diabetes is stunning in its incidence and represents a severe public health concern. Approximately 90% of clinical diabetes is of the type 2 variety, and it affects 9% of the world's population and 10% of the U.S. population. Furthermore, throughout the U.S., it is a significant cause of kidney malfunction, blindness, and amputation. Obesity and chronic inflammation are closely linked with type 2 diabetes. In recent years, however, infection involving *Staphylococcus aureus* bacteria has also been associated with the onset of type 2 diabetes.

Treatment for diabetes can be somewhat different depending upon whether the patient has type 1 or type 2 diabetes. For type 1 diabetes, treatment lasts a lifetime of the patient and includes activities like daily insulin injections, monitoring the sugar concentration in the blood, and eating a proper diet with regular exercise. The daily insulin dosage will invariably depend upon the individual situation for each patient.

For type 2 diabetic patients, treatment involves the management of the illness. This includes maintaining a low weight, eating a proper and healthy diet, exercising regularly, monitoring blood sugar concentrations, and perhaps medication such as insulin and other medications. These other medications may be used for decreasing glucose synthesis in the liver and enhancing the body's reaction to insulin so that the insulin is used efficiently. Some medications will stimulate more insulin production by the pancreas. A more recent medication is represented by a class of drugs called SGLT2 inhibitors, which are used to prevent the uptake of sugar into the blood. These medications inhibit the activity of a glucose transporter (called SGLT2) in humans.

2. *First, let's talk about sugar–how is sugar related to diabetes first of all, and then how sugar is related to insulin?*

In general, insulin is a protein hormone that regulates the appropriate levels of sugar in the blood. In diabetes, however, blood sugar levels are elevated, producing symptoms of the disease.

In type 1 diabetes, elements of a patient's own immune system will attack their own body. This so-called autoimmunity is not a normal process. In this case, it's the patient's insulin-producing cells, called beta cells (β-cells) of the pancreas, which are targeted for attack and are destroyed. The pancreatic β-cells have also been referred to as the islets of Langerhans. The attacking autoimmune cells are the individual's own cytotoxic T-lymphocytes (CTLs), which are a form of white blood cells that are generally used by the body's immune system to target and destroy harmful antigens. In the case of diabetes, however, the autoantigens are the individual's own useful, life-necessitating, pancreatic cells, and their destruction by the auto-CTLs is a severe pathological process. These autoimmune system cells, the auto-CTLs, invade the pancreas and turn on a patient's own macrophages, a condition known as insulitis.

The macrophage activation, in turn, stimulates an immune system-based reaction, called a delayed-type hypersensitivity (DTH) process. During the DTH response process, small messenger protein molecules, called cytokines, are released and result in the synthesis of so-called auto-antibodies. This is an abnormal process in which the type 1 diabetic patient's own pancreatic cells are targeted for destruction because the self-antibodies (auto-antibodies) that were produced are specific for the patient's own pancreatic β-cells.

The auto-antibodies can turn on an immune system component called complement, which in turn breaks apart the β-cells into cellular debris. Another part of the destructive process involving the β-cells by the immune system is called antibody-dependent cell-mediated cytotoxicity (ADCC). Whatever the case, complement, or ADCC, the pancreatic β-cells are destroyed, and insulin levels in the blood drop down to abnormally low levels. Consequently, blood glucose levels are elevated, and type 1 diabetes ensues.

In type 2 diabetic patients, their levels of blood insulin are average or maybe even somewhat elevated. However, such type 2 diabetes patients are non-responsive to the blood insulin, which is a condition called insulin resistance. The end result is that blood glucose levels become abnormally elevated.

The type 2 diabetes ailment is also associated with a component of chronic inflammation, which are specific messenger molecules called cytokines. These cytokines are small protein molecules, and there are many of these that are involved in the immune system. In our case, the two cytokines that are of prime importance are called tumor-necrosis factor-alpha (TNF-α) and interleukin-6 (IL-6). The IL-6 and TNF-α cytokines trigger a process called a signal transduction pathway, sometimes called a signaling cascade.

Signaling cascades in general function to activate a physiological system by using an amplification process in which one molecule can activate ten other molecules, and each of these 10 molecules can, in turn, activate 10 more molecules, and so on. The end consequence is a massive physiological function that may be turned on, or perhaps turned off, depending on the process in question. In our case involving type 2 diabetes, one cascade is turned on, and another is, thus, turned off.

The signaling cascade turned on by TNF-α, and IL-6 cytokines is called JNK, for c-Jun N-terminal kinase. Activation of the JNK cascade turns off the insulin receptor signaling (IRS) process. The IRS is customarily supposed to respond to the blood insulin but doesn't in type 2 diabetes. Thus the body is unresponsive to insulin (insulin resistance), and blood glucose levels accumulate to abnormally high levels, producing type 2 diabetes.

3. I have heard the insulin is a type of key that unlocks the door, so to speak. Is this metaphor or analogy correct?

You are spot on with respect to your key-door insulin assessment. Insulin acts in a manner that is akin to a key. The proverbial door, in our case, is a protein that resides embedded in the membranes of fat and muscle cells and is referred to as the glucose transporter, known as GLUT4. That is, the door is GLUT4. Without actually entering the cell, the insulin key works to increase the entry of the GLUT4 transporter door into the cell membrane, where the GLUT4 door can then facilitate the entry of glucose from the blood through the channel hole of the GLUT4 transporter and into the cell for metabolism of the intracellular glucose.

The lock referred to in this particular scenario is another membrane-bound protein called the insulin receptor. Activation of this lock opens up several doors. When extracellular insulin binds to its dedicated receptor (the lock), several doors are opened. The first cellular door opening involves the insertion of the GLUT4 glucose transporter that I mentioned above. The insulin key binds to the insulin receptor lock mechanism and opens up the glucose transporter door. This process permits entry of glucose into the cells so that glucose can be broken down biochemically for the generation of energy. This is a normal life-maintaining process.

This insulin-glucose connection involves certain signal transduction processes. One process is called the phosphoinositide 3-kinase (PI3K) pathway, and its activation by insulin receptor binding by insulin results in the activation of protein kinase B (PKB), which, in turn, permits GLUT4 to move into the plasma membrane of the cell. This GLUT4 transporter (door) insertion into the membrane allows the cell to increase the uptake of glucose. Thus, it's the body's mechanism for lowering blood glucose.

Insulin opens up other doors. These doors serve other important cellular functions. Two of these important doors are discussed in further detail below.

A second consequence (another door) of insulin activation of the PI3K pathway is the triggering of the enzyme activity of glycogen synthase in the liver and muscle. This enzyme activation by insulin involves, however, a different intermediate called glycogen synthase kinase (GSK3). In this process, glycogen synthase is activated by the GSK3. Thus, excess glucose that enters the cell (e.g., via GLUT4) is stored in the form of glycogen.

Another door, a signal transduction process that's activated by insulin and its receptor binding, is called the receptor tyrosine kinase system. Here, the insulin receptor binding by insulin leads to a series of phosphorylation events at the actual insulin receptor itself, the receptor part that's on the inside-facing side of the cell. This so-called auto-phosphorylation (putting phosphates upon itself) of the insulin receptor leads to the activation of a cascade called mitogen-activated protein kinases (MAPK), sometimes called the MAP kinase cascade, which in turn ultimately leads to the turning on of the gene expression systems of over 100 different genes! One grand end-result of this insulin-activated cascade system is the growth of the cell.

Now, I've mentioned above several distinctive ways in which insulin regulates the cellular entry and metabolism of glucose, like in the liver, muscle, and fat cells. Oddly enough, however, glucose can actually regulate the release of insulin from pancreatic cells. In this process, glucose first enters the pancreatic β-cell via a GLUT2 transporter. The glucose then gets metabolized by glycolysis, the Krebs cycle, and undergoes oxidative phosphorylation to generate ATP energy. The ATP then prevents the exit of potassium ions (K^+) from the cell by closing K^+ channels. This K^+ transport inhibition depolarizes the membrane of the pancreas cell, which in turn activates calcium ion (Ca^{2+}) entry into these cells via their dedicated Ca^{2+} channels, called voltage-gated calcium channels. The increased entry of calcium results in the release of insulin from the cell. The insulin had been stored inside vesicles within the pancreas cells. The calcium influx causes the intracellular insulin-containing vesicles to move to the membrane and fuse with it, thus, allowing the secretion of insulin from the pancreatic cells.

4. *Now I have also heard about pre-diabetes and hypoglycemia and hyperglycemia. How do physicians test for this?*

Hypoglycemia is characterized by a lower than normal level of glucose in the blood, and hyperglycemia represents a higher than normal blood glucose level. Both of these glucose levels are considered abnormal. Prior to the development of type 2 diabetes, a phenomenon called insulin resistance can first emerge. In this type of pre-diabetic situation, the patient will require more and more insulin to mediate its biological effects, such as those alluded to above, like the GLUT4 transporter membrane insertion, enhanced glucose uptake into cells, increased glycogen production, etc.

During the initial stages prior to the type 2 diabetes onset, the β-cells of the pancreas are actually able to accommodate the increased requirement for insulin in order to maintain normal levels of blood glucose. Eventually, however, the body will not be able to compensate for the insulin resistance, and the body now enters a so-called metabolic syndrome stage. Others may refer to this stage as syndrome X. In any case, it represents an intermediate state of affairs that is prominent just prior to the onset of type 2 diabetes.

Patients with metabolic syndrome will exhibit obesity, a higher than normal blood pressure, elevated lipid content in the blood, and elevated levels of blood glucose (hyperglycemia). This latter situation can be tested for by physicians by performing a so-called glucose tolerance test. During this test, individuals with metabolic syndrome will have a more difficult time trying to clear glucose from their blood. These patients also have differences in their blood proteins, such as elevated fibrinogen molecules, indicating an abnormal ability with their blood clotting activities. Another abnormal blood protein is C-reactive peptide, indicating that these metabolic syndrome patients exhibit a higher than normal inflammation.

5. *What are the signs and symptoms of Type I and Type II diabetes? And how do they relate to hypoglycemia and hyperglycemia?*

The symptomology of both types of diabetes, type 1 and type 2, is characterized by excessive thirst, frequent urination (the medical term for this condition is polyuria), and considerable water consumption by the patient (the medical term is polydipsia). These symptoms are the result of an overabundant secretion of the sugar glucose into the urine of a patient, which is a medical condition referred to as glucosuria or sometimes glycosuria.

The signs and symptoms of hypoglycemia, low levels of blood glucose, can involve anxiety, tiredness, shakiness, paleness of the skin, sweating, hunger, a feeling of irritability, and an irregular heartbeat (arrhythmia). Prolonged hypoglycemia can further lead to more serious symptoms, such as confusion, difficulty in seeing clearly, seizures, and unconsciousness. These sorts of symptoms of hypoglycemia can be related to diabetes during treatment when a patient is having trouble adjusting their insulin intake.

The signs and symptoms of hyperglycemia are similar to those of hypoglycemia in that they, too, involve hunger, thirstiness, blurred vision, as well as an additional tingling sensation in the patient's feet. The patient may also exhibit headache, fatigue, and frequent urination. Both type 1 and type 2 diabetes patients can exhibit the signs and symptoms of hyperglycemia.

6. *Let's link diabetes and insulin to organs in the human body– what are the specific organs involved?*

As I mentioned above, insulin is produced by pancreatic β-cells (called islets of Langerhans) and that glucose plays an important role in regulating this insulin production by the pancreas. Let's take a look at this relationship in a normal scenario that occurs after the consumption of a meal. Nutrients such as amino acids and sugars in the gut enter the blood and then go to the liver. This presence of glucose is a situation that stimulates the pancreas to produce insulin and to secrete it.

The secreted insulin, in turn, now regulates the intracellular concentration of glucose in fat cells (called adipose tissue), the liver, and in muscle, by reporting the status of glucose in the blood. If the glucose concentrations in the blood are higher than normal, insulin then reports this blood-sugar occurrence and controls the fat, liver, and muscle cells to increase the uptake of glucose, thus lowering the blood glucose to normal levels. Normal levels of glucose are observed to range between 70 and 100 mg/100mL of blood.

In muscle and fat cells, the uptake of glucose, as mediated by the effects of the insulin, results in increased glucose metabolism, and glucose-6-phosphate (G-6-P) is, thus, produced. From this key starting point metabolite, the G-6-P, it can take one of a variety of fateful biochemical routes. Any excess G-6-P that is not used in the muscle can be stored as fat within the adipose tissue.

In liver cells, insulin also regulates the glucose uptake, but in these cells, the G-6-P generated from the excess intracellular glucose that is not used degradatively by glycolysis can then be stored in the form of glycogen.

In brain cells, glucose supplies the energy for neuronal functions. Insulin works in the brain to supply a continual dose of glucose. This is a critical function, as depletion of brain glucose can be quite detrimental to this important organ. Additionally, insulin works in the brain to thwart the hunger feeling by acting on the hypothalamus.

This process works in the following manner. In certain brain cells called orexigenic nerve cells of the arcuate nucleus, insulin binds to the insulin receptor, which prevents the production of a protein called neuropeptide Y. On the other hand, in so-called anorexigenic nerve cells of the brain, insulin binding to its own receptor turns on the production of an α-melanocyte-stimulating hormone (α-MSH), also called melanocortin. Then, the hunger feeling is, thus, alleviated.

Let's take a look now at the disease process. In the case of untreated diabetes, an abnormal process, insulin may be absent (type 1), or the body may be unable to respond to insulin even though it can be present in the blood, i.e., insulin-resistance occurs (type 2). In this type 2 insulin-resistant case, the organs and tissues are affected in ways fundamentally different from that seen after a meal in a normal individual. In essence, the body behaves in a fashion similar to that of prolonged fasting in these uncontrolled type 2 diabetic patients.

The lack of insulin (type 1) or unresponsiveness to the insulin (type 2) results in the cells being unable to mediate the uptake of glucose to use as a fuel for making ATP. This condition can result in a severely detrimental consequence. Cells need glucose in order to survive. Instead, the glucose is aberrantly shunted for excretion, rather than being taken up normally to (and by) the tissues. The resulting lack of cellular glucose requires that the energy for cellular life must now be obtained by other means. Other sources of cellular energy include glucose stored as glycogen in the liver and a little bit left in the muscles. But the main source of energy stores includes a large amount present within fat cells of adipose tissue. It is this latter alternate source of energy, the fatty acids of the adipose, which now constitutes the grand bulk of the required cellular energy.

In untreated diabetics, the fatty acids are now metabolized for energy. The fatty acids are, therefore, broken down by a biochemical pathway called β-oxidation. This β-oxidation process results in the production of massive amounts of a central metabolite called acetyl-coenzyme A (acetyl-CoA), which is then converted into large quantities of ketone bodies, acetoacetate, and β-hydroxybutyrate.

Each of these new metabolites can have unfavorable outcomes in diabetic patients. Let's examine a couple of these metabolic fates, and we'll start with the ketone bodies.

In patients with untreated diabetes, the excess amount of ketone bodies produced is called ketosis. If the ketone bodies are in the blood, it's called ketonemia, and if present in the urine, ketonuria. Ketosis causes the liberation of new protons and results in an excessive condition of acidity, overwhelming the buffering capacity of the blood's bicarbonate system. The consequence of this acid production is a lowering effect on the pH number in the blood, a condition called acidosis. The combination of ketosis and acidosis is often referred to as ketoacidosis.

Further, the acetoacetate can be readily converted to acetone, which is a very small lighter-than-air type of molecule. The acetone may, therefore, be exhaled by diabetic patients, and occasionally, such patients will smell of acetone in their breath; sometimes, the acetone breath is mistaken for alcohol breath. When combined with a very high blood glucose level, acetone breath, and a consequent confused mental state, the untreated diabetic patient is prone to misdiagnosis of alcoholism, rather than of the more appropriate diagnosis of diabetes.

7. *Finally, a bit about Banting–I know he was born in Canada and spent some time in World War II. Can you give us a brief summary of his life and work?*

Frederick Grant Banting was born on the 14th day of November in the year 1891 to Methodist parents Margaret Grant and William Thompson Banting. The Banting family owned a farm near the town of Alliston, Ontario, Canada. Young Frederick was the youngest of five siblings. He completed both elementary and high school in Alliston. After high school, in 1911, he enrolled in Victoria College at the University of Toronto, where he majored at first in divinity. During the course of his undergraduate studies, in 1912, Banting switched his major concentration in order to focus on the study of medicine, and he consequently enrolled in the Faculty of Medicine, a medical school that was also housed at the University of Toronto.

Banting's decision to become a physician was based on two life-changing events that transpired around him. First, he witnessed a roof downfall in which two workers were injured, and Banting was said to have quickly sought help. The responding physicians to the scene were reported to have a calming effect in a seemingly calamitous situation, a response which deeply impressed Banting. The second influential event in Banting's decision to become a medical doctor was the death of one of his very close friends, named Jane, whom Banting watched slowly pass away from the effects of diabetes at the age of 14 years. Banting viewed Jane's untimely death as needless and resolved to study the pathological nature of diabetes.

While in medical school, in 1915, Banting briefly served in an ambulance corps of the Canadian Army Medical Service as a private and later as a sergeant. Dr. Banting earned an M.B. degree (bachelors of medicine) in 1916 after the faculty at the University of Toronto established an accelerated program, allowing medical students, such as Banting, to graduate one year earlier than scheduled.

Dr. Banting held a post as a physician at Granville Hospital, England, until World War I broke out, and he was ordered to serve as a battalion medical officer, in 1918. During Banting's deployment, he was wounded in the battle at Chambrai, earning the Military Cross medal as a result of his valor during the incident. After the war, Banting moved to Toronto, where he worked as a physician intern at the Christie Street Hospital for Veterans, in 1919. Then, in 1920, Banting moved to the Hospital for Sick Children, also in Toronto, Canada. During this time, Banting held a part-time teaching post as a professor at the University of Western Ontario. One of his noteworthy lectures was on the topic of the pancreas, in which his background preparation for the lecture made him a noted expert on the organ. In 1922, Dr. Banting took his M.D. degree from the University of Toronto.

Back in 1920, Banting had formulated a hypothesis that islet cells of the pancreas secrete a substance that could improve the outcome of diabetics. In 1921, Dr. Banting began experiments in the laboratory of Dr. John J. R. Macleod, a professor who was initially skeptical of Banting's idea but nevertheless allowed him (Banting) use of his (Macleod's) facilities, and use of the expertise held by a young laboratory assistant Charles Herbert Best. At the time, Mr. Best had been a recent college graduate who had majored in biochemistry and physiology and was a medical student who had later on taken his doctorate of science (D.Sc.) degree, in 1928. It turned out to be a fortuitous collaboration in 1921 because Dr. Banting provided expert surgical skills, and Mr. Best had expertise in measuring sugar levels in animal blood and urine samples. It has been reported that as they progressed through their collaborative work, each investigator eventually acquired an astute proficiency in each other's mode of expertise (surgery versus physiology).

Meanwhile, in the laboratory, in 1921, Dr. Banting and Mr. Best first ligated the pancreatic ducts in anesthetized dogs, leaving the pancreas to atrophy. From these atrophied pancreases, Dr. Banting and Best made a pancreatic extract material and injected it into another dog who had had its own pancreas surgically removed weeks earlier. This pancreas-free dog had been clearly suffering the artificially induced effects of diabetes, as she (the dog was named Marjorie) had had no pancreas. But with the pancreatic extract injection, Marjorie improved her behavioral condition within the hour, and her blood sugar levels had increased as a result of the extract injection.

The active ingredient in the pancreatic extract was called "isletin" by Dr. Banting because the material that was involved in effectively treating Marjorie had been derived from the islet cells of the pancreatic organ. We now know that the islet of Langerhans consists of β-cells, which produce insulin.

We also know that α-cells (i.e., alpha-cells) of the islet of Langerhans make glucagon, which is synthesized in response to low blood glucose and which in turn lowers insulin production. The δ-cells (delta-cells) of the pancreatic islet of Langerhans produce somatostatin, which inhibits production of insulin and glucagon and which regulates other molecules such as growth hormone and thyroid hormone.

Unfortunately, Dr. Banting's isletin extract was only temporarily successful. The laboratory dogs who had undergone the pancreas removal by using surgery (i.e., pancreatectomy) and were later improved by the injected isletin extract needed more of the life-improving substance. In fact, it also seemed that these diabetic dogs needed the isletin on a continual basis. Dr. Banting had further learned that fetal and newborn animals harbored greater concentrations of pancreatic extracts and that cattle slaughterhouses routinely discarded the embryos of pregnant cows who were going to slaughter. Thus, Dr. Banting was able to obtain these cow embryos (instead of letting them be discarded) as a source of the pancreatic isletin-containing extracts.

Using bovine-derived isletin extracts in the laboratory, Dr. Banting and Mr. Best found that they could improve the behavioral and physiological effects of pancreatectomized dogs, just as well. They recorded in their laboratory notebooks that on July 30, 1921, diabetic dog number 410 who had been injected with the cow isletin showed a dramatic lowering of blood glucose!

Dr. Banting and Mr. Best later repeated the experiment in dog number 92 and found similar outcomes. These findings were to change the course of history. Insulin had been discovered!

Thanks to the investigative work of Dr. Banting, human beings with diabetes could, for the first time in history, actually survive in the face of its terrible effects. Because of insulin, diabetics could live! Moreover, because of Banting's daily insulin, diabetics might possibly be able to lead normal lives. Countless millions of lives have been affected in the most positive way. Accordingly, I consider the discovery of insulin a historic medical achievement of epic proportions.

8. *What have I neglected to ask about diabetes and its relationship to insulin and the discoveries of Banting (and his colleagues?)*

In their notebooks, Dr. Banting and his medical student assistant Charles Best recorded the magnitude of the difficulties encountered in conducting their famous insulin-discovering experiments. For example, the surgical removal of the dog pancreas required a laborious two-step process and which often resulted in many of their laboratory dogs dying from post-surgical infections. The physiological blood-sugar data required careful calculations.

Dr. Macleod had been absent from his laboratory during the summer of 1921 when Dr. Banting and Mr. Best were conducting their famous insulin-discovering experiments. Banting and Best had accumulated a wealth of data. Upon returning to his laboratory, however, Dr. Macleod had challenged their behavioral and physiological data, and he also necessitated further experimentation, in order to confirm their findings. Apparently, Dr. Banting took this response by Dr. Macleod as a personal insult, and the rift it produced would last a lifetime for both biomedical scientists.

Dr. Macleod soon focused his efforts on developing isletin for human use. Furthermore, he changed the name of the life-giving isletin to insulin, a term which had been derived from Latin meaning island. Dr. Macleod collaborated with Dr. James Collip to purify insulin for the treatment of human diabetics.

Another controversy had arisen between Drs. Banting and Macleod. The issue this time had been whether Macleod deserved equal credit for the insulin discovery. Dr. Banting claimed that Dr. Macleod had not participated in their day-to-day experiments during the summer of 1921, while Dr. Macleod countered that he had provided continual guidance during the entire summer that the experiments had been performed.

When, in 1923, the Nobel Prize in Medicine or Physiology had been awarded to both Drs. Banting and Macleod, Banting was chagrined about the Nobel nod to Macleod. Dr. Banting felt that Dr. Macleod did not deserve credit for their insulin discovery. Dr. Banting was further annoyed that Charles Best had been entirely ignored by the Nobel committee, and he shared his half of the prize money with Best. Countering Dr. Banting's annoyance about the Nobel, Dr. Macleod publically announced that Dr. Collip deserved credit just as well, and he then shared *his* (Macleod's) half of the Nobel Prize money with Collip.

Dr. Banting had been the first Canadian and youngest individual at the time, at the age of 32, to receive the Nobel in his category, physiology, or medicine. His discovery has saved the lives of countless millions over the many years since the breakthrough had occurred. However, Dr. Banting had certain aspects of his personal life which were to be publically scrutinized, such as a courtship with, the marriage to, and the divorce from, in 1932, Marion Roberson, after 8 years of marriage. The couple had had one child, William, born in 1929.

In 1934, King George V knighted Dr. Banting. Sir Banting later married Lady Henrietta Elizabeth Ball, in 1939. That same year, Sir Dr. Banting volunteered for active duty in the Royal Canadian Army Medical Corps during World War II. While traveling to England on the 20th night of February, in 1941, the bomber that Banting was flying in, a Lockheed Hudson, went down shortly after takeoff near the eastern coast of Newfoundland. Severely injured, Sir Dr. Banting died of his injuries the next day, on the 21st day of February, in 1941, at the age of 49 years.

For more information go to:

https://www.youtube.com/watch?v=V0_9LzAYLRY
https://www.youtube.com/watch?v=JA7jVqYOf2k
https://www.youtube.com/watch?v=kVG7xlY7xVg

Chapter 5

KONRAD BLOCH – CHOLESTEROL AND FATTY ACID METABOLISM

1. *Professor Varela, Konrad Emil Bloch was born in Germany and studied in Munich – then what happened?*

A 1964 Nobel Laureate in Physiology or Medicine, Dr. Bloch was a famous biomedical scientist who discovered how cholesterol was made naturally in the body. On the 21st day of January, in 1912, Konrad Emil Bloch was born to Jewish parents Fritz (father) and Hedwig Striemer Bloch (mother) in the town of Neisse (presently Nysa), Germany, in the then eastern Prussian province of Silesia, presently Poland.

In Munich, Germany, Bloch was an undergraduate student majoring in chemistry at the Technische Hochschule (technical university). While a university student young Konrad was inspired by a great professor and scientific investigator, Dr. Hans Fischer, who had just earned a Nobel of his own, in 1930, for his work on hemin, hemoglobin, and chlorophyll. It was Prof. Fischer who influenced young Bloch to have an interest in studying the chemistry of naturally occurring molecules, such as fatty acids. As your question alludes, however, there was, at that time, a rather serious problem.

In 1934, Konrad Bloch had just received his so-called Diplom-Ingenieur degree in chemistry when the dean told him that Prof. Hans Fischer could not accept Bloch into his laboratory as a graduate student. Bloch later learned that the dean had lied to him.

No doubt because of Nazi Germany's racial laws, signed into legislation in the early 1930s, the real reason for his rejection had been entirely different than mere rejection by a prominent scientist. Instead, Bloch's graduate school application at the Technische Hochschule was nefariously denied because he was, of course, of Jewish origin. Thus, Konrad Bloch needed to find a new graduate school, and he needed one *quickly* as it turned out, because the German Reich movement was spreading rather swiftly.

Thus, seeking alternatives, Bloch made an inquiry of Prof. A. Butenandt, of the Technische Hochschule at Danzig. Unfortunately, Bloch's plea for graduate school in Danzig was refused there, too.

Next, Bloch sent an application to Prof. F. Kögl, of Utrecht University, at The Netherlands, and Bloch was rebuffed, as well. While this more recent rejection may seem to have been quite unfortunate at the time, because acceptance would have meant being able to leave Germany, it turned out to have two silver linings to it.

First, Holland became occupied by the German Nazis only a few months after his rejection. Thus, even if Bloch had moved there, he would have been trapped in Europe by the Nazis, and it might have been impossible, therefore, to escape the holocaust. Second, in Prof. Kögl's laboratory, they had claimed to have made two rather fantastic discoveries, one pertaining to new plant hormone, called "heteroauxin" purified from horse urine, and the other discovery pertaining to D-amino acids purified from proteins sampled from tumor tissue. Both of these "fantastic discoveries" turned out to have been faked by a laboratory assistant in Kögl's laboratory. The scandal had become public only after World War II had come to an end.

Meanwhile, back in the mid-1930s Nazi Germany era, it was clear to Bloch that he was no longer welcome to pursue graduate education in Germany. Being aware of the anti-Semitic nature of the environment in Germany due principally to Adolf Hitler, his Nazi Party followers, and to the sympathetic general public, Bloch felt that he had no choice but to leave Germany, for good.

Escape from Nazi-occupied Europe, however, did not happen for Konrad Bloch until 1936. The pathway out for Bloch took place by another route.

With Prof. Fischer's blessing, Konrad Bloch found a new position as a laboratory assistant at the Swiss Research Institute at Davos, in neutral Switzerland. In Prof. Frederic Roulet's laboratory there, Bloch was put to work in resolving a conflict.

One idea held that cholesterol could be purified from the lipid material in the human tubercle bacillus, the bacterium called *Mycobacterium tuberculosis,* and the causative agent of tuberculosis. The other idea, supported by the great scientist Dr. Erwin Chargaff, held that such was not the case, that there was no cholesterol in *Mycobacterium tuberculosis*. That is to say, it was not clear whether the bacteria had cholesterol.

Bloch's first experimental work had shown that Prof. Chargaff had been correct. Bloch failed to find cholesterol in the tubercle bacilli. The negative result was disappointing but true. It was never published. Bloch was still trapped in Europe!

Bloch's next project at Davos, in 1935, was to conduct phospholipid chemistry in order to prepare a compound called phosphatide from the *Mycobacterium tuberculosis* bacteria. He was supposed to follow the protocol as devised by Prof. Rudolph J. Andersen, from Yale University. When Bloch's preparation showed more phosphorous and much less nitrogen (in fact, no nitrogen) than was expected, he wrote to Dr. Anderson for advice on what to do next. Dr. Anderson's reply was that Bloch's preparation was probably better than his. The reply from Yale provided the needed courage on Bloch's behalf to write again to Dr. Anderson for the daring purpose of asking him for a job. In his 1987 memoirs, published in the prestigious *Annual Review of Biochemistry*, Bloch writes what happened next.

In his 1987 review, Bloch reveals that, in 1936, he received two immediate replies from Yale. The first letter was from their dean congratulating him on his acceptance as a laboratory assistant in the Biological Chemistry department at their School of Medicine, and the other letter flatly stating that there were absolutely no funds available for the job offer at Yale.

Nevertheless, Konrad Bloch arrived as an immigrant to New Haven, Connecticut, in the U.S., in December of 1936, with his life's savings, which were good enough to live on for a month, but nevertheless making good his escape from Nazi-occupied Europe.

In essence, the immigrant traded his life's savings for his life.

2. *I understand his Ph.D. was from Columbia University in New York City– no mean feat– what did he study there, and what was his major focus?*

Obtaining a graduate education at Columbia University is indeed an impressive accomplishment. Konrad Bloch's Ph.D. from the prestigious institution, however, took a rather circuitous route.

Before having left Europe for good, Bloch had followed the advice of his boss Dr. F. Roulet and attempted to use the work that he (Bloch) had already performed at the Swiss Research Institute in Davos. You'll recall above that Bloch's work at Davos had been carried out in a way that was much improved over the originator of the protocol that was first developed at Yale. The result of Bloch's methodological approach was that he had purified the true product, phosphatidic acid, rather than the expected but elusive (and incorrect) phosphatide from the tubercle bacillus lipid material.

The work, however, left Bloch forever scarred.

You see, Bloch had actually injected himself with the phosphatidic acid preparations, one from the human tubercle bacillus into his left arm and the other from cow tubercle bacillus into his left arm. The injection into the left arm produced a reaction and a scar, two inches in diameter, which stayed with Bloch for the remainder of his life!

Reminiscing about the incident late in life, the elderly Dr. Bloch realized how greatly naïve the younger version of himself had been, apparently not giving a thought back then, in 1936, to the fact that his tubercle bacillus had stayed alive after multiple exposures to the chemical acetone!

Despite the scars, or maybe because of them, Bloch's work at Davos, Switzerland, was published in two peer-reviewed scientific journals. Dr. Roulet's idea that these published works, Bloch's first two scientific articles, might suffice for a Ph.D. project, was put to the test. According to the plan, Bloch would enter graduate school at the University of Basel, in Switzerland, and submit his two papers to the graduate committee for acceptance as a Ph.D. thesis. The plan failed to work.

Bloch's Ph.D. thesis work in 1936 at Basel was rejected by all faculty members of the committee. It had been deemed "insufficient." It was a terrible blow because he now had to go to another school and start all over again!

Years later, returning to Basel as a Nobel Prize Laureate and keynote speaker, he presented a seminar at the same institution and couldn't resist relating this earlier incident to his captivated audience. Interestingly, his host's curiosity at Basel was piqued, and after the seminar, he decided to look up the old records of the now famous 1936 thesis rejection. In the archives, Bloch's host found that the unanimous rejection, in reality, took the form of only one faculty member of the graduate committee having actually voted no. The policy was that if one member voted no, then the rejection was considered unanimous. The lone dissenter had been dissatisfied with the thesis because, in Bloch's two publications, he had failed to cite the dissenter's own papers!

Back at Yale, in early 1937, Dr. Anderson, who was instrumental in providing Bloch the opportunity to escape Nazi Germany as an immigrant to the U.S., had given Bloch more advice. The good professor Anderson told Bloch he wouldn't learn much at Yale and that he should, therefore, go to Columbia and study under Prof. Hans Clarke.

Along with a letter of recommendation that Dr. Fischer in Germany had provided to Bloch, he also provided some advice, which was basically to seek the advice from the distinguished Prof. Max Bergmann, who had studied under Dr. Fischer and had currently been at the Rockefeller Institute for Medical Research, in New York. The great Profs. Bergmann and Anderson were in complete agreement: Bloch should go to Hans Clarke's laboratory at Columbia.

The interview with Dr. Clarke ended in acceptance into graduate school at Columbia University. Bloch attributed his acceptance, perhaps very likely in jest, to the fact that he played the cello, and that Dr. Clarke, who appreciated chamber music, warmly welcomed the new cellist.

Bloch conveyed the good news of his acceptance to his parents and to Profs. Anderson and Bergmann, at which point Bergmann conveyed further good news. Dr. Bergmann told Bloch that he was aware of a promising funding source for Bloch's graduate education!

The source of this funding for graduate school was Dr. Leo Wallerstein, in charge of Wallerstein Laboratories, Inc. Dr. Wallerstein had become quite wealthy, having invented a method for clarifying Lager beer using proteolytic enzymes. The lucrative nature of the invention made Dr. Wallerstein a noted philanthropist who was especially interested in helping young scholars and scientists who were refugees trying to escape war-torn Europe and Nazi Germany. Bloch was awarded a one-year Wallerstein graduate fellowship for graduate study at Columbia.

Unlike the case with the unforgiving Basel graduate committee, Dr. Clarke was happy to accept Bloch's first two papers as sufficient for partial fulfillment of a Ph.D. thesis, but Columbia's policy was that at least *some* of the graduate work had to be performed at Columbia proper. Thus, Dr. Clarke assigned another small project to Bloch.

In Clarke's laboratory at Columbia, Konrad Bloch was charged with making several derivatives based on *N*-alkyl-cysteine, in order to measure how labile the sulfur content was in the products. The project went well, except that at one point, an important product, called *N*-methyl-cysteine hydrochloride, failed to turn into visible crystals, as had been expected. It was considered a setback.

However, with sufficient incubation time being allowed, the expected crystals managed to surface! Now, it was a cause for celebration!

Apparently, prominent scientists, one being the famous Prof. Vincent du Vigneaud at Cornell, had also tried to obtain the important *N*-methyl-cysteine crystals and failed. A gleeful Bloch happily provided the du Vigneaud laboratory at Cornell with some Columbian crystals to use as starter material for the Cornell group. A forever grateful Dr. du Vigneaud paid a visit to Columbia University and thanked Bloch in person.

The *N*-methyl-cysteine work performed at Columbia, along with the phosphatidic acid work performed at Davos, was deemed sufficient for a graduate thesis, and Konrad was granted a Ph.D. from Columbia University, in 1938.

3. *Life took him to Harvard and eventually to the Nobel Prize – can you retrace some of his achievements along the way?*

The road to Harvard was also circuitous. After taking his Ph.D. from Columbia University, in 1938, under Prof. Clarke, the newly minted Dr. Bloch worked briefly with Max Bovarnick in the same lab trying to synthesize a so-called "super hormone," that is, one that took a thyroxin derivative and used it to load up with lots of iodine atoms and phenyl rings. It was hoped that the massive end-product would have potent biological activity. Unfortunately, the super hormone product had no activity.

Next, Dr. Rudolf Schoenheimer, another Columbia University faculty who had been trained earlier with Prof. Anderson at Yale, offered Dr. Bloch a job with him. Prof. Schoenheimer was a young genius who invoked a method for tracing radioactive isotopes through biochemicals in order to elucidate metabolic pathways, an important area of biomedical research. He put Dr. Bloch in charge of making radioactively labeled creatine to trace the nitrogen-15 isotope to creatinine. Next, Dr. Bloch was tasked with attempting to elucidate the biosynthetic pathway for creatine. However, before the second project regarding creatine biosynthesis could be finished, Dr. Bloch received an offer he couldn't refuse.

Dr. Bloch took a higher-paying job in New York at the Mount Sinai Hospital Cancer Research center. It paid twice the salary he had been making at Columbia, and he needed the money in order to afford getting married to Lore Teutsch. A year later, however, Dr. Schoenheimer provided a counteroffer, matching the New York salary. Dr. Bloch had recalled how happy and productive the work had been in Schoenheimer's laboratory, and he eagerly returned to Columbia in 1940.

It is back at Columbia, where Dr. Schoenheimer had asked Dr. Bloch to study cholesterol synthesis now. The question put to them was, where did the oxygen in cholesterol come from? That is, did the oxygen come from water or molecular oxygen (i.e., O_2)? As brilliant as these two hypotheses were (water versus O_2), the project went nowhere. Unfortunately, the mass spectroscopy methodology that was badly needed in order to measure the incorporated oxygen atoms into cholesterol hadn't been invented at the time.

Then, to make matters worse, a terrible disaster happened.

Although Dr. Schoenheimer was a genius, he was also a manic depressive, and on September 11, 1941, he committed suicide. In his wake, he left behind mayhem and uncertainty in the laboratory.

Following the advice of Dr. Hans Clarke, the group that had been left behind thus chose to finish the remaining projects and then study whatever they might so desire afterward. The problem was, however, that no one had actually been in charge of the individual projects in Dr. Schoenheimer's laboratory. It was not certain who would take over each of the various projects. After much discussion, Dr. Bloch got the so-called lipid project; and Dr. D. Rittenberg had gotten the protein synthesis project, while Dr. D. Shemin got the amino acid project.

However, Dr. Bloch had soon thereafter lost all interest in pursuing the oxygen origin question for cholesterol. Another laboratory group from Germany had found that the hydrogen and oxygen atoms in acetate were readily converted into sterols. Dr. Bloch focused, instead, on examining cholesterol as a source of bile acids and steroid hormones. He continued with this area of study at the University of Chicago, where he took on an academic post as an assistant professor in their Biochemistry department. During this time, he also began a systematic evaluation of the reactions that made cholesterol, using acetate, of course, as a starting point. The cholesterol synthesis work, though labor-intensive and time-consuming, nevertheless, proved to be fruitful.

In 1954, Dr. Bloch, an established investigator in his own right, moved to Harvard. In his 1987 memoir, Dr. Bloch wrote that he had no reason to leave Chicago, except that the Bloch family had long lived to go to the big city. Probably another reason to leave Chicago was that Dr. Bloch's salary would be endowed, and he would thus become the new Higgins Professor of Biochemistry, a prestigious position at a prestigious institution.

Back in Chicago, before the untimely death of Prof. Schoenheimer and with the knowledge firmly in hand that the starting point for making cholesterol was the 2-carbon molecule called acetate, Dr. Bloch had invoked the labeling approach to study cholesterol synthesis. It proved to be a daunting task because cholesterol had 27 carbon molecules! Using radiolabeled acetate as a starting point, they found that at least half of the carbons in cholesterol came from acetate.

Besides acetate, another clue to making cholesterol was shark fat.

The 1926 work of Prof. Harold John Channon at University College, London, showed that when laboratory test animals were fed a preparation of shark oil called squalene, cholesterol levels increased, indicating that squalene was an intermediate, probably between acetate and the cholesterol end product. Furthermore, in 1934, Prof. Robert Robinson at Oxford had hypothesized that the shark squalene could form a circle upon itself, a process known as cyclization, to form the ring-based cholesterol structure. It was an intriguing idea.

Meanwhile, the cholesterol synthesis experiments of Prof. Bloch continued in the Chemistry department at Harvard, after his move to Cambridge, Massachusetts, in 1954.

Prof. Robinson had proposed a rather specific mechanism for circularizing the squalene to form cholesterol in one step. But when Prof. Bloch and his colleague Dr. Robert Woodward considered the cyclization phenomenon, they felt that another intermediate called lanosterol would be formed, instead, of cholesterol. Using radiolabeled acetate, they found that the appropriate radioactive carbon of the acetate ended up in lanosterol, as predicted, demonstrating that the so-called Bloch-Woodward mechanism that squalene circularized to form lanosterol was correct. Furthermore, it showed that the Robinson proposal that squalene circularized to make cholesterol was inaccurate.

In 1965, Prof. Konrad Bloch shared the Nobel with Prof. Feodor Lynen, in the category of Physiology or Medicine.

The path from Munich to Harvard and the Nobel had been circuitous indeed.

4. *Bloch apparently shared the Nobel Prize in Physiology or Medicine back in 1964– interestingly enough when the Beatles were arriving on American shores with Feodor Lynen. Who was Lynen, and how did they come to collaborate?*

Professor Feodor Lynen shared the Nobel Prize with Prof. Bloch in 1964. Dr. Lynen was housed at the prestigious Max-Planck Institute for Cell Chemistry. It's not entirely clear that these two biomedical investigators collaborated together. Each investigator had somewhat distinctive interests. Prof. Bloch's interest was primarily concerned with the metabolism of cholesterol, while that of Prof. Lynen was in the area of lipid and amino acid metabolism.

The main scientific connection between Profs Bloch and Lynen was acetyl coenzyme A (acetyl CoA), an important molecule described by the famous Nobel Laureate Fritz Lipmann. At Harvard, Prof. Lipmann delineated the biochemical conversion of pyruvate, the glycolytic oxidative breakdown product of glucose, to acetyl CoA, which is a central metabolite.

In Prof. Bloch's case, acetate was converted to acetyl CoA, and it could combine with acetoacetyl CoA to form 3-hydroxy-3-methylglutaryl CoA (HMG-CoA) and about 30 more biochemical steps later, cholesterol was made in the end. Acetyl CoA was the starting point, and Prof. Bloch's interest was, thus, a biosynthetic process.

In Prof. Lynen's case, acetyl CoA was formed after the breakdown of lipids. The enzyme lipase participates in fat breakdown and releases free fatty acids, which are long hydrocarbon chains. The fatty acid breakdown releases acetyl CoA molecules. The acetyl CoA was the endpoint of fatty acid breakdown, and Prof. Lynen's interest was, thus, a degradative process.

During the process of fatty acid breakdown metabolism, two carbons are cleaved off of the long-chain fatty acids, in a step-by-step series of biochemical reactions. Such fatty acid molecules can be quite lengthy, anywhere, on average, of about 16 carbons, sometimes shorter or longer, depending on the lipid composition. For example, a fatty acid that consists of 16 carbons along the chain will, therefore, yield 8 molecules of acetyl CoA. Each acetyl CoA molecule contains two carbons. The fatty acid breakdown pathway is called beta-oxidation and is often denoted as β-oxidation.

If the fatty acid chain consists of an odd number of carbons in the chain, acetyl CoA molecules are still produced, but eventually, a three-carbon version will also be made, called propionyl CoA which has to be handled somewhat differently, biochemically speaking. Propionyl CoA can be converted to a succinyl CoA, which can then be further metabolized.

The end commodities of fatty acid breakdown, e.g., acetyl CoA and propionyl CoA, are oxidized by the famous Krebs cycle, also known as the citric acid cycle or the tricarboxylic acid cycle, a pathway for which Sir Dr. Hans Krebs shared the Nobel Prize, in 1953, with Prof. Lipmann.

5. *Cholesterol and fatty acid metabolism seem to be the main thrust of their work. Why is this stuff so important, and did it serve as any kind of foundational work?*

Cholesterol is important for several reasons. First, it is known to be acutely involved in cardiovascular disorders such as atherosclerosis and coronary artery disease. These conditions can, in turn, lead to increased risks of stroke and heart attacks. Associated with this, certain genetic diseases are known in which cholesterol concentrations in the blood are hyper-elevated, leading to serious medical conditions. These issues are enormously important in biomedical science.

While the reduction and maintenance of cholesterol in the blood to healthy levels is a major objective in human cardiovascular medicine, cholesterol may also serve useful purposes. Thus, another reason cholesterol is important is the role it plays as a starting point, a precursor if you will, for the synthesis of signaling molecules, such as steroid hormones. Among these biomolecules include cortisol, estradiol, progesterone, and testosterone.

A fourth reason cholesterol is important is that when it is incorporated into the insides of biological membranes, which surround living cells, cholesterol serves to regulate the fluidity of the membranes. Another justification for the relevance of cholesterol is that in the skin, it serves as a precursor to the synthesis of vitamin D using ultraviolet light from the sun in order to do so. Vitamin D, in turn, plays a role in controlling the levels and biochemistry of calcium and phosphorous. Cholesterol is also an important precursor in the formation of bile salts, which in turn are useful for emulsifying dietary fats and in inhibiting the growth of potentially dangerous microbes, especially certain Gram-positive bacteria.

Fatty acids are important for several reasons. First, fatty acids can be used as a sort of energy storage system in living beings. The storage form of lipids consists of molecules called triacylglycerols. These triacylglycerols consist of a glycerol backbone connected to three long-chain fatty acids. Another reason fatty acids are important is that they can be used as a biological fuel, i.e., energy for conducting living purposes. When an individual needs biological energy, it can be obtained from the stored lipids.

Another important aspect of fatty acids is that they are the staring-points for the biosynthesis of phospholipids, which in turn can be used to make biological membranes that surround living cells. Without biological membranes, there would be no life, and fatty acids play an important role in maintaining this life process.

Fatty acids can also be used biochemically to modify proteins. Fatty acids can be attached to certain proteins in order to alter their structure and, thus, their functions. This is an important way to regulate the activities of proteins.

In cancer, fatty acid metabolism is altered in such a way that fatty acid synthesis is enhanced. This is because when tumor tissue is produced, the cancer cells being made need membranes to surround them, and fatty acids are needed to make the membranes.

Pathologically, cholesterol and fatty acids can work together. A diet rich in both cholesterol *and* fatty acids can result in greatly enhanced formation of atherosclerotic plaques, which can block coronary arteries, reducing oxygen-rich blood flow to the heart, and increasing the risk of strokes and myocardial infarctions, i.e., heart attacks.

6. What have I neglected to ask about this famous scientist?

While Prof. Bloch's prime interest of study was focused on cholesterol biochemistry, as mentioned above, there were several other areas that held his investigative curiosity, as well. For instance, while Prof. Lynen's focus was on fatty acid hydrolysis, Dr. Bloch's focus, in contrast, was in the biosynthesis of fatty acids. Regarding this latter focus, Dr. Bloch took advantage of microbes, such as bacteria and yeasts, to study fatty acid production.

He found out from several of his colleagues that these kinds of microbes could easily be made into mutant versions that exhibited important properties that could be exploited for the study of lipid metabolism. For instance, Prof. Bloch used microbial mutants to examine the oxygen requirements for the synthesis of the fatty acid called oleic acid from stearoyl CoA and oleoyl CoA precursors.

Dr. Bloch was a key investigator in the discovery of an important protein called acyl carrier protein, ACP. The ACP molecules were demonstrated to be important in making fatty acids. Many of the precursor intermediates formed during fatty acid biosynthesis had ACP molecules attached to them. During their studies, it was found out that another research group headed by Dr. Roy Vagelos was working along the same lines, studying the ACP processes, as well. After agreeing to meet at a scientific conference over cocktails, the two groups decided that instead of partaking in a race to the finish, each group would instead focus on separate projects so as not to duplicate their efforts. Thus, Dr. Bloch's group studied the production of unsaturated fatty acids under oxygen-free conditions while Dr. Vagelos's research laboratory focused on studying the process of fatty acid chain elongation.

Using mutant microbes, Prof. Bloch also managed to learn about the biochemistry of unsaturated fatty acids, such as olefinic acid, in lactic acid bacteria like *Lactobacillus*. There were conflicting ideas regarding the production of olefin, an unsaturated form of fatty acid. One idea was that it formed because of an oxidative dehydrogenation mechanism versus the notion that olefin production involved a dehydration step of so-called β-hydroxy acids. To support their contention, bacterial *Escherichia coli* mutants were used to purify the necessary enzyme responsible, called β-hydroxydecanoyl thioester dehydrase, which they colloquially, perhaps affectionately, referred to simply as their "dehydrase."

In Dr. Bloch's continued study of the β-hydroxydecanoyl thioester dehydrase enzyme, it turned out to produce a rather startling discovery!

To better examine the so-called dehydrase enzyme, Dr. Bloch's laboratory needed its substrate in order to do so. However, the required substrate, 3-hydroxydecanoyl thioester, was not available commercially for purchase. So they set about to make necessary substrate in their laboratory, which turned out to be an arduous painstaking, but fortuitous, effort!

First, they found a mixture of contaminating molecules in their substrate preparation. The mixture included not only the necessary substrate but also a confounding inhibitor molecule! The Bloch laboratory managed to purify each of the compounds in the mixture, including the pure substrate, but also another substance called 3-decynoyl thioester, which, when purified to homogeneity, inhibited the dehydrase enzyme! Shockingly, the dehydrase enzyme MADE this confounding inhibitor! That is to say, by making its own specialized inhibitor, the enzyme committed suicide!

Dr. Bloch called this phenomenon "enzyme suicide!"

On the 15th day of October, in the year 2000, he died from congestive heart failure at the age of 88 years. His beloved wife, Lore, passed away 10 years later, at the age of 98 years. The Bloch couple had had two children, Peter and Susan, plus 2 grandchildren.

For future investigation:

https://www.youtube.com/watch?v=gG8ETypjbp4
https://www.youtube.com/watch?v=dX-gKZKGdls

Chapter 6

SANTIAGO RAMÓN Y CAJAL – NERVOUS SYSTEM STRUCTURE

1. *Professor Varela – a name that is almost synonymous with the nervous system is a Spaniard – Santiago Ramón y Cajal – where and when was he born and when did he go to school?*

Prof. Shaughnessy, I think you will greatly appreciate the life and science of the very famous Santiago Felipe Ramón y Cajal, who is considered by many a biomedical neuroscientist as one of the founding fathers of neuroscience. A great deal of literature has been written about and by Ramón y Cajal. He was a prolific writer in his time, both popularly as well as scientifically.

The famous Dr. Ramón y Cajal is well known for having discovered the neuronal structure called the synapse, the connection between neurons. He is also famous for having formulated the so-called neuron theory, the idea that the brain, the nervous tissue, is composed of discrete, separate neurons, as opposed to the inaccurate theory that the brain is a system of fused cells.

Dr. Ramón y Cajal wrote in his best-selling autobiographical memoir "*Recollections of my Life*" that he was born on the first day of the month of May, in the year 1852, in a small Spanish town called Petilla de Aragon, which was situated in the region called Navarre, in the province of Zaragoza, near the town of Sos del Rey Católico, Spain. Dr. Ramón y Cajal attributes his later successes as a scientist directly to both of his parents.

Santiago's father, Dr. Justo Ramón Casasús, was a country doctor and surgeon, who later became a professor of applied anatomy. Santiago's mother was Antonia Cajal, who is described rather fondly by her grateful son. Dr. Ramón y Cajal also wrote that according to her siblings, his mother in her younger days was a beautiful, vibrant, and caring young woman who later as a mother became devoted to her son. He described how she fretted over his safety as he went on his many outdoor hiking excursions. The son described his father as possessing an astonishing proclivity for memory recollection, a strong work ethic, a firm believer in perseverance and, from a positive standpoint, ambition. He conveyed that his father could recite entire written works about pathology on command. He also recalled his father having to overcome a profound array of adversity in order to acquire his dream of becoming a surgeon.

Dr. Ramón y Cajal's childhood education started in a small town called Valpalmas. However, his father homeschooled him on various subjects, such as reading, grammar, French, mathematics, geography, and physics. Even while away in Madrid at medical school, his father managed to provide instruction for young Santiago by correspondence. He recounted one terrible day when his elementary school at Valpalmas had been struck by lightning, killing the parish priest, who had been struck directly, and injuring the schoolmistress. Another event recounted by young Ramón y Cajal was a lunar eclipse of the sun, accurately predicted to occur in 1860. The event transformed young Santiago because it provided an everlasting trust in science, which he learned was terrific enough to predict such astronomical phenomena. I think many young beginning scientists share a similar sort of wonderment with the natural world.

At the age of 10, Ramón y Cajal was sent to a boarding school, a college for wayward children, and run by Esculapian friars in Jaca, Spain. In 1864, arrangements were made for 12-year old Ramón y Cajal to transfer to another school, this one at Huesca. It was later reported by Ramón y Cajal that his grades at both institutions while passing in all subjects, were still less than stellar. Thus, in order to focus his idle time on more positive aspects, his father arranged for Ramón y Cajal to begin an apprenticeship under the auspices of a barber during the third session of his bachelor's degree program while in secondary school at Huesca. Acquiring failing grades the following year, in 1866, Ramón y Cajal's father then arranged for entry into an apprenticeship as a shoemaker.

Another intervention by his father at hand, it was decided that, in 1868, young Ramón y Cajal would now take up the subject of osteology, the study of bones. The topic intrigued him, especially when accompanied by midnight excursions to deserted cemeteries in order to acquire the requisite anatomical specimens!

Invoking the "learn-by-doing" method of education, young Ramón y Cajal developed an acumen for anatomical knowledge. Further, he applied his expertise in drawing to conduct his studies. Prior to this, Ramón y Cajal's zeal for drawing had been a point of conflict between himself and his father. Instead, it was now a point of connection between the father and son collaborators.

Successfully completing the requirements for his bachelor's degree Ramón y Cajal then enrolled in a preparatory school for an additional year, taking courses in natural history, physics, and chemistry, before entry into medical school. It is at this point that the 17-year old Ramón y Cajal became a serious student and successfully completed the required prep courses for the study of medicine.

In 1870, he enrolled in medical school at the University of Zaragoza. He devoted himself to the classical study of anatomy, performing dissections on human cadavers guided by open books and making careful drawings during the course of study. During the latter part of his second year, he had generated an extensive anatomy portfolio and became a dissection assistant, which took a great deal of his time. Regarding this, Ramón y Cajal recounted an anecdote.

Apparently, he had been publically chastised for his lack of attendance in a course on obstetrics, taught by Prof. Ferrer, who was put out by Ramón y Cajal's absences during the lectures. Ramón y Cajal replied that his dissection work had precluded any pleasure of prof. Ferrer lectures, but that he (Ramón y Cajal) was, nevertheless, quite well versed in the course material. Calling his bluff, Prof. Ferrer made Ramón y Cajal actually go to the board in front of the class during the lecture in order to provide for all in attendance the origins of the fetal membranes. As requested, Ramón y Cajal proceeded to do exactly that, clearly drawing on the board every membrane of the blastoderm, complete with their individual stages, umbilical vessels, and the allantois, etc. and accurately including the arrows with their physiological explanations, within the diagram. With Ramón y Cajal's acumen of the topic publically demonstrated for all to see, Prof. Ferrer and the students were astounded. After the incident, Prof. Ferrer had been converted to the ingeniousness of Ramón y Cajal and gleefully excused all future attendance requirements for the duration of the course.

Ramón y Cajal confesses in his memoirs that he had been supremely lucky that day. It had been the only topic he had been well-versed in because it had also been covered during the course of his dissections. He further writes that had prof. Ferrer asked him about *any other topic whatsoever* from the obstetrics course, the good professor would have discovered his (Ramón y Cajal's) complete ignorance of the entire remainder of the course material.

Nevertheless, Ramón y Cajal flourished while in medical school, and he took his medical degree in June of 1873, obtaining the title of licensure in medicine, earning honors in the field of anatomy.

2. *Apparently, in his youth, Ramón y Cajal was somewhat of a rapscallion. Any interesting early stories?*

A self-proclaimed rapscallion, Dr. Santiago Ramón y Cajal wrote in his famous memoirs that when he was young, his parents and teachers, with varying degrees of success, had to have an unprecedented amount of patience with him.

At the age of 10 years in boarding school at Jaca, he described bullying by students and dreadful mistreatment by teachers involving beatings, isolation, humiliation, and starvation as various modes of punishment. He further conveyed that school curricula at Jaca was taught by rote memorization. According to Ramón y Cajal, neither the draconian punishments nor the teaching methods produced their respective desired effects upon him at Jaca. He found several ways to escape confinement in order to find food at his uncle's nearby house, and he figured out how to return to his routine confinement without detection, for a relatively large number of days. Eventually, his scheme was discovered, and talk of permanent dis-enrollment for young Ramón y Cajal was bandied about, until his father intervened with a letter of reply, imploring the authorities to relax the harshness of their treatment towards his son.

Not surprisingly, considering the interruption in educating Ramón y Cajal with the vicious cycle of behavior-punishment, he failed to study effectively. In fact, he writes that he had lost interest in learning the subjects. With his professors at Jaca ready to flunk him outright, his father arranged for an independent assessment of his academic performance by professors from the nearby Institute of Huesca, who had not been aware of Ramón y Cajal's behavioral history at Jaca. Just as readily, the Huesca faculty independently gave him passing marks after having graded the same work.

His transfer the next year to school at Huesca was arranged. While his teachers were significantly less draconian than their counterparts had been at Jaca, his fellow students at Huesca were, unfortunately, more harsh in their bullying. Perhaps finding solace in the surrounding beauty of Huesca and its countryside, Ramón y Cajal filled many pages of his sketchbook with drawings of butterflies, trees, rocks, streams, and in particular, flowers.

Ramón y Cajal reported that he had drawn every flower he could find, but had heard of rare specimens that were not a part of his sketchbook portfolio. It is, thus, with his drawings of rare flowers that Ramón y Cajal recalls two memorable incidents at Huesca, both events of which dealt with attempted flower thefts.

The first incident with flower theft occurred when Ramón y Cajal and two of his classmates made a nighttime raid and scaled the wall of a garden containing a coveted specimen, the rose of Alexandria, desirable because of its colors, suitable for drawing, as well as, incidentally, for its fragrance. Almost immediately, the trio of would-be flower thieves were discovered and chased, with Ramón y Cajal eventually making good his escape. His two companions, however, were caught and, consequently, beaten rather severely by their two capturing gardeners.

The second incident transpired when Ramón y Cajal attempted a solo flower heist in another garden, this time in that of a railway station, which harbored another fine flower specimen, tea roses, suitable for drawing because of its shape. This time the raid was made in broad daylight, and having scaled the fence, Ramón y Cajal stole the exquisite flower and scaled back the same wall, where a railway official was waiting. As what occurred with the first attempted flower heist, another chase ensued. Ramón y Cajal lost his chaser but fell in a quagmire of slimy mud while attempting to jump a ditch. Several witnesses who became sympathetic to the hapless young Ramón y Cajal stuck in the mud pulled him out, and, being clothes-washers, proceeded to wash his slimy clothes while he huddled incognito behind a nearby willow tree. It is at this point that the railway chaser finally caught up with the alleged flower thief. With the spectacle of Ramón y Cajal dirty and half-clothed, the official could only burst out laughing, choosing not to pursue the matter, if not also concerned with sliming his own clean uniform. Ramón y Cajal related that his foul-smelling, muddy, and slimy state proved to be an invincible suit of armor against further prosecution.

The next year of school, back at Huesca, this time accompanied by his younger brother, Pedro, the Ramón y Cajal brothers undertook rock-throwing with the aid slingshot devices and became proficient, if not accurate, in their aiming. One incident, in particular, was conveyed in his memoirs regarding a stone-hurtling battle with another group of kids in which police were caught in the crossfire and injured. The story is told that the ringleaders, Ramón y Cajal among them, were hidden for a few days inside the home of a schoolmaster, who had had a prior grudge with the police and chose, thus, not to aid them.

Another rock-throwing battle that same year involved a beating of young Ramón y Cajal by another victim caught in the crossfire, this time by a mountaineer who had been herding a train of mules. According to Ramón y Cajal, the mountaineer incorrectly attributed a stray stone striking him directly to the visible young boy. Protesting his innocence while the purported real wrongdoers were hiding from view, the disbelieving mountaineer gave young Ramón y Cajal a sound thrashing and then went on his way. Vowing revenge for receiving an unjust punishment, the young Ramón y Cajal shadowed the mountaineer, and when conditions were ripe, he delivered a fresh barrage of stones upon him. A complaint that was consequently filed with the police led nowhere, as the identity of Ramón y Cajal was unknown.

Nevertheless, many of the local villagers were actually very well aware of Ramón y Cajal and of his stone slinging reputation. Schoolgirls his age were aware, too, especially of one girl in particular named Silvería Fañanás García, all of whom would flee for fear of his accurate stone slinging. Ramón y Cajal would recount how this same girl would later marry him in 1879, having three sons and four daughters together.

3. *Apparently, one of his significant contributions was his study of the structure of the cortex of the brain. How did he become involved in this?*

Dr. Ramón y Cajal was already a full professor at the University of Valencia, having established himself already in the scientific world, dealing with the field of histology when in 1887, he paid a historic visit to Dr. Luis Simarro, a friend and colleague. Dr. Simarro was himself well established as a noted neurologist and psychiatrist. He was the first investigator to introduce the new silver chromate staining method of Golgi.

Dr. Camillo Golgi was a prominent investigator and professor of histology who was housed at the University of Pavia, where he developed the famous staining technique of nervous system tissue, in1873. Dr. Golgi would share the Nobel with Dr. Ramón y Cajal, in Medicine or Physiology, in 1906.

Dr. Simarro had been using the technique to study brain tissue. During that fateful visit in 1887, when Dr. Simarro showed his Golgi-inspired slides to Dr. Ramón y Cajal, he was immediately impressed with the slides he saw.

Upon returning to his own laboratory back at the University of Valencia, Dr. Ramón y Cajal immediately invoked the Golgi staining method and instructed his laboratory personnel to do the same. Thus, Dr. Ramón y Cajal's laboratory began a systematic study of the cerebellum, the cerebrum, the spinal cord, the olfactory bulb, and the retina, among other tissues, of young animals and of embryos. It is at this point where Dr. Ramón y Cajal made a tremendously important discovery.

Using the staining method of Golgi, Dr. Ramón y Cajal found that nervous tissue consisted of individual, discrete elements that may be in physical contact with one another but were nonetheless separate entities. He further found that long nerve cells had ends, further supporting the notion that nerve cells were distinctive individuals.

Importantly, Dr. Ramón y Cajal had discovered that nervous system cells were not fused with each other, which had been an incorrect notion believed by Dr. Golgi and by virtually all other neuroscientists at the time.

Based on his Golgi staining observations, Dr. Ramón y Cajal went on to postulate the neuron theory, which stated that the brain consisted of individual neurons and not fused cells. In a sense, Dr. Ramón y Cajal had discovered the neuron, the individual nerve cell. Thus, Dr. Ramón y Cajal established the neuron as a fundamental unit of the brain.

4. *Histology seems to have been another area of interest for this Nobel Prize winner– what exactly do scientists mean by this, and what were his contributions?*

The field of histology has to do with the study of tissues that encompass living beings. In order to visualize cells of living tissue in the microscope, the specimen must often be stained with colorful chemicals in order to do so. Such histological work frequently entails acquiring tissue samples from organisms, carving the tissue samples into very thin slices, fixing or embedding the tissue slices onto microscope slides, staining the fixed tissue slices with various chemicals, and using various modes of microscopy to visualize the cells of the tissues.

In modern times, the sophistication involved with histology is incredible, involving the observation of the various cellular activities in tissue that's still alive or in observing various cellular components as they go about their life-giving activities. Medical histology is a vital field devoted to the study of pathology, such as is seen in cancer or other medical diseases.

Dr. Ramón y Cajal can be considered as one of the founding fathers of neuroscience. This is because his main contributions in this realm had to do with his histological studies regarding the neuroanatomy of the central nervous system (CNS), which in turn consists of the brain and spinal cord. The CNS relays electrical sensory signals between itself and the peripheral nervous system (PNS) and the body's muscular system. The CNS receives these external sensory stimuli and interprets them in order to make decisions and instruct the neuromuscular system to conduct behavioral responses.

The CNS represents one of the most complicated biological systems ever known. Although the neuroscientists in modern times regularly make great strides on a routine basis, they nevertheless have much work remaining to do with respect to how the CNS functions at a fundamental level.

5. *His artistic talents bode him well– in terms of his drawings. What has he contributed? Professor Varela, in an attempt to get high school students and even college students to delve more deeply into the lives of these famous scientists, I have listed a few YouTube videos–I hope they meet with your approval!*

When he was young, Dr. Ramón y Cajal had been an aspiring artist, drawing as many subjects as he could, even getting himself into quite serious trouble in order to do so, not only with his father but also with the authorities, in some cases. As a drawer, he clearly had a burgeoning talent. His interest in drawing as a career was a point of contention between young Santiago and his father. He experienced telling adventures attempting to steal rare flowers in order to draw them for his portfolio. At the point of exasperation, the elder Dr. Ramón y Cajal introduced his son to the macabre study of human anatomy, a new interest in which young Ramón y Cajal could apply his drawing talent to and of which he took to heart. The new intellectual pursuit changed his life.

As an independent investigator, Dr. Ramón y Cajal produced amazing drawings of neuroanatomical tissues, clearly drawing neuronal branches emerging from the spinal cords of laboratory animals. The artistic and scientific output of drawings by Dr. Ramón y Cajal was legendary, working every day and night, foregoing vacations, etc. in order to continue his work.

The voluminous work of Dr. Ramón y Cajal is inspiring. As your question regarding the YouTube videos attests, young people in modern times have (re)discovered his awe-inspiring work. I think this is a warmly welcomed opportunity for aspiring young scientific investigators. It is especially relevant given that while so much is known regarding the brain and spinal cord, that a tremendous amount of its physiological, cellular, biochemical, and molecular knowledge of its basic function is still largely unknown and even unexplored.

Dr. Ramón y Cajal's drawings also make for great art, and a great deal of microscopic-based images in the scientific realm can certainly be envisaged as artistic. I think this is one of the main points to be made regarding Dr. Ramón y Cajal and the YouTube videos that you identified.

On many occasions, artists trained as such can be called upon to construct visual graphics depicting biological structures and their cellular mechanisms. Artists are needed to help scientists convey the mechanistic details of various physiological processes during public presentations or in their publications in the literature. While it is unclear to what extent YouTube as a venue for young people will continue to be an important medium as the current generations continue to age, it is clear that there is a tremendous amount of room for art and science to become linked together. Regarding this linkage, like many great scientists, Dr. Ramón y Cajal was many generations ahead of his time. Below is an example of his extraordinary talent.

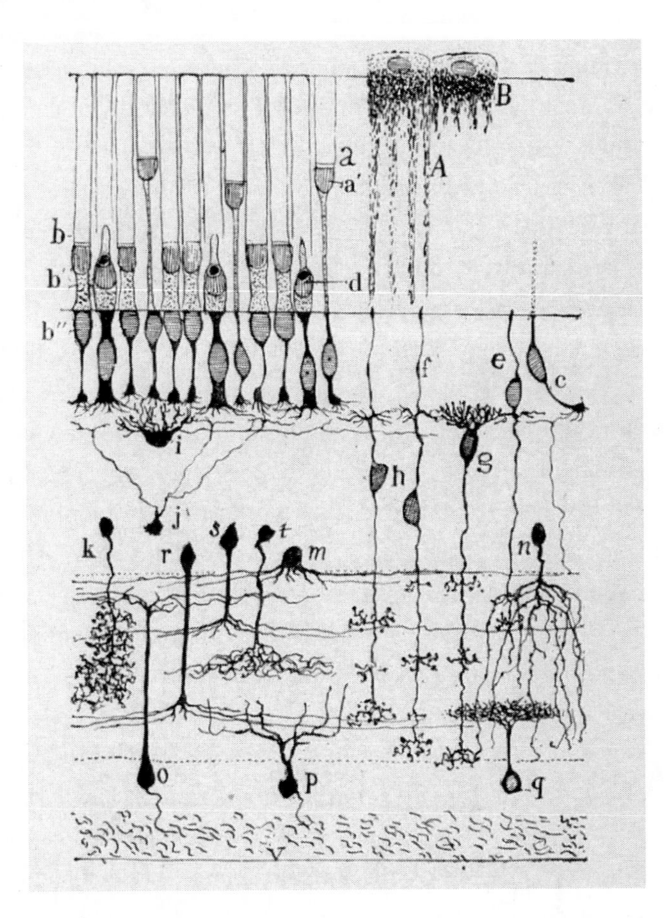

6. As I understand, he won the Nobel Prize– what was this for?

In short, Dr. Ramón y Cajal earned the Nobel Prize, in 1906, in the category of Medicine or Physiology. He shared the prize with Dr. Camillo Golgi, who had invented a method for staining tissues, using a silver chromate chemical to do so. Dr. Ramón y Cajal used this Golgi technique to study more closely CNS cells and tissue. He discovered that the CNS was composed of separate nerve cells, now called neurons. The implications of the so-called neuron theory were profound. It immediately suggested that the brain and spinal cord were made up seemingly of billions of separate cells. Due to Dr. Ramón y Cajal's work, it now became known that the CNS is an extremely complicated organ from an anatomical perspective. Furthermore, this complicated structural nature of the nervous system, in turn, indicated that there is an extremely complicated functional nature with correspondingly complex sets of cellular and molecular mechanisms associated with it. The profound ramifications of this structural-functional and mechanistic insights would forever change the way neuroscientists would view the nervous system.

Once the concept of the individual neuron had been postulated by Dr. Ramón y Cajal and had become accepted (albeit slowly), then further insightful advances in neuroscience became possible. The study of nerve function was now a possibility. Investigators could now research how nerves work, how signals could be generated, transmitted, and received by and between neurons. Due to the pioneering work of Dr. Ramón y Cajal, many functional aspects of the brain and spinal cord fell into place. The electrical signals between neurons, called action potentials, became a focal point of study by the neuroscientists. The field of neuroscience exploded. Today, many thousands of scientists have specialized in the field.

7. Can you summarize his contributions to the field of medicine?

In addition to determining the Nobel-winning notion that nerve cells, neurons, are discrete entities and not fused into a giant neuro-filament bundle, he also determined that neurons were connected to each other by forming synapses. Stated differently, one nerve cell consisting of its cell body called soma and an extended axon structure where its end, called a presynaptic terminal, would connect to the next (separate) neuron by forming a synapse with the so-called post-synaptic end of that second neuron. Further, Dr. Ramón y Cajal postulated that these pre- and post-synaptic neurons weren't actually physically connected. Instead, based on his investigative studies in his laboratory, he theorized that these synapses, which he called "connexions" consisted of spaces where these connected nerves weren't actually touching each other with their respective membranes. He found these connexions throughout the brain and spinal cord and even in peripheral nerves. He showed these various connexions as occurring in so-called Purkinje nerve fibers, which serves inhibitory functions in certain cases.

Later studies of these so-called connexions showed that pre-synaptic nerve terminals would release packets of neurotransmitters, such as small molecules like acetylcholine, or norepinephrine, which would move across the space of the synapse to reach the post-synaptic end of the associated neuron to continue the electrical impulses across the pathway of a particular neuronal system. In some cases, the electrical impulse was excitatory, causing a certain function to occur, or inhibitory, such as seen in Purkinje cells, thus, causing the inactivation of a function. Other studies showed neuromuscular junctions in which a certain type of neuron, called collaterals or reflex motor by Dr. Ramón y Cajal, would innervate a muscle to cause it to contract or perhaps relax its contraction.

In terms of embryonic development of the brain, Dr. Ramón y Cajal found growing nerve ends, called axonal growth cones. These growth cones had endpoints to them, ends of nerves, which he interpreted as meaning that nerve cells were contiguous and not fused, i.e., not continuous, with each other. In modern times, the growth of nerve endings during brain development is an extensively studied field in neuroscience. He had further postulated that growth cones were guided by gradients of chemicals, showing a behavior called chemotaxis. This area is of particular importance as knowledge of its growth mechanism might pave the way for reconnecting severed spinal cords after traumatic accidents occur in which patients are paralyzed. Severed neurons in the CNS do not reconnect, and knowledge of axonal growth-cone-making connections between neurons during development is a promising avenue.

Dr. Ramón y Cajal also studied, in his words, the "less important sympathetic system of the intestines." Later, investigators, however, were to find that his studies into the topic were of great importance as it helped explain how the gastrointestinal tract conducts its contractions as regulated by the function of smooth muscle cells. Dr. Ramón y Cajal reported that he studied new types of cells in this arena, and as a tribute to him, one of these cell types has been named interstitial cells of Cajal, each, in turn, having different sub-categories, such as intramuscular interstitial cells of Cajal, or myenteric interstitial cells of Cajal.

8. What have I neglected to ask?

For aspiring scientists, Dr. Ramón y Cajal wrote a popular book called "*Advice for a Young Investigator*." The book is a frank treatise on pragmatic aspects for young scientists. His book is filled with plenty of practical advice on many aspects of scientific research. For example, the book includes instructions on how to write scientific papers or how to be an effective teacher. When he had also written in his personal memoirs about the early education he named not only his teachers' various mistakes, he named his teachers.

Apparently, in 2005, an asteroid or minor planet, 1.4 km in size, was named after this great scientist: "Ramonycajal asteroid number 117413," and its orbit has been definitively calculated. I'm not sure if asteroid Ramonycajal 117413 is actually slated to interact with or even come close in any way near to the Earth, but it is most certainly known that Dr. Ramón y Cajal has made a huge impact on the knowledge of our brains.

Dr. Ramón y Cajal's color drawings have been exhibited in art shows and showcased in museums. His work has been inspirational to artists worldwide. As your YouTube inquiry above indicates, his work will no doubt continue to make influential contributions to generations of artists and scientists alike and to be a positive inspiration for anyone who learns about him.

Dr. Ramón y Cajal passed away in Madrid, Spain, on the 17th day of October, in 1934, at 82 years of age.

For future study and to learn more about this amazing man, go to:

https://www.youtube.com/watch?v=pBd7AJk1drY
https://www.youtube.com/watch?v=x7k6r7AtH3Q
https://www.youtube.com/watch?v=72IPPIt5iMw

Chapter 7

RENATO DULBECCO – VIRUSES AND CANCER

1. *Professor Varela, someone who has contributed a good deal to our understanding of the relationship of viruses and cancer, was Renato Dulbecco, originally of Italy. What do we know about his early years?*

Dr. Shaughnessy, I think you'll greatly appreciate knowing about this remarkable scientist, Dr. Renato Dulbecco. As a world-renowned and pioneering microbiologist, molecular biologist, cancer biologist, and biomedical scientist, Dr. Dulbecco discovered that DNA tumor viruses could infect and transform normally working cells into tumor cells.

In 1975, Prof. Dulbecco shared Nobel Prize in physiology or medicine with Howard Temin and David Baltimore for their works dealing with the interactions between cellular genetic material and tumor-causing viruses. Drs. Temin and Baltimore studied how RNA tumor viruses transformed cells, discovering the famous reverse transcriptase enzyme in the process.

Dr. Renato Dulbecco was born to parents Maria and Leonardo Dulbecco, on the 22nd day of the month of February, in 1914, just before the Great War. Like his mother, Maria Virdia, who was from southern Italy, in the region called Calabria, Renato was born in its capital called Catanzaro, also known as the city with two seas. His father, Leonardo, a civil engineer, was from northwestern Italy, along the coastal region of Liguria, Italy. Shortly after his birth, the Dulbecco family moved to Cuneo and to Torino (Turin), and then later to Imperia, also in the region of Liguria, Italy.

It is in Imperia, Italy, where young Renato attended elementary and high schools. He was recognized during this time as being brilliant. In 1930, at the age of 16 years, Renato entered university at Torino, where he majored in pre-medicine, an interest inspired by an uncle who was a surgeon. After his first year in university, however, Dulbecco had developed a fascination with the biological sciences, thus, choosing instead to concentrate his studies in the discipline of gross anatomy and pathology. Consequently, he chose to work in the research laboratory of Prof. Giuseppe Levi, a noted expert in nervous tissue anatomy and histology. During this time as a student assistant in Dr. Levi's laboratory, Dulbecco met two strongly influential friends, Salvador Luria and Rita Levi-Montalcini, each of whom became quite prominent biomedical scientists and Nobel Laureates in their own rights. Dulbecco graduated from the University of Torino, taking his undergraduate degree, a B.S., in pathology, in 1932, and later his medical degree, an M.D., in 1936.

2. *Apparently, his early life was impacted by World War I and World War II– what was his involvement like, and how did these events impact his ability to study?*

During World War I, Dulbecco's father was drafted into the military, serving in Imperia, Liguria, in Italy. It is thus here in Imperia where young Renato spent a great deal of his youth, being raised and educated. It provided an opportunity for Renato to develop his interests in mathematics and physics, during which time it is said that on his own, he had built a functional seismometer. During the summer vacations from school, Renato spent a great deal of time at the beach. The Great War had solidified his roots in Imperia in the long term and provided him with otherwise unprecedented opportunities.

World War II had a somewhat different impact on Dulbecco. First, after obtaining his doctoral degree in medicine and prior to the start of the Second World War, he had been called into military duty where he served as a medical officer and soon after was discharged as an Army doctor in 1938.

However, with World War II looming ahead, he was drafted once again in 1939, when he was sent to the French front and then to the Russian front. During a Russian offensive, in 1942, Dr. Dulbecco was severely injured, taking several months to convalesce from his injuries. After his recovery, he was sent home.

Shortly after Dr. Dulbecco's arrival back home to Italy from his military duty, Mussolini's fascist government had collapsed, and the country of Italy had been occupied by the German forces. At about this time, Dr. Dulbecco had chosen to side with the United States and English allies, hiding in a small village called Piemonte and joining forces with the Resistance movement against the German Nazis. As a physician in the Resistance, he tended to the wounded and participated briefly in local political activities.

3. *Like many other research scientists, he traveled to the U.S to study and research. Can you trace some of his institutional affiliations?*

It is during this time, after the Second World War was over, that Dr. Dulbecco chose to gain more education, focusing this time on physics and working in the Torino University laboratory of Dr. Levi, alongside Dr. Levi-Montalcini. At some point during this experience, Dr. Dulbecco realized that a dream of his was to learn all about microbial genetics using radiation!

It was a new scientific field that his friend Dr. Luria, who was briefly visiting the Levi laboratory in the summer of 1946, but who had been studying at his home base in Indiana, in the U.S. Consequently, a promising opportunity for Dr. Dulbecco's dream of studying phage genetics with radioactive mutagens would soon present itself. Thus, with the history-altering invitation by Dr. Luria to work with him, and the equally historic encouragement by Dr. Levi-Montalcini, Dr. Dulbecco moved to Bloomington, Indiana, in 1947, sharing a tiny laboratory with young and brash graduate student by the name of Jim Watson.

Dr. Dulbecco's work at Indiana was fruitful as he became a dedicated virologist. He obtained interesting data using ultraviolet light to convert bacteriophages, viruses that infected bacteria, from an inactive state to an infectious state, discovering a process he and Dr. Delbrück called phage photoreactivation. The work confirmed the earlier studies of Dr. Albert Kelner, who had studied fungi and *Escherichia coli* bacteria, finding that light exposure improved recovery of the fungi and bacteria from radiation and UV light damage, respectively. Dr. Dulbecco's confirmation was ground-breaking work because the mechanism of phage induction was an intensely studied field of molecular biology. It is about this time that Dr. Dulbecco was inducted into the so-called "Phage Group." The membership was exclusive and was said to be devoted to the study of phage genetics.

Dr. Dulbecco's phage induction work with UV light caught the attention of a great scientist and a pioneer of molecular biology, Dr. Max Delbrück, who was housed at the California Institute of Technology (Caltech), in Pasadena, California, in the U.S. The famous Dr. Delbrück soon after offered Dr. Dulbecco a job at Caltech as a senior research fellow. In 1949, Dr. Dulbecco moved to California, continuing his studies of the phages.

In 1952, Caltech promoted Dr. Dulbecco to the rank of associate professor, and in 1954 he became a citizen of the U.S. In 1955, he was promoted to the rank of full professor at Caltech.

At Caltech, the early 1960s, Dr. Delbrück introduced Dr. Dulbecco to a new idea. A benefactor had bestowed a handsome monetary gift to Caltech if new studies could be conducted in the field of animal viruses. Dr. Dulbecco accepted the challenge and used the funding to develop a new plaque assay technique for animal viruses successfully. The plaque assay had initially been known for the phages, and many of those in the Phage Group had put to use in fantastically successful ways to discover genetic operon induction and negative regulation of gene expression, etc. The animal virus-based plaque assay developed by Dr. Dulbecco now permitted unprecedented advances in this new and vital area of biomedical science, just as had been enjoyed with the phage viruses! One could now study ways to make vaccines, like that for polio, or to learn how viruses caused cancer. Many new possibilities for innovation within the biomedical sciences had opened!

Dr. Dulbecco had a new graduate student, Howard Temin, and a postdoctoral fellow, Dr. Harry Rubin, both of whom had had an interest in the famous Rous Sarcoma virus. Their work inspired Dr. Dulbecco to study cancer biology. He invoked the plaque assay to culture viruses that conferred polio and cancer. He also studied the polyomavirus, which caused mice tumors and the simian virus 40 (SV40), which caused leukemia in animal primates, discovering the stages of lytic infection and of tumorigenic transformation in mammalian cells in culture.

In 1962, Dr. Dulbecco moved to the Salk Institute for Biological Studies in a suburb of San Diego, California, called La Jolla, where he had the notable rank of a senior research fellow. In 1972, Dr. Dulbecco then moved to London, England, where he became director of its prestigious British

Imperial Cancer Fund Laboratories and where he had an opportunity to study human cancer biology.

After receipt of the Nobel in 1975, Dr. Dulbecco moved back to the Salk Institute for Biological Studies, in La Jolla, in 1977, becoming a distinguished research professor and later its acting president, in 1988 and its permanent president, in 1992. He retired in La Jolla in 2006.

4. *Behind every great man is a woman, and as I understand, his wife Maureen worked with him in the lab. What was he studying and what were some of his preliminary findings?*

Maureen Rutherford Muir was Renato's second wife, marrying in 1963. They had a daughter named Fiona. They had met each other at Caltech, where Maureen had been working as a research associate in the laboratory of Dr. Harry Rubin. But when Dr. Rubin decided to move to Berkeley, Maureen had not liked the idea of moving again. So Dr. Rubin casually suggested she work in Dulbecco's lab, and that's how she and Renato started working together, starting in 1962.

Maureen Dulbecco had assisted with Renato's experiments in the laboratory for a number of years. She was also a stabilizing force, as well as a supportive partner and confidant for Dr. Dulbecco. They stayed married for almost 50 years, until his death on the 19th day of February, in 2012, three days before his 98th birthday. As of this writing, Maureen Dulbecco is still alive, living in California.

Prior to all of this, Dulbecco had been married first to Guiseppina Salvo, his first wife, in 1939, and the couple had had two children, a son named Peter and a daughter named Maria Vittoria. Renato and Guiseppina had divorced earlier in 1963, shortly before his second marriage, to Maureen.

5. *Further, he also worked with some of the great minds of the times – can you list a few and tell us about their collaborative efforts?*

In 1947, Dr. Dulbecco started work with the famous Dr. Salvador Luria and studied phage genetics, introducing him to the burgeoning field of virology, expertise which would serve him extremely well in later years. Dr. Luria also introduced Drs. Dulbecco and Rita Levi-Montalcini to each other. In later years, Dr. Dulbecco attributed much of his successes with his career directly to both her encouragement and advice. A truly dedicated biomedical scientist, Dr. Levi-Montalcini, would earn the 1986 Nobel Prize in medicine or physiology for her work with the growth of nerves.

In Dr. Luria's laboratory, Dr. Dulbecco also met Dr. Hermann Joseph Muller, whom Dulbecco attributes as having provided him with an expertise in the field of genetics. Dr. Muller had received the 1946 Nobel Prize in physiology or medicine for his work with genetic mutations in fruit flies by radiation.

As I mentioned earlier, starting in 1952, Dr. Dulbecco worked at Caltech with the great pioneer of molecular biology, Dr. Max Delbrück, who had personally invited Dulbecco to join them in California. At Caltech, Dr. Delbrück taught Dr. Dulbecco about the scientific method as well as about the importance of attaining biological goals for the pursuit of biomedical research. That is, he taught Dr. Dulbecco what scientific topics were of vital importance for closer study. Drs. Delbrück and Luria would go on to share the 1969 Nobel Prize in physiology or medicine with Alfred D. Hershey, for their own pioneering scientific works.

Dr. Delbrück further provided an opportunity for him to explore the biology of animal-based viruses, whereupon Dulbecco and another great scientist and German World War II refugee, Dr. Marguerite Vogt, worked together to develop the plaque assay technique for quantifying poliovirus, the causative agent of polio. The work was seminal because it provided, for the first time, a means for investigators to quantitate infectivity for animal-based viruses, and it thus permitted new advances in animal viruses and cancer research. Drs. Dulbecco and Vogt also conducted many studies pertaining to the tumorigenic viruses and the transformation of normal cells into tumor-growing ones, like cancer.

In 1965, Dr. Dulbecco had offered Dr. David Baltimore a job to work at the Salk Institute. Additionally, Dr. Dulbecco had admitted young Howard Temin to work in his laboratory as a graduate student. Dr. Dulbecco had also hired a new postdoctoral fellow, Dr. Harry Rubin. It was both Drs. Temin and Rubin who would introduce Dr. Dulbecco to the virtues of studying the biology of cancer. The trio Drs. Baltimore, Temin, and Dulbecco would share the Nobel, in 1975.

6. *The Nobel Prize – what was he actually awarded the Nobel Prize for – and how did it contribute to our understanding of cancer?*

In the early 1960s, Dr. Dulbecco had been interested in the mouse polyomavirus, a DNA-based virus, which causes rodent cancer. Dr. Dulbecco's studies showed that the DNA of the virus somehow actually inserted itself into the genome of mice cells! The work had profound implications for cancer transformation of normal cells. One of these notions was that cellular transformation into cancer involved the incorporation of a viral genome into the DNA of the animal genome! The integrated virus DNA into the rodent DNA must in some way cause the normal mouse cell to grow abnormally in rodents, causing cancer.

In 1968, Dr. Dulbecco worked with Dr. Joseph Sambrook to demonstrate the actual incorporation of virus DNA into the genome of the host cell. They postulated that the newly integrated viral DNA brought with them new genes, which in turn caused the cell to be carcinogenic. Together, the various works demonstrated that viral DNA could cause cancer. These scientific works were worthy of the Nobel Prize for Dr. Dulbecco.

The Nobel work of Dr. Dulbecco permitted significant advancements in the area of polyomavirus infection and cellular transformation to cancer. The process starts with the virus protein called VP1, for viral protein number one, and its binding to the host animal cell, which has a viral receptor for VP1 called ganglioside GM1 on the cell's surface. The polyomavirus that's bound to the cell now undergoes internalization into the host cells by a process called endocytosis, and a host cell protein, called caveolin, facilitates this viral entry into the cell. Next, the virus, which is now in the cellular cytoplasm, enters the insides of the endoplasmic reticulum where the virus is then transported into the inside of the cell's nucleus. In the nucleus, the virus is uncoated in which the DNA-based genome is separated from the encompassing capsid protein, releasing the viral DNA in the nucleus!

Next, as predicted and shown by Dr. Dulbecco, the viral DNA is actually integrated into the genomic DNA of the soon-to-be transformed cells. The newly inserted viral DNA encodes a couple of genes that confer the transformational event in the host cells. The genes fall into a class of so-called oncogenic proteins, such as the large T antigen protein, and the lesser-known middle T antigen. Together, these viral DNA elements are known as the transforming genes. They work on their targets, one of which is known as p105 or Rb protein, short for retinoblastoma protein.

Whatever name one chooses to call it, the function of Rb is to suppress tumors by regulating the cell cycle in mammal-based cells. Under normal circumstances, the Rb protein turns off a transcription factor that's needed for cell division. When cell division is supposed to occur on a normal basis, the Rb protein is instead phosphorylated, which results in the ungluing of the transcription factor and thus allows the cell cycle to occur for growth of the cell.

However, under tumorigenic conditions, the virally introduced large T antigens bind to and inactivate Rb! This abnormally releases the transcription factor and thus allows the cell cycle to proceed and tumor cell growth to occur!

7. *A generalization question– his work was typically with animals– how was he able to generalize from his work to the human species?*

In short, animals and humans share similar cellular machinery targets for the same sorts of viruses. This is because humans have a rather large number of homologs (evolutionarily shared) in common. Thus, the push for a generalization from Dr. Dulbecco's animal cancer virus work to that in humans was an easy one to make, and much evidence has already been found for just such an association. As an example, in 2008, it was discovered that the so-called Merkel cell polyomavirus (MCPyV) could bind to and infect human Merkel cells, which are human skin-based mechanosensory cells. Merkel cell cancers of the skin, called carcinomas, though rare, nonetheless, are due to an infectious association with the MCPyV viral microbes!

These human-specific MCPyV viruses also integrate into the human host genome DNA and express large T antigens. Remarkably, however, the mechanism of cellular transformation by MCPyV in humans appears to mimic in a much similar fashion that mode of transformation of normal monkey cells infected with the SV40 and their resulting viral oncogenesis. That is, many aspects of the cell transformation mechanism were discovered to be evolutionarily conserved between humans and the lower animals!

Incidentally, you'll recall that Dr. Dulbecco had studied the SV40 in monkeys. Early studies by other laboratories that had supposedly implicated SV40 infection and human tumors suffered terribly from widespread contamination of cultured cells with laboratory strains of the SV40 virus.

The problem was so serious that Dr. Dulbecco was driven to invoking terribly outrageous behavior in order to convince naysayers that SV40 did not cause human cancer. Although he did not ultimately follow through on his threat, in order to show that SV40 wasn't a cancer causer, he had seriously considered drinking a sample of the SV40 virus!

Today, the SV40 virus is no longer thought to be a factor in causing human tumors.

While evidence has shown that SV40 itself is not carcinogenic nor tumorigenic in humans, there are similarities, nevertheless, in their respective molecular mechanisms of neoplastic transformation in monkeys and humans. These similarities have to do with the function common to the large T antigen in both types of life systems.

After earning the Nobel, Dr. Dulbecco moved on to the study of human and rat breast cancers. This newer work led to discoveries involving the development of mammary tissue and of breast cancer originating from stem cells. The Dulbecco laboratory also learned about new gene expression programs in human breast cancer and in learning new ways to improve the method for detection, an improvement over that observed by the problematic expression data associated with the microarray systems.

8. What have I forgotten to ask about the relationship between genetics, viruses, and cancer?

In 1986, at the age of 72, Dr. Dulbecco wrote a seminal perspective in the prestigious journal *Science*. In his article, he wrote at length about the difficulties that he and other investigators had encountered in attempting to clearly identify the major types of cells involved cancer and with developmental biology. He wrote that in order for biomedical scientists to make any sense of the types of cells involved and the roles they played in each of these two important biological systems, one must, therefore, know the genes that are actively turned on when they are conducting their respective biological functions. Thus, the best way, he said, to understand these two processes, cancer, and development was to determine their genes involved. This meant one needed to undergo the labor-intensive processes of mapping and sequencing of the entire human genome; that is to say, one must establish the human genome project and find *all* of the genes!

At first, he was widely criticized for having proposed to determine the whole human genome simply for the sake of knowing its genes and their sequences. Soon afterward, however, the commentary turned in favor of just such an endeavor. While other prominent investigators were touting the same genomic virtues at the time, Dr. Jim Watson, among them, the human genome project was started shortly after Dr. Dulbecco's far-reaching ideas were published.

Many of the methodologies required in this massive undertaking required that the human genome be broken up into many pieces and that those pieces be inserted into viruses! The human genome was finally officially completed by publication, in 2003, and Dr. Dulbecco lived to see its genomic fruits.

Recently, genome projects have been concerned with determining cancer genomes. One well-known cancer, the so-called HeLa cell, a particularly insidious cancer, was completely sequenced in 2013. The genomes of many more cancer cell types are being determined, as well. The information gathered from these cancer genomes will permit biomedical scientists to learn how these cancers start and, importantly, how to stop them, perhaps by finding vulnerable targets inherent in them.

For additional information go to:

https://www.youtube.com/watch?v=NRNr6ZYE00I
https://www.youtube.com/watch?v=xA_xE_tKdOU
https://www.youtube.com/watch?v=cL6mhK8wm74

Chapter 8

GERTRUDE B. ELION – GOUT TREATMENT WITH ALLOPURINOL

1. *Professor Varela, one very famous female bioscientist, was Gertrude B. Elion. Where and when was she born, and where did she go to school?*

Prof. Shaughnessy, the preeminent biomedical scientist Gertrude Belle Elion and Nobel Laureate in medicine, was quite famous amongst her peers after discovering innovative scientific approaches for the development of novel chemotherapeutics. Her work had far-reaching positive consequences stemming from her contributions towards a vast array of scientific disciplines, such as immunology and tissue transplantation, and from her contributions towards treatments for medical diseases such as leukemia, gout, leishmaniasis, and herpes infections.

Elion was an American, born in New York, NY, on the 23rd day of January, in 1918 to Jewish parents Robert and Bertha Cohen Elion. Elion's father was a dentist who took his dentistry degree from New York University and had emigrated to the U.S. from Lithuania. Her mother had emigrated to the U.S. from Russia, in what is present-day Poland, in 1911.

The Elion household has been described as an environment rich in intellectual pursuits, filled with voracious reading activities by all members of the small family. The family members had devoted themselves to the study of topics ranging from history, classical literature, biographies, and fiction to the discipline of poetry.

Elion's elementary education occurred in the Bronx, in what was then considered a suburb of New York City. Young Gertrude Elion was exceptionally bright. As she progressed through the elementary and junior high school years, she had been repeatedly moved up, having skipped a total of 4 years by the time she entered the girls-only Walton High School, in New York.

The collapse of the economy after the stock market crash of 1929 figured prominently in her choice of higher educational institutions post high school. Elion entered Hunter College, an all-women college, primarily because the institution offered free tuition. At 19 years of age, Elion graduated from Hunter College in 1937, taking her undergraduate degree in chemistry and with the institution's highest honors, Phi Beta Kappa and *summa cum laude*.

As a newly minted chemist with her undergraduate degree in hand, she applied to over a dozen different graduate schools, each within their various chemistry Ph.D. programs. Unfortunately, despite her academic credentials, she had been rejected by every single graduate school, each one stipulating that no funding had been available to her.

Having difficulty landing employment in a chemistry laboratory, primarily because such scientific environments at the time were not terribly friendly to female scientists, Elion consequently went to secretarial school. Elion found the situation discouraging.

A short time later, she had managed to land a scientifically-based position, albeit a temporary one-semester position, in a laboratory. With that position now over in due course, she then took on a non-paying voluntary position in a company devoted to the development and production of pharmaceuticals. After working half-a-year developing a diagnostic kit, her supervisor was permitted to actually pay Elion, an amount that was $12 weekly. After another year, she was paid $20 weekly and had managed to save enough money for graduate school, entering the master's program in a part-time manner at New York University. Meanwhile, Elion taught chemistry and physics at the high school level in New York's public school system. She took her master's degree in chemistry from New York University in 1941.

Due to a shortage of male chemists during World War II, Elion managed to secure a quality control position with a food company, analytically testing foods, such as pickles and mayonnaise, for their various qualities. She later reflected that the experience helped her to gain valuable lessons with new instrumentation.

Then she turned her attention to a new job housed in New Brunswick, New Jersey, at Johnson and Johnson, where she became a laboratory assistant charged with developing new antimicrobial sulfa drugs, the sulfonamides, an endeavor she considered quite worthy. Unfortunately, a reorganization within the company led her to seek other avenues in pursuit of her dream to conduct scientific research.

Her first golden opportunity had started in 1944 with Dr. George Hitchings, who was in charge of a research division at Burroughs Wellcome Research Laboratories. She started out by studying the organic chemistry of nucleic acids. Her work with purine chemistry and spectrophotometry instrumentation lead to the publication of her first paper in a scientific journal.

The work with nucleic acids inspired Elion to pursue a doctorate. Sadly, Elion never received her Ph.D. degree, despite having received numerous honorary doctorates many years later, after bestowment of the Nobel, in 1988.

Needing to make a living on her own, she worked during the day and studied for her Ph.D. degree during the evenings at the Brooklyn Polytechnic Institute. She spent two years commuting several days during the week between Brooklyn by subway and her home in the Bronx.

Then, the dean of the college had unceremoniously announced to her that serious Ph.D. students had to devote their full time to the pursuit of the doctorate. Unable to simply give up her current employment, she was forced to quit graduate school, on a permanent basis. When she looked back at the incident in her later years, she had written that she had had no regrets about the incident.

2. *Her name seems to be inextricably linked with the excruciating condition known as gout. How did she first become involved with gout?*

Elion's involvement in gout studies began first with her interest in the biochemistry of nucleic acids. This nucleic acid work consisted of synthesizing pyrimidines and purines and separating the various intermediates from each other by purifying each of the intermediate components. It was laborious work, involving many chemical steps in the process.

In the course of her work, Elion focused on, in particular, a compound known as 6-MP (short for 6-mercaptopurine), as it was simpler to make chemically-speaking, and it seemed to have interesting properties. For instance, the 6-MP compound showed promise as an immunosuppressive agent and, importantly, in treating leukemia. Unfortunately, the potentially useful 6-MP agent was later observed to be less effective against leukemia as patients seemed to experience relapses despite undergoing an initially promising clinical 6-MP treatment.

In an effort to improve the anti-leukemic nature of the 6-MP, Elion and others began a series of unprecedented studies involving the analysis of the agent's pharmacokinetics and metabolic behaviors. It was hoped that if Elion and colleagues could get a handle on the molecular targets and mode of action for the 6-MP compound, one might be able to improve its clinical performance.

During the course of this new work, Elion found that 6-MP had been broken down in an oxidative manner to a product called thiouric acid by the activity of a now very famous enzyme called xanthine oxidase. It seemed, therefore, that if this degradative enzyme could be stopped, it could save the 6-MP from an unfortunate oxidative breakdown and thus possibly maintain its anti-leukemic nature. Therefore, the search was on for any potential inhibitors of the xanthine oxidase. Such enzyme inhibitors might possibly restore the therapeutic efficacy of the 6-MP.

Elion tried an enzyme inhibitor candidate called 4-hydroxypyrazolo (3,4-d) pyrimidine, known famously as allopurinol. This xanthine oxidase inhibitor had been made in the lab by a colleague of Elion, named Elvira Falco. While the allopurinol appeared to work well toward leukemia both in laboratory mice and in human subjects, the therapeutic index in humans remained disappointingly unaffected, indicating that the blood levels of the allopurinol worked at a concentration that could be toxic to the patient without a concomitant improvement in treatment efficacy. It was a disheartening finding.

The disappointment encountered with the allopurinol against leukemia and with immunosuppression was alleviated with another potential benefit. Elion reasoned that if the allopurinol was so effective in inhibiting the xanthine oxidase enzyme, the compound might then lower the toxic levels of uric acid in the blood. Gout patients experience a significant problem of having higher than normal levels of uric acid, a painful condition known as hyperuricemia. Thus, allopurinol was studied by Elion for its potential to improve the problematic gout condition by possibly lowering the excess blood concentration of the uric acid.

The early physiological studies of the allopurinol were a success. Elion and colleagues found that the allopurinol treatment in human studies resulted in reduced levels of uric acid in blood serum and in the urine. The allopurinol treatment for gout was approved by the FDA in 1966.

3. Some researchers link the eating of too much red meat with gout. What if any is the relationship between way too much red meat and gout?

Meats and other protein-containing foods such as seafood and poultry have high concentrations of purines, a type nucleic acid consisting of nitrogenous bases adenine and guanine. In humans and other organisms, the biochemical breakdown of purines during catabolic metabolism results in the production of excess amounts of uric acid in the blood, a disorder known as hyperuricemia, and it leads to the gout ailment.

Gout is a painful disease characterized by a form or type of arthritis in the joints. The overabundance of the blood levels of uric acid produced by the oxidative metabolism of purine may lead to the deposition of the uric acid crystals in the joints, which then leads to the symptoms of gout.

The symptomology of gout includes the classic hallmarks of inflammation at the arthritic joints, namely, pain or tenderness, redness, heat, and swelling at the affected joint areas. The uric acid crystal buildup at the joints during hyperuricemia is a prime cause of gout symptoms.

4. In general, the big toe of the foot– specifically in the joint is affected. What causes this?

The abnormally high amounts of the uric acid in the blood lead to the settling of uric acid crystals in the joints, like those of the foot and in the big toe, causing gout. It seems that the joints of the big toe represent a commonly affected area, although gout can manifest itself in other joints of the body such as in the fingers, wrists, elbows, as well as in the knees and ankles. The big toe seems to be a common gout location. This is because the big toe is cooler in temperature than in the rest of the body. The cooler temperature, in turn, allows the uric acid crystals to remain stable and embedded in the toe joints, causing the classic gout symptoms there.

5. *Now, treatment seems to be the idea that individuals should stop eating red meat. Will this be successful?*

According to the Centers for Disease Control and Prevention (CDC), there are several avenues to the prevention and treatment of gout.

One avenue is pain management. Typically, when gout symptoms acutely flare-up, anti-inflammatory agents are recommended. These involve agents that may be steroidal or non-steroidal in nature. Non-steroidal anti-inflammatory agents include ibuprofen, for instance, and steroidal agents include the corticosteroids.

Another avenue involves the prevention of uric acid buildup of crystals in the blood by taking Elion's allopurinol. The allopurinol treatment also prevents the development of a pathological structure known as tophi, present within the skin tissue. Tophi consist of hardened uric acid crystals that accumulate just under the skin layers, causing gout flare-up problems for the patient.

A third avenue involves preventing gout flare-up with alterations in diet and lifestyle. These alterations may include avoidance of meats and consuming less of the types of foods that are rich in the purines. Foods that are relatively lower in purines or do not trigger flare-ups include vegetables, whole grains, legumes, and certain fruits. It is also reported that coffee and certain vitamin supplements lower the gout risk. Lifestyle changes include consuming less alcoholic beverages and lowering one's body weight with diet and exercise. The CDC also recommends avoiding or limiting the intake of diuretic medications that are linked to high blood levels of uric acid.

6. *Gertrude Elion seems to have discovered that the treatment of gout is with allopurinol. So what exactly is allopurinol, and how does that work?*

Allopurinol is a biochemical molecule that specifically targets and inhibits the xanthine oxidase enzyme. This enzyme takes typically the purine substrate called hypoxanthine and converts it to uric acid. Oddly enough, allopurinol is also a substrate of the xanthine oxidase. But instead of making uric acid, the allopurinol is converted by the enzyme to oxypurinol, which in turn binds too tightly to the active site of the reduced form of the enzyme, preventing it from doing any further biochemistry until the enzyme is later somehow re-oxidized, at which time the oxypurinol will be released from the inhibited enzyme.

The allopurinol inhibition of the xanthine oxidase enzyme results in the purine metabolism making xanthine and hypoxanthine, instead of the notorious uric acid. The xanthine and hypoxanthine are water-soluble and are, thus, less able to form the confounding pathological crystals than is with the case of the uric acid, which does form the painful gout-associated crystals. Thus, because of the allopurinol, xanthine and hypoxanthine are readily excreted, without producing crystals, and importantly, without producing gout.

7. *What were some of her other discoveries, and is she still alive and researching?*

In addition to her discovery of allopurinol as a treatment and preventative agent for gout, Gertrude Elion was also crucial to the discovery of the allopurinol as an immunosuppressive agent, which was needed for successful graft and tissue transplantation. Elion was also a key figure in the discovery that the allopurinol was somewhat useful for the treatment of childhood leukemia.

Together with her colleague Dr. George Hitchings, Gertrude Elion was also acutely involved in the discovery of the anti-viral agent called acyclovir, which was effective against infectious diseases like oral and genital herpes. The acyclovir therapy was further shown to be useful in addressing cancer that was also causally associated with the herpes viruses. Her anti-viral work was demonstrated to be helpful in addressing AIDS due to HIV infection.

Elion was also an essential scientist during the discovery of the antibacterial agent called trimethoprim. This antimicrobial agent was shown to target specific building block-associated metabolic enzymes involved in nucleic acid biosynthesis, such as the xanthine oxidase, as well as dihydrofolate reductase. Both of these critical enzymes and others play essential intermediary metabolic roles in making necessary biochemical building blocks, which in turn are then required for the production of essential amino acids and nucleic acids, for instance. These building blocks are essential to life.

Sadly, Gertrude (Trudy) B. Elion is no longer with us. She passed away on the 21st day of February, in 1999, at the age of 81 years.

8. What have I neglected to ask?

Gertrude Elion, a child of immigrant parents, never married, nor did she have any children of her very own. Interestingly, while she did not have or raise children, she nevertheless had, through her scientific work, profoundly positive effects on countless millions of other people's children. Furthermore, she never acquired a Ph.D. degree of her own, an honor that is routinely bestowed to the vast majority of male colleagues without much commotion, and apparently without any complaint by their peers and supervisors. Elion did not appear to have that same consideration. Despite the fact that her well-documented academic performances in university and her absolute brilliance repeatedly demonstrated in the research laboratory, she was instead readily discouraged early on in her pursuit of science as an independent investigator and was instead encouraged to serve in menial and even non-paying jobs. It is, thus, a true testament to her extraordinary resilience that she was able to be as hugely successful as a scientist while working in climates that were not terribly conducive to females or even to persons of Jewish origins. It is truly remarkable that Gertrude Elion was able to rise above the fray.

For more information go to:

https://www.youtube.com/watch?v=2EzoTSQlxnM
https://www.youtube.com/watch?v=meqAC16EN1w
https://www.youtube.com/watch?v=UMXxk7cx66k

Chapter 9

GERALD EDELMAN – ANTIBODY STRUCTURE

1. *Professor Varela, we have all heard about the immune system, which protects us. Someone closely associated with it is Dr. Gerald Edelman, who, like a lot of other scholars we have studied, was interestingly enough born in New York City, probably at the height of the stock market crash in 1929. What do we know about his early life?*

Gerald (Gerry) Maurice Edelman was an American biomedical scientist who specialized in the structural protein biochemistry of antibodies, developmental biology, and neurobiology. Dr. Edelman shared the 1972 Nobel Prize in Physiology or Medicine with Dr. Rodney Robert Porter for having determined the structural nature of the antibody molecule.

Edelman was, as you pointed out, born in New York City, in the Queens borough, Ozone Park, in the U.S. His parents were Anna Freedman and Edward Edelman on the first day of the month of July, in 1929, just prior to the crash of the stock market and the ensuing Great Depression of the 1930s. Edelman's father was a physician, and his mother was an insurance agent. The Edelman family was known to partake in intellectual pursuits, such as art, literature, and music.

The child Edelman had wanted to become a concert violinist as one of his earliest interests. He was particularly interested in the music composed by Wolfgang Mozart. Young Edelman attended the New York public school system, from kindergarten through to high school, attending John Adams High School in Queens. His interest in music was serious, having studied under a famous music teacher Albert Meiff. During this time, however, while in high school, Edelman, perhaps influenced by his father, decided to pursue medicine as a career. Another account holds that Edelman discovered that performing was not necessarily of interest to him, after having performed a sonata in front of an audience. Thus, he tried composing music and learned fairly quickly that he felt he had no talent for music composition. The decision to become a scientist instead emerged soon after this early realization.

He graduated from high school in 1946. After high school graduation Edelman attended Ursinus College, a private liberal arts institution which was located in the small town called Collegeville, in the state of Pennsylvania, in the U.S. Choosing to focus his major studies in the field of chemistry, Edelman took his undergraduate degree with honors (magna cum laude) in 1950.

During the same year, Edelman married Maxine M. Morrison, and the couple remained married until his death on the 17th day of May, in 2014, at 84 years of age. Together, the Edelman's had three children.

After graduation from college, in 1950, Edelman was accepted into medical school and enrolled in the School of Medicine at the University of

Pennsylvania, receiving his M.D. degree in 1954. Newly minted, Dr. Edelman became an intern at the Johnson Foundation for Medical Physics, at the University of Pennsylvania, for approximately one year, until 1955. Next, Dr. Edelman moved to Boston, Massachusetts, for further internship training at the famous Massachusetts General Hospital. His official title at Mass General was medical house officer.

2. *Again, like many other Nobel Prize winners, he spent time in the military. What do we know about his work during that time frame?*

Dr. Edelman's military service commenced during the same time frame as his medical internship years, in 1955. After a year interning at Mass General, he joined the U.S. Army Medical Corps. He spent the next two to three years stationed in Paris, France, serving at the officer rank of Captain at a military hospital and spending time in a nearby hospital attending to civilian patients.

During this military service, Dr. Edelman practiced general medicine. He was known to have visited with thousands of patients and delivered countless infants. Interestingly, and fortunately for the rest of us, it is also the same time frame in which he acquired an interest in immunology and, in particular, the antibodies. The new interest stemmed partly from his observations with the then cutting-edge modern molecular biological research conducted at the nearby Sorbonne.

Another source has posited that his interest in antibodies arose because he had read a book on the subject of immunology. He read that exposure to antigens, i.e., foreign agents such as microbes or non-self-substances, in the body provoked the production of the antibodies, which then presumably neutralized the potentially pathogenic effects of the invading foreign antigens. He had further noticed that while a great deal of information was known about the antigens, very little, however, was known at the time about the nature of the antibody itself. This unknown aspect piqued his interest in antibodies and immunology.

3. *Apparently, he earned both the M.D. and the Ph.D. Any ideas as to how this came about?*

As a military medical officer serving in post-World War II France, Dr. Edelman, with an M.D. in hand, was a practicing physician, seeing both military and civilian patients, between 1955 and 1958 when he was honorably discharged from the Army. His interest in the field of immunology had been sparked during this stretch, and it is at this point during his career that he decided to pursue additional formal education.

He chose to acquire another doctorate, this time, the Ph.D. Consequently, Dr. Edelman, the M.D., applied to the Ph.D. graduate program at the Rockefeller Institute for Medical Research, concentrating on immunology. He entered the research laboratory of Prof. Henry G. Kunkel, a prominent immunologist in his own right. In Prof. Kunkel's lab, Dr. Edelman focused his attention on separating apart the various immunoglobulin chains that constituted the antibody molecule.

In 1960, he took his second doctoral degree, becoming Gerald M. Edelman, M.D., Ph.D. The graduate thesis work he conducted for this second doctoral-level degree would start the pathway to the Nobel Prize.

4. *His name is linked to the Rockefeller Institute, again in New York City–what kind of work did he do there?*

At the time, Dr. Edelman, an M.D., undertook graduate-level studies and conducted a thesis project for his Ph.D. at the Rockefeller Institute, known today as Rockefeller University. He successfully defended the thesis project and took his Ph.D. in 1960. That same year he accepted a new position as assistant dean of graduate studies until about 1963 when he became associate dean. Then, in 1966, he was promoted to full professor until 1992, when he retired from the university and moved to the Scripps Research Institute, in La Jolla, California, in the U.S.

Starting with his graduate thesis studies, Dr. Edelman focused his attention on the antibody molecule, wanting to study its structure from a chemical standpoint, using chemical-based tools to do so. Towards this, he first elected to treat the antibodies with chemical agents that broke apart certain bonds known as disulfide bridges that kept the antibody molecule together. One of these chemical agents is called beta (β)-mercaptoethanol. These disulfide bonds consist of two sulfur atoms that are connected to each other. When the disulfide bonds are broken, the sulfur atoms come apart, releasing the rest of the larger molecules that are connected to them along with the sulfur atoms. The chemical process of breaking disulfide bonds with reducing chemicals, such as the β-mercaptoethanol, is called reduction. Next, he treated the broken up antibody molecule parts with an alkylating agent, such as dithiothreitol (DTT), in order to keep the individual broken-up parts from re-associating back together. He had to keep the individual antibody parts separated from each other. Next, he isolated the individual antibody parts from each other by using a biochemical technique called gel filtration. The technique permitted Dr. Edelman to determine the molecular sizes of the antibody parts.

He discovered that the original intact antibody molecule consisted of two large (i.e., heavy) peptide chains and two small (i.e., light) peptide chains. Thus, the graduate student Dr. Edelman found that the antibody molecule consisted of 4 peptide molecules: two heavy chains and two light chains. He further discovered that each of the heavy chains had massive molecular weights of about 50,000 Daltons, and the light chains were each about 22,000 Daltons. It is this work that was to start the process on the road to the Nobel Prize.

Later on, throughout the 1960s, still at Rockefeller, he was able to determine the so-called primary structure of the antibody chains. The primary structure consists of the sequence of amino acids along a protein chain. At the time that he had learned the amino acid sequences of the heavy and light chains of the antibody, it had been the biggest molecule ever to have been sequenced in such a manner. It was a monumental effort.

By combining the results of his studies with those of Dr. Rodney Robert Porter, then at Oxford University, a molecular model of the antibody was proposed in 1969. Professor Porter would shortly become Dr. Edelman's 1972 co-Nobel Laureate in the Physiology or Medicine category, for correctly having deduced the proper antibody structure. The achievement was of enormous importance, not only to immunologists but also to biochemists, cell biologists, microbiologists, and molecular biologists. The rapidity of the Nobel bestowment to Drs. Porter and Edelman, so soon after the structural discovery of the antibody, became known is a testament to the immense importance of the work.

5. *His name is linked with the following fields: biophysics, protein chemistry, immunology, cell biology, and neurobiology. Could you perhaps link his most important investigations with each one of these areas?*

Dr. Edelman's research experiences did indeed touch upon several seemingly disparate fields of study. I shall briefly summarize his connections to each of these areas.

His involvement with the field of biophysics started in 1954, when he focused on medical biophysics at the University of Pennsylvania, working in the research laboratory of Prof. Britton Chance, a biophysical and medical biochemist. It turned out to be the very first research experience that Dr. Edelman had gained in his scientific career. Working under Dr. Chance, Dr. Edelman participated in the spectrophotometric analysis of an important protein called cytochrome *C* peroxidase in mutant yeast microbes. The enzyme is involved in the oxidative phosphorylation process of the respiratory chain, a system for generating biological energy in the form of ATP. The work was of tremendous importance because it confirmed the enzyme-substrate association, as originally predicted by another great biochemist Dr. Leonor Michaelis.

Dr. Edelman's protein chemistry work involved his studies, during the 1960s, on the antibody structure, using chemical means to split apart the various peptide chains by exploiting reducing compounds that would disrupt disulfide bridges that held the chains together and then using alkylating agents that would block the broken bonds in order to prevent the chains from coming together again. This type of protein chemistry work was a main staple in the toolbox of techniques used by biochemists and protein chemists. Working with such a gigantic molecule as the antibody, it required an enormous amount of work. Furthermore, the determination of the primary amino acid sequence of the protein chains required a firm knowledge of the protocols necessary for peptide sequencing. Sequencing the amino acids along a protein chain was a laborious process.

The protein chemistry work of Dr. Edelman comes hand-in-hand with that of immunology. The antibody molecule is one of the most important proteins ever known, especially when one considers that they confer the acquisition of immunity against pathogens, cancer, and against any foreign agent that invades the body. Incidentally, antibodies are also referred to by protein chemists and immunologists alike as immunoglobulins because, at the molecular structural level, the chains have globular configurations to them. That is, the antibodies consist of a set of globs!

Hence, antibodies are also frequently called immunoglobulins, or Ig, for short. The antibodies are the prime fighters of cancer and microbial pathogens, and exposure to these types of antigens represents the onset of potentially serious diseases. The antibodies, induced after antigenic exposure, thus provide protection and immunity to these antigens. Therefore, Dr. Edelman's discovery of the antibody (immunoglobulin) structure will, no doubt, continue to be of great importance. Consequently, Dr. Edelman's name will forever be connected to immunology.

During the 1970s, Dr. Edelman started a new line of research. This effort involved the study of the cellular and molecular mechanisms that controlled the growth of biological cells. He also studied cellular developmental biology of multicellular organisms. He concentrated on those embryonic systems which connected cells to each other, a phenomenon known as cell-cell interactions. The type of cells he focused on consisted of developing neurons, which function in the brain. Thus, as he became a cell biologist, he also became a neurobiologist.

This cell biological and neurobiological work of Dr. Edelman ultimately led to his discovery of a new type of cellular glue, i.e., molecules that held cells together. These molecules are known as cell adhesion molecules. The discovery of these cellular glue-like molecules has been regularly included in textbooks involving both the fields of cell biology and neurobiology alike.

Expanding upon the neurobiological work, he later paid attention to the functioning of the brain, proposing a new idea to explain how the brain develops and organizes its neurons. The mechanism is known as neuronal group selection. He became well known for his contributions to the field of neuroscience; as a result, he shed new light on the biological mechanisms of consciousness.

6. *The Nobel Prize – was apparently shared with a Rodney Porter – what exactly did they win the Nobel Prize for?*

Together, Drs. Edelman and Porter shared the 1972 Nobel Prize for their work involving the structural elucidation of the antibody molecule. We discussed the antibody work of Dr. Edelman above, which encompassed breaking up the four various peptide chains, two heavy and two light protein chains, that make up the antibody, in determining the molecular sizes of these chains, and in determining the amino acid sequences along the antibody chains.

Dr. Porter's work with the antibody structure determination took a different track than that of Dr. Edelman. In the Porter laboratory, they added an enzyme called papain to an antibody molecule and broke it into three separate fragments. Two of the three antibody fragments were identical in size and correctly presumed to be identical in nature. These two fragments were discovered to bind to the antigens. Even when broken up into their pieces, the fragments could specifically and tightly bind to their dedicated antigens. Thus, these two fragments were referred to as Fab, for antibody fragments that perform antigen binding. It was the first time it became known that an intact antibody could bind to two molecules of antigen. It was also found that the Fab fragments contained the entire complement of light chains but only part of the overall heavy peptide chains.

The third fragment was distinct from the two identical Fab fragments, and it was shown that this third distinctive part could readily precipitate into a crystallized form. Hence, this third antibody fragment was called Fc, meaning a fragment that crystallizes easily. The Fc fragment consists of the rest of the heavy chains, but without any of the light chains. Later work showed that the Fc part of an antibody participates in performing other functions associated with humoral immunity and in communicating with certain components of innate immunity.

7. *I lifted a phrase from his bio – perhaps you can help me understand it. "In his most recent work, he and his co-workers have been investigating the "fundamental cellular processes of transcription and translation in eukaryotic cells." First, what are eukaryotic cells? And what exactly is meant by these terms?*

Strictly speaking, a eukaryotic cell harbors a nuclear membrane that surrounds an internal nucleus. The nucleus resides inside the cell of the eukaryote, surrounded by the cell's cytoplasm. The term eukaryotic means the true nucleus. The nucleus, in turn, harbors the cell's chromosomal DNA contents of a cell's genome, plus associated proteins involved in, for instance, nucleic acid synthesis, regulation of gene expression, and in chromosomal DNA packing, among other constituents. In general, organisms that are eukaryotic in nature are considered to be higher organisms, i.e., higher than, let's say, prokaryotes, which do not harbor such cellular nuclei. Such prokaryotes include the bacteria and the archaea.

Dr. Edelman's contributions to this eukaryotic field include his findings related to transcription, i.e., RNA synthesis, and to translation, i.e., protein synthesis. The Edelman laboratory was key to making new DNA promoters that helped to enhance gene expression, i.e., turning on transcription and translation of DNA-based genes. The DNA promoter elements encoded so-called ribosome binding sites that, when transcribed into RNA, the ribosome binds this RNA site in order to facilitate greater translational efficiency. This work has become of major importance within the newer bioinformatics-based discipline of proteomics, which deals with the entirety of the protein collections within a cell, or a tissue type, or of an entire living being. Dr.

Edelman's work with eukaryotic molecular biology is also of fundamental importance to genomics. The research study of genomics is concerned primarily with genomes and their relationships to their evolution, function, and structure, including the physical mapping of the genes harbored with the genomes.

8. Why study antibody structure?

The short answer to your question is if one knows the structure of a molecule, then one may also understand its function. While this tenet may not be applicable to all molecules of known structure, it is most certainly true in the case of the antibody structure. The antibody is a central player in the overall immune system. The antibody forms the basis of the so-called humoral immunity. One of the four humors, originating from ancient medicine, is blood, and antibodies are made by plasma cells which can reside in the blood. Later on, these humoral factors, the antibodies, were also known as Bence-Jones proteins, then later as antitoxins, and more recently as immunoglobulins.

In the natural world, antibodies confer immunity, i.e., protection from a second exposure to a possibly pathogenic antigen, after having been exposed to the antigen the first time. Knowledge of antibody structure and its mechanisms of production can also be used to produce certain antibodies with highly precise binding sites for certain antigens of interest. Such highly specific antibodies can, in turn, be used to detect and purify these interesting antigens for further study.

Interestingly, the number of antigens, these so-called non-self-entities, is vast. They can number into the billions, and yet our genetic programming, with only a mere approximately 33,000 human genes, has the capability to produce precisely specific antibodies that, on the whole, can recognize and bind to virtually any or all of these countless antigens! Thus, one type of molecule, the antibody, has this astonishing heterogeneity.

As mentioned above, the Fab portions of an antibody, whether intact or in fragments, can bind to antigens in a precise manner. The antigen-binding sites of the Fab are made up of both light and heavy chains, and each Fab section is thus variable in their structures in order to accommodate their binding specificity to the vast array of available antigens. In theory, every antibody molecule is unique for a given antigen, and one basis for this astounding heterogeneity is the variable sections inherent in the Fab segments of the antibody.

Such antigen binding by the Fab sections of an antibody serves to neutralize the potentially pathological effects of the antigens. Some Fab parts of the antibody can participate in actually oxidizing bound antigen, resulting in their destruction. The Fab part can undergo an agglutination process, which can, in turn, be exploited experimentally to determine, for instance, one's blood type, or to diagnose an infection, or even to detect tumors. Yet, with such extreme variability in their mode of antigen binding, the same molecule has retained a remarkable consistency with its other parts!

The Fc part of the antibody structure is amazingly conserved—it is considered constant. Furthermore, the Fc has its own set of functions associated with it. For example, the Fc directly participates in inducing inflammation, enhancing phagocytosis, turning on the complement cascade, recruiting natural killer cells against cancer or virus-infected cells, and helping an antibody from a pregnant mom cross her placenta in order to confer passive immunity to her baby in utero.

In summary, the antibodies will continue to be of remarkable importance to the worlds of immunology, protein biochemistry, and biomedical science. The relevance of the antibody will most definitely be a long-lasting one. It is my opinion that biomedical scientists are only beginning to tap the marvelous potential of these antibodies.

9. The study and control of cell growth– why is this important in the big scheme of things?

All living cells grow to various extents. Some cells can become specialized in their functions, perhaps to produce certain biomolecules for immunity, or to produce necessary hormones and other communication-based molecules, etc. Even single-celled organisms will grow, producing more numbers of cells. Cell growth is a basic life process. Certain cells with desirable functions, such as synthesizing needed molecules, can be encouraged to grow extremely efficiently in order to maximize the production of important products. Such growth processes are important for biotechnology and in the cellular-based industries.

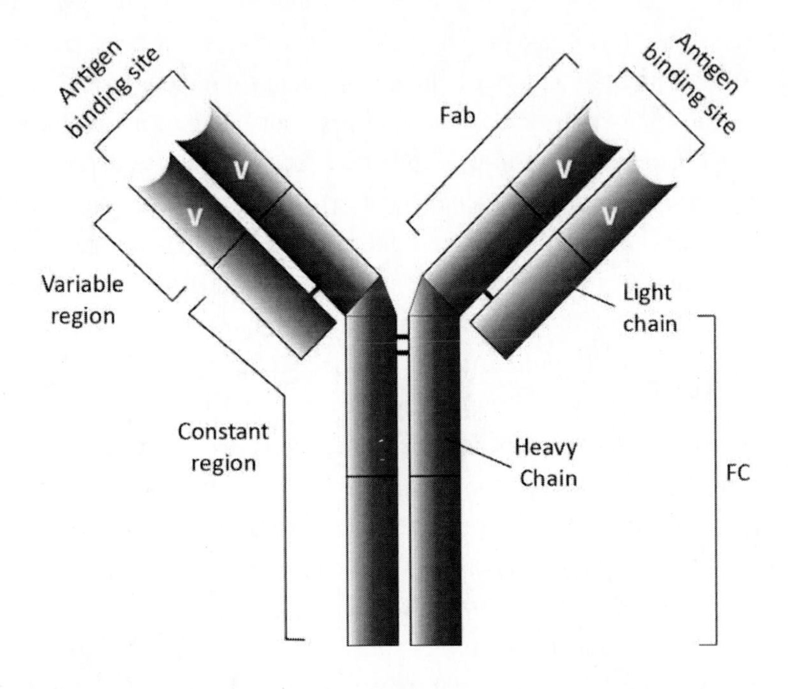

Normal cells will grow when it is necessary. Further, such normal cells will stop growing when required to do so. Living systems have developed sophisticated molecular mechanisms for controlling when to start and stop such cellular growth. This area is of great importance in the field of developmental biology, such as in producing an intact living organism from a fertilized egg.

On the other hand, certain cells, the tumorigenic type, come to mind, may not permit themselves to be subjected to these normal growth control mechanisms. The tumors may consequently grow in an uncontrollable manner. Such uncontrolled tumor growth can lead to a potentially more serious type of cell growth, namely, that of the malignant kind. Malignancy involves the movement of parts of the overall tumor mass within the body to other parts of the same body and resulting in abnormal cellular functioning. Interruption of normal cellular functioning by malignant tumor masses can not only be detrimental, causing morbidity but can also be deadly. Therefore, circumventing malignancy, by studying cell growth control systems, is a crucial goal of cancer biology research, an important field within the biomedical sciences.

10. What have I neglected to ask about this great scientist, investigator, and Nobel Prize winner?

Dr. Edelman's body of scientific literature is immense, having published over 500 articles in the technical journals. He also penned numerous popular books, many of which dealt with the functioning and evolution of the nervous system.

In an interview, released as a series of the so-called *Web of Stories*, Dr. Edelman relates many aspects of his life, complete with many delightful anecdotes that are not covered here. I highly recommend that our readers spend the time to watch these enjoyable, if not humorous, stories!

For more information go to:

https://www.webofstories.com/playAll/gerald.edelman?sId=15743

Chapter 10

JOSEPH GOLDSTEIN – CHOLESTEROL

1. *We have all heard that nasty word—cholesterol, and it sends shivers and shakes into our minds and spines. However, what exactly IS cholesterol, where does it come from, what does it do? Moreover, what can we do about it?*

Indeed, the term cholesterol evokes a sense of fear amongst the masses of people, especially those who are concerned about their heart health. Cholesterol is widely known to be involved in coronary artery disease, such as atherosclerosis. This type of heart disease involves the arteries that supply oxygen-laden blood to the heart. These coronary arteries are blocked to varying degrees by atherosclerotic deposits containing cholesterol and fats. The numbers of human deaths every year is staggering, both at the national level, in the U.S., where it is the number one cause of mortality, and on a worldwide scale.

Cholesterol, an organic molecule, is a biochemical steroid in its nature. In humans, cholesterol is obtained as part of the regular diet, but it is also made in the liver.

In the liver, the starting molecule for the biosynthesis of cholesterol is called acetyl-coenzyme A (i.e., acetyl CoA), which will have been made from our dietary intake of sugars, protein, and fats, during metabolic catabolism. During the cholesterol synthesis, several molecules of acetyl CoA are condensed with each other to make a vital precursor called 3-hydroxy-3-methylglutaryl-CoA (HMG-CoA). Then, the HMG-CoA is converted into another metabolite called mevalonate. From mevalonate, the cholesterol molecule will be biosynthesized in a pathway that requires over two dozen additional biochemical reactions.

The enzyme that catalyzes the biochemical conversion to mevalonate is called HMG-CoA reductase. This enzymatic step is a crucial committed stage, and it is regulated naturally in the body. The enzyme, however, is also a good target for regulation by pharmaceutical drugs, the statins being an example that comes to mind. The statin drugs will target the HMG-CoA reductase enzyme to prevent the overproduction of the cholesterol.

Combined with diet and exercise, the levels of blood cholesterol can usually be kept in check. In the case where a patient is suffering from hypercholesterolemia, a condition where the blood cholesterol levels are abnormally elevated, the statins and other cholesterol-reducing medicines may be utilized.

Incidentally, it may interest our readers to know that while cholesterol certainly has its pathological circumstances, there are also positive aspects to this famous molecule. While cholesterol is generally found within the cell membranes of individuals, it serves a regular physiological role in regulating the fluidity (i.e., flexibility versus rigidity) of these membranes at the molecular level. It is also a metabolic precursor to the biosynthesis of certain steroid hormones, such as cortisol, estrogen, and testosterone. Another interesting fact is that cholesterol can be converted to vitamin D by the action of ultra-violet light in the skin of humans.

2. *Now, LDL and HDL – I look at my blood work, and I use the memory device – LOUSY DL and Healthy DL – but what is DL? So what do these terms mean?*

The LDL and HDL acronyms refer to low-density lipoprotein and high-density lipoprotein, respectively. Both of these biomolecules are found in the body, and they serve to carry cholesterol throughout the various regions of the body. Using your amusing vernacular, lousy, the LDL is indeed lousy because LDL transports cholesterol from the liver to the tissues like the heart, where cholesterol, together with fats, can build up in the coronary arteries to occlude them, increasing the risk of heart attacks. The occluded or blocked coronary arteries are prevented from providing needed oxygen to the heart, causing an increased risk of heart disease. A heart that is deprived of its oxygen may create a situation where the cardiac muscle is damaged or where heart muscle cells may even die.

On the other hand, the HDL, the "healthy DL" as you so aptly put it, serves to carry the cholesterol to the liver. This cholesterol transport to the liver is a necessary, healthy process. Excess cholesterol that's brought to the liver by the HDL can, in turn, be degraded. For example, cholesterol in the liver can be converted to bile acids or a compound called coprostanol, which can then be excreted from the individual. Alternatively, as I mentioned above, cholesterol can be converted into any of a variety of useful hormones, or to vitamin D, or sent to the cell membrane.

Obviously, then, one would (or should) like to optimally have their lousy DLs as low as possible and their healthy DLs correspondingly as high as possible.

3. *How does one go about balancing the healthy and unhealthy? And is the American diet utterly CRUMMY?*

If one wishes to harbor healthy levels of cholesterol, then a proper diet is indicated. Such a diet is low in both cholesterol and certain fats. Fats, especially those that are saturated, serve to maintain potentially unhealthy blood cholesterol levels. Thus, a low saturated-fats diet is essential. Second, exercise helps to get the blood circulation going to healthy levels. The practice helps better to supply oxygen to the tissues to keep them healthy. If diet and exercise do not keep the cholesterol and saturated fat levels down, then chemotherapy may be indicated. This is where cholesterol-reducing drugs can come into play.

The short answer to your question about the poor quality of the American diet is: yes. While one's version of a healthy diet may vary in detail from individual to individual, a consensus amongst clinicians seems to be that a healthy diet is rich in fruits, vegetables, nuts, legumes, fish, polyunsaturated fatty acids, and low in carbohydrates, saturated fats, and processed foods. The American diet is crummy because of overeating during meals, excessive snacking between meals, and consumption of so-called fast-foods, much of which are rich in unhealthy saturated fats and cholesterol.

4. *Now, who was Joseph Goldstein, and where was he born? (I understand he is still alive).*

Dr. Joseph Leonard Goldstein has been a world-class medical geneticist, biochemist, and 1985 Nobel laureate, sharing the honor with Dr. Michael Stuart Brown, for their discovery that cellular receptors for LDL serve to reduce the levels of blood-laden cholesterol. Goldstein was born in Sumter, South Carolina, in the U.S., on the 18th day in the month of April, during the year 1940. His parents were Isadore and Fannie Alpert Goldstein. His parents were owners of a clothing store. He was raised as a child in

Kingstree, S.C., in the U.S. As of this writing, he is presently 79 years of age.

5. *His early years and medical training– where did he receive his education and under who – and what got him studying cholesterol?*

Goldstein attended elementary school and a small high school (about 60 enrolled students) in Kingstree, S.C., the latter of which was known to be an all-white school that was steeped in segregation. A central topic of interest for Goldstein included chemistry, and he attributed this scientific interest to his high school science teacher.

After high school graduation, Goldstein went to a private, liberal arts institution called Washington and Lee University, which was located in Lexington, Virginia, in the U.S. Majoring in the discipline of Chemistry, Goldstein took his undergraduate degree, with highest honors, *summa cum laude*, in 1962.

After graduating from university, Goldstein enrolled in medical school at the Southwestern Medical School Health Sciences Center, which was part of the University of Texas, in Dallas, TX, in the U.S. While in medical school, Goldstein became interested in the area of academic medicine. He has attributed this new interest to a medical school teacher and mentor Dr. Donald W. Seldin, who at the time was the departmental chair of Internal Medicine. Dr. Joseph L. Goldstein took his M.D. degree in 1966.

The newly minted Dr. Goldstein then moved from Dallas, TX, to Boston, Massachusetts, in order to take up a new post as an intern and later a medical resident at the prestigious Massachusetts General Hospital, where he stayed until 1968. It is at Mass General where Dr. Goldstein first met Dr. Michael Brown, both of whom became friends and scientific collaborators.

After the conclusion of his residency training at Mass General, in 1968, Dr. Goldstein moved to Bethesda, Maryland, in the U.S., where the National Institutes of Health (NIH) had been housed. Dr. Goldstein became a clinical associate studying molecular genetics at the National Heart Institute in the NIH research laboratory of the famous Prof. Marshall W. Nirenberg, who in

1968 became a Nobel Laureate with Dr. Har Gobind Khorana and Robert W. Holley, for their solving of the genetic code.

At the NIH, Dr. Goldstein participated in the clinics, where he and Dr. Brown had first encountered patients who presented with the genetic disease called familial hypercholesterolemia (FH). The severe medical condition much interested Dr. Goldstein and his good friend and collaborator, Dr. Brown, who had also moved to the NIH, working in the laboratory of Prof. Earl Stadtman, studying the chemistry of enzymes. Encountering these FH patients was the prime spark that started their Nobel Prize-winning cholesterol work.

6. *I understand he worked with a Michael S. Brown– what do we know about this chap?*

Biomedical scientists Brown and Goldstein shared the Nobel Prize in physiology or medicine in 1985 for their collaborative work on cholesterol biochemistry. The scientific duo had first met while they had been young medical interns at Mass General in Boston, MA. Thanks to their pioneering studies, countless millions of lives have been saved from the ravages of coronary artery disease.

Michael Stuart Brown was born in Brooklyn, New York, in the U.S., on the 3rd day of April, in 1941. His parents were Harvey and Evelyn Brown. Having been raised in Wyncote Pennsylvania, Brown went to Cheltenham High School and attended the University of Pennsylvania, where he took his undergraduate degree in Chemistry in 1962. He then attended the School of Medicine at the University of Pennsylvania, and he received his M.D. degree in 1966.

After interning at Mass General, Boston, MA, where he met Dr. Goldstein, Dr. Brown moved to the NIH in 1968. Dr. Brown worked in the laboratory of Dr. Earl R. Stadtman, focusing on the biochemistry of enzymes. Next, Dr. Brown moved to Dallas, Texas, where he studied the HMG-CoA reductase enzyme at the University of Texas Southwestern Medical School.

In 1974, Drs. Goldstein and Brown shared a research laboratory, choosing to combine their previously independent laboratories into one collaborative lab. The move was to result in astonishing research successes. Together, the research teams wanted to focus on FH disease in order to solve the problem of high blood cholesterol.

The Goldstein-Brown researchers found out that cells from humans have in their membranes the LDL receptors, which function to lower the cholesterol levels from the blood and that in the FH patients, these LDL receptors were lower than usual. Thus, the cholesterol concentrations in the blood of the FH patients were abnormally high, leading to the severe condition of hypercholesterolemia.

7. *On some T.V. commercials, I hear them talking about "genetics" and blaming genetics on high LDL. Is there any truth to this?*

Indeed, it is true. The Goldstein and Brown research laboratory discovered the LDL receptor in the membranes of cells from FH patients with hypercholesterolemia. They found that the gene which encodes the LDL receptor in humans with the FH condition was defective, leading to lower than normal levels of this receptor. In examining more closely the nature of the defect, they discovered the mechanism of the LDL receptor's disappearance from the cellular membranes. This mechanism is referred to in the textbooks as receptor-mediated endocytosis. As the LDL ligand binds the receptor on the membrane, the membrane invaginates and pinches off to form an intracellular vesicle enclosing the LDL receptor within the internalized endosome. With the LDL receptor missing from the plasma membranes of cells, the LDL-cholesterol builds up and collects in the blood and its vessels. This is especially troublesome in the arteries that feed blood to the heart, the so-called coronary arteries. The LDL-cholesterol build-up in the blood may result in the formation of atherosclerotic plaques in the vessels, which block the flow of oxygenated blood to the heart, increasing the risk of heart attacks.

8. *Apparently, they have won a number of prizes for their work– can you name a few?*

Drs. Goldstein and Brown made their Nobel Prize-worthy discoveries relatively early on in their careers, and they consequently garnered a significant number of other accolades. Each of these awards is bestowed to investigators for making substantial scientific contributions to the biomedical sciences.

One, in particular, is the Albert Lasker Award, 1985, for basic medical research, which is considered by many to be a preamble to the Nobel Prize. The Lasker prize was established in the mid-1940s by Albert D. Lasker, who was a prominent advertising magnate and a dedicated philanthropist. Another leading accolade is the Warren Alpert Prize, 1999, which is awarded by its associated Foundation and is run by a committee composed of biomedical scientists at Harvard Medical School. Another distinguished honor is their inclusion as Fellows, in 1991, into the prestigious Royal Society. This Royal Society Fellows list, established in 1663, has a large number of world-renowned scientists, such as Isaac Newton, himself, plus Albert Einstein, Francis Crick, Dorothy Hodgkin, and Tim Hunt, to name only a few. One of my favorites is the Herbert Taylor Research Award in 2005, established in 2004 by the American Society for Biochemistry and Molecular Biology (ASBMB). The ASBMB-based award was given to both scientists for their excellent contributions in the areas of biochemistry and molecular biology. One last tribute is the National Medal of Science, which is bestowed by the president of the U.S. and was given to Drs. Goldstein and Brown in 1988.

9. *Goldstein and Brown did work on the SREBP family of "membrane-bound transcription factors." What does SREBP stand for, and why is it important?*

The acronym SREBP stands for sterol regulatory-element binding protein, and Drs. Goldstein and Brown discovered it in the early 1990s. The pathway to its discovery began in 1933, when a biomedical scientist by the name of Dr. Rudolf Schoenheimer, sealed laboratory mice in bottles with plenty of air and fed the mice a diet that completely lacked cholesterol. The jars then exhibited a higher cholesterol content.

But when Dr. Schoenheimer sealed his lab mice in the jars and gave them food with plenty of cholesterol in it, he found that the mice inside the jars did not produce any additional cholesterol. These findings suggested (1) that mice, and by extension other animals like humans, can make cholesterol on their own and (2) that when cholesterol is already present in sufficient amounts, it prevents the further biosynthesis of additional cholesterol, i.e., that cholesterol production was regulated by cholesterol. Such a regulatory mechanism is known as feedback inhibition by the product that's made at the end of the pathway.

This is where the SREBP mechanism discovered by Drs. Brown and Goldstein comes into play. This SREBP discovery of theirs was performed in the early 1990s, after they had received the Nobel, in 1985. First, they had purified the SREBP family of proteins. The SREBPs are DNA-binding factors that turn on the gene expression programs for a variety of new genes, making a set of proteins that function in making cholesterol and fatty acids. Since the activation of gene expression by the SREBPs are at the level of transcription, i.e., RNA synthesis is turned on for a variety of genes, the SREBPs are also referred to as transcription factors. In general, transcription factors bind to promoter elements on DNA and turn on the transcription of specific genes.

Drs. Brown and Goldstein found that members of the SREBP family are bound to the membrane of the intracellularly located endoplasmic reticulum (ER) but in an inactive form. When cholesterol levels are low, however, the SREBP comes out of the membrane. The newly loosened SREBP molecule moves to the Golgi complex, where it is cut into two fragments and becomes active as a putative transcriptional activator. Next, the freshly activated SREBP moves to the nucleus of the cell, where it binds to its DNA and stimulates the gene expression of elements that encode enzymes for cholesterol biosynthesis. One essential protein is the HMG-CoA reductase, which then proceeds to make the needed cholesterol in the ER.

When cholesterol levels are too high in the blood, the SREBP is kept in an un-fragmented state, thus maintaining itself in an inactive form. The genes that encode cholesterol and fatty acid biosynthesis consequently are not expressed.

10. Apparently, Goldstein has been involved with the Salk Institute and the Rockefeller University in New York City. What kind of work did he do at these excellent places?

In 1983, Dr. Goldstein was elected as a so-called non-resident fellow for biological sciences at the Salk Institute, which is located in La Jolla, California, in the U.S. One activity that Dr. Goldstein partook in at the Salk Institute was that of a symposium presenter at the 40th anniversary of the founding of the famous institution.

In 2015, Dr. Goldstein became a life-long member of the board of trustees at the Rockefeller University. The institution was established in 1901 by the oil magnate and philanthropist John Davison Rockefeller.

Along these lines, Dr. Goldstein also became a member of the board of trustees for the Howard Hughes Medical Institute, established by another wealthy entrepreneur Howard Hughes, in 1953. Each of these institutions is laden with many prominent biomedical scientists. A great deal of biomedical research is conducted at these institutes.

11. Goldstein seems to be a model of someone who has done a great deal of clinical research and investigation. What would you say are his most significant accomplishments? And how does he seem to be able to discern such important factors and variables and discoveries?

The discovery of the LDL receptor was a tremendously important finding. His involvement in the scientific breakthrough of its regulation, its feedback mechanism for controlling cholesterol biosynthesis via the SREBPs, constitutes another hugely significant mark on the biomedical science field. This more recent discovery has led directly to the saving of countless millions of lives from the detrimental effects of heart attacks.

Another significant discovery by Dr. Goldstein that I have not yet mentioned is that of Scap.

Scap stands for SREBP cleavage-activating protein. Like the SREBP, the Scap molecule is also an ER-associated protein. But the Scap is also associated with the SREBP, as well. Together, they form a complex called SREBP-Scap. The membrane-bound SREBP-Scap complex in the ER functions as a sensor of cholesterol levels. The Scap molecule aids in the feedback regulation of the cholesterol biosynthesis.

It is my contention that Dr. Goldstein's medical training in the clinical field is the prime factor in his discernment regarding what is essential from a biomedical standpoint. Obviously, studying medical diseases is vital for discoveries of underlying cellular and molecular mechanisms. Knowledge of such fundamental life-associated machinery is then critical for its manipulation in order to realize effective treatments. With heart attacks still being close to number one as a leading cause of morbidity and mortality, if not number one itself, the work of Dr. Goldstein and others in this area of biomedical science will continue to be of great importance, possibly for generations to come.

For additional information on Dr. Goldstein go to:

https://www.youtube.com/watch?v=Nlqst3DegfM
https://www.youtube.com/watch?v=nzYpbQInFmY
https://www.youtube.com/watch?v=7-vaio1fFy0

Chapter 11

JOHN B. GURDON – STEM CELLS

1. *One individual who not only won the Nobel Prize but was named "Sir" in Great Britain was Sir John B. Gurdon. He was born in England– but apparently had some very early difficulties. Tell us about his early education.*

Sir Dr. John Bertrand Gurdon, a 2012 Nobel Laureate in Medicine or Physiology, was born in the small rural village of Dippenhall, in Hampshire county (now Surrey), England, on the second day of October, in the year 1933. John's parents were Marjorie Byass and William Nathaniel Gurdon, a banker with a substantial inheritance from an endowment.

John Gurdon's earliest educational experience was based on a sort of home-schooling instruction, complete with private tutors. John and his older sister Catherine had been shipped to England's countryside during World War II, as this region of the country, southern England, was a prime target for German Blitz bombing.

In a keynote memoir, published in the prestigious *Annual Reviews* series devoted to cellular and developmental biology, Dr. Gurdon writes about his early schooling at a preparatory school, Edgeborough, which apparently neglected to teach him the biological sciences before his entry into Eaton, a prestigious college preparatory school, at age 13, where biology was not taught there, as well, until 15 years of age. His experiences at Eaton were less than desirable. First, he was bullied by classmates, and he was staunchly discouraged by his teachers to pursue the academic discipline of biology.

Gurdon's main interests at the time appeared to be moths and butterflies, a passion he had had since early childhood. Thus, upon graduation from university at Oxford, he eagerly applied to their Entomology program for graduate school. His application for a Ph.D. school was rejected.

Thus, in 1956, he applied instead to Oxford's graduate program in Embryology, and his application was accepted! As a newly minted 22-year old graduate student, Gurdon entered the research laboratory of Prof. Michail Fischberg. It was here in Dr. Fischberg's laboratory where young Gurdon learned the technique of transplanting cellular nuclei from the embryos of frogs, known as *Xenopus*, into living host eggs! In 1960, John B. Gurdon took his Ph.D. degree from Oxford.

2. *Interestingly enough, there are some records of some of his instructors expressing some doubt that he would ever make it as a scientist. Do we have some records of his early evaluations?*

John Gurdon's biology instructor at Eaton is recorded to have described John's plan to become a biological scientist as "ridiculous" and a "sheer waste of time" not only for John but especially for his future Biology teachers! According to another source, an interview he gave to a reporter,

Gurdon placed academically at the very bottom of about 250 students of his Biology course at Eaton.

At the age of 15, his academic performance at Eaton was so appalling, he was accordingly told that he had absolutely no abilities whatsoever to undertake any sort of academic subjects in any kind of depth, and he was consequently placed in a classroom with other students who were at the bottom, like himself. In this new class, however, he was placed at the bottom of even that class. In fact, he was ranked at the very bottom of the entire school!

Furthermore, he was told by his teachers that there was no sense in trying to make a career out of anything having to do with science, as he was just "no good" at it. He was made, therefore, to study Latin and ancient Greek, instead of Biology, not because he had any acumen for those topics but because there were extra teachers available to teach them. He was made to abandon a topic he loved, Science, for now focusing on topics that held no interest for him.

He was given a year to try to get back into his science-based courses, a discipline in which he had held a life-long passion. He later recalled that he felt sorry for his parents, who had then paid his tuition money for all of this trouble.

The educational ordeal had been brutal, and its effects long-lasting.

The negative student evaluation by the teacher was to be framed and shared with the world. The student, Dr. John Gurdon, in later years, was himself to provide an assessment of his own about his former teacher.

Soon after the Nobel, Sir Dr. John Gurdon had recalled that the discouraging teacher, the one who had placed him at the bottom of his class and had recorded his scientific career options as "hopeless," was, in fact, a terrible teacher in that he had taught the material incorrectly. Much of the course material delivered by the teacher was factually wrong!

Thus, many years later Sir Dr. Gurdon was to candidly note in an interview regarding his Nobel Prize that he had, on the contrary, felt quite fortunate during that time in Eaton, because he was no longer under auspices of such a terrible teacher—it had been, instead, a great relief for him to have been removed from the course.

To make matters worse, however, when the time arrived to consider higher education at university, Gurdon was informed in no uncertain terms that while he was undoubtedly welcome at Oxford University, it was nevertheless under the proviso that he NOT concentrate his studies in Latin or Greek, as he appeared to have performed less than adequately in these subjects on his entrance examinations.

He was permitted, however, to concentrate on learning Zoology, the study of animals, at Oxford. Unfortunately, with his lack of a proper secondary preparation in the biological discipline, Gurdon had to spend an extra year of study to make up for the deficiency. Nevertheless, he took his undergraduate degree from Oxford, majoring in Zoology.

Gurdon's troubles with his previous preparatory education plagued him as he applied to graduate school. His undergraduate record was less than stellar, and he was rejected from the Ph.D. program in Entomology at Oxford but later accepted in the Embryology Department, where he successfully completed all requirements for the doctorate, in 1960. The thesis work was to lead ultimately to the Nobel.

3. *The family motto "Virtus viget in arduis" (virtue thrives in adversity) is interesting in that Sir John Gurdon had to undergo a great deal of adversity and difficulty during his life. Tell us about some of the adversity he had to face?*

The Gurdon family follows a long and distinguished aristocratic ancestral line. As you pointed out, the family motto is "*virtus viget in arduis*" (Latin for virtue flourishes in adversity), which originates as far back in history as 1199 A.D. The Gurdon family name goes back to this ancient time in England, with his earliest known ancestor, Bertrand de Gurdon, and to ancient France, to about 1400 A.D, with a one Jean de Gurdon as another known ancestor.

As you noted in your previous question, John Gurdon's early educational experience was fraught with "disaster" and had been an exceedingly appalling predicament for him. The experience left him traumatized for many years to come, openly speaking of it in blunt terms, even after the Nobel.

While his first foray into his Ph.D. thesis project was met with technically challenging laboratory protocols, trying unsuccessfully at first to perform nuclear transfer between somatic cells of the *Xenopus* frogs, Gurdon nevertheless persevered and eventually overcame each of the technical obstacles. Part of the problem was dealing with, as he referred to it, a "jelly-like" type of material that emerged during his experiments and was impenetrable to his micro-injection needles. Fortunately, the problem was solved when a new microscope, one that was fitted with a new UV lamp on it, was purchased. When the scope's UV lamp was turned on to low wavelength emissions, the UV light dissipated the jelly, making it possible to conduct the micro-injections of the nuclei.

After successfully attaining his Ph.D. he had yearned to obtain postdoctoral training in the laboratory of the famous Dr. Renato Dulbecco but was apparently turned away by the departmental head because Dr. Gurdon did have a firm foundation in the field virology, the study of viruses. Thus, Dr. Gurdon accepted a postdoctoral position at the California Institute of Technology (Caltech) working under Prof. Robert Edgar, studying the genetics of bacteriophages. He found the work unsatisfying and resigned after only one year.

Another source of adversity had to do with Dr. Gurdon's early animal cloning work in graduate school. He was roundly criticized for the work, even by investigators who had developed the methodology that Gurdon had made use of but having arrived at the exact opposite conclusions that Gurdon had reached. Fortunately, Gurdon's experimental system had been strongly supported by a reportable genetic marker, which the other laboratory did have not have available at the time.

This particular criticism aside, Gurdon's cloning work was then condemned by none other than his former lab mate, Dr. Jim Watson, perhaps rightly, as foreseeing a shocking situation that was akin to eugenics. The controversy came to a head later with the cloning of a well-known animal, a sheep named "Dolly." Dr. Watson derisively asked whether we were next going to see a clone of new "Einsteins or Raquel Welches." While biomedical scientists decry such human cloning, the work of Gurdon generated an air of hysteria. Not even Gurdon was advocating such a thing, of course, but other cell biologists were thinking out loud, based on Gurdon's frog cloning work, about possibly cloning lower mammals. One merely needed to make the next leap to the cloning of humans!

Another bout with adversity had to do with the stem cells, the use of which many non-scientific groups criticized, especially with the embryonic type of stem cells. The stem cells made excellent progenitors for potential development into clinically useful tissues or even organs, but the idea was much criticized as unethical. These criticisms waned with the later finding by Dr. Gurdon's co-Nobel Laureate, Dr. Shinya Yamanaka, who managed to develop an experimental system for converting non-embryonic mature stem cells back to immature primitive stem cells, without the need for any sort of embryos. This particular criticism, i.e., a putative need for embryos to get stem cells, had been an unnecessary one from the very start, because actual embryos were never actually needed. Immature stem cells could always have been obtained directly from placental tissue, i.e., the tissue that is routinely discarded after every single birthing process anyway.

4. *From Eton to Oxford to Cambridge – he seemed to make the rounds of the best schools in England. What did he study at each university?*

Eaton, at the time of Dr. Gurdon's tenure, was an elite boarding school that was geared to the preparation of young students for entry into university. At the age of 15, Gurdon was enrolled at this institution, and his stay there was unsettling. He experienced bullying by students and terrible teaching by teachers. His passion for science was almost stymied by being forced to learn other topics that he found neither interesting nor of significance. Misunderstood from the very beginning of his entry to Eaton about his aptitude for biological science, he was removed from his science courses and made to study Latin and ancient Greek. The experience was so profoundly adverse that he was said to have actually framed one of his negative student evaluations by a teacher from the Eaton years.

At Oxford, Gurdon took his Ph.D. degree in 1960. It had been an elegant and groundbreaking thesis project. As a graduate student there, he gained expertise in transplantation methodology of cellular nuclei in laboratory frogs called *Xenopus*, creating the first clone of a genetically identical frog, and demonstrating in an elegant fashion the ability of a cell to multiply and make each of the various somatic cell types of an animal. He had found that a transplanted nucleus could remember where it had come from and direct the production of an embryo-specific to its origin rather than its host. The host cells had been reprogrammed!

When his former graduate advisor, Dr. Fischberg, left Oxford, Dr. Gurdon was asked to replace him. He accepted the offer and became an assistant lecturer in 1962.

At Cambridge, Dr. Gurdon became a group leader, in 1971, of the Cell Biology Division at the institution's Medical Research Council's Laboratory for Molecular Biology. It was (and still is) a world-class and prestigious research facility. In 1983, Dr. Gurdon was promoted to full professor supported by the John Humphrey Plummer endowment, becoming the Plummer Professor of cell biology at Cambridge's Zoology Department. Then, in 1990, he became a departmental chair at the Wellcome Trust Cancer Research Campaign sponsored Institute of Cancer and Developmental Biology. In 2001, this institution was renamed to The Gurdon Institute.

One notable field of study at Cambridge by Dr. Gurdon was his pioneering work with RNA. In Dr. Gurdon's laboratory work, they used microneedles and injected the oocyte egg cells of their frog *Xenopus* with certain strings of RNA. The RNA-injected oocytes could actually use the RNA to make proteins as directed by the egg's translational machinery! This methodology is still widely used to this day to study the physiological properties of proteins expressed in the *Xenopus* oocytes.

5. *By the same token, he seemed to encounter a lively life– traveling from New York to California on the famous Route 66. What did he encounter along the way?*

The Route 66 trip taken in 1960 by the newly minted postdoctoral fellow Dr. Gurdon epitomizes an excellent example of the sort of activity one expects from an adventurous-minded spirit. He was taking the road trip from New York to California, in order to start his new position as a postdoc in the Caltech laboratory of Prof. R. Edgar, to study phage genetics. The new postdoc offer had been inspired from a visit to the Fischberg lab by the very famous Dr. George Beadle, 1958 Nobel Laureate, for his work pertaining to the notion that a gene specifies an enzyme—the so-called "one-gene one-enzyme" hypothesis.

Dr. Gurdon had purchased a used Chevrolet car for the cross-country road trip. Driving along the historic Route 66, Dr. Gurdon paid visits to various scientific luminaries. One such luminary was the notable Dr. Alexander Brink at the University of Wisconsin, at Madison, U.S. As a result of the visit, Dr. Gurdon became lifelong friends with Dr. Brink and his wife, Joyce, and for many years after the road trip, he would periodically visit the Brinks at their second home in Florida during the winter times.

Also visited by Dr. Gurdon during his historic Route 66 road trip was the famous Dr. Robert Briggs, who was housed at the University of Indiana, in Bloomington, in the U.S. Working with Dr. Thomas J. King, Dr. Briggs had been involved in developing nuclear transplantation techniques, a protocol of which Dr. Gurdon had effectively used in graduate school at Oxford.

Also, at Indiana, during the famous Route 66 sojourn, Dr. Gurdon met Dr. Tracy M. Sonneborn, who was to elegantly work out the genetic behavior involved in the cellular differentiation inside the nucleus during the developmental stages in organisms of the *Paramecium* and *Tetrahymena* genera. In his memoir, Dr. Gurdon recalled how all members of the Sonneborn lab had picked up smoking of the pipe, as sort of an unspoken and endearing dedication to their research mentor.

6. *Behind every successful man is a woman– and how did his wife contribute to his academic and professional success?*

In 1962, Jean Elizabeth Margaret Curtis and John Gurdon met in Oxford, England, soon after his arrival to a post as assistant lecturer in their Zoology department. The couple had sired two children, a daughter named Aurea and a son named William. When Dr. Gurdon accepted the prestigious position of Mastership at Magdalene College in 1985, Jean Gurdon took it upon herself to make sure that she entertained each and every undergraduate at the college. In so doing, she would invite twenty undergraduates at a time to a weekly Sunday lunch, prepared by herself. She also acquired an amicable affiliation with each of the college's personnel. Together with Dr. Gurdon declining pay for the Mastership and with Jean's support, both teaching and administrative duties were minimized, and it permitted time to focus on scientific research. The end result of these activities was that Magdalene College at Cambridge enjoyed a high degree of faculty and staff morale during their tenureship.

7. *British university systems are quite different from U.S. systems– and apparently, Sir John Gurdon had to navigate a number of administrative concerns as well as research and teaching concerns. What do we know about all this?*

Taking the advice of the famous Dr. Max Perutz, who headed the MRC Laboratory of Molecular Biology, in Cambridge, Dr. Gurdon declined to accept a professorship offer at Cambridge's Zoology department. The post would have been a prestigious one for Dr. Gurdon, as it had once been occupied by another famous scientist by the name of Sir Alan Hodgkin. However, Dr. Perutz had advised Dr. Gurdon that such an undertaking would most certainly kill his research program because he would be largely "crippled by university administration."

Interestingly, while Dr. Gurdon was at the Wellcome CRC Institute, he had expanded the laboratory facilities with collaborator Prof. Ron Laskey by inviting others to participate in the collaboration, namely, Drs. Michael Akam, Martin Evans, Janet Heasman, and Chris Wylie. It was a monumental undertaking, requiring significant alterations in administrative duties. The research team decided to invoke the successful management style of Dr. Perutz. First, the team established a chairmanship structure, rather than a directorship. Next, they recruited younger promising scientists to become group leaders, giving these investigators opportunities to flourish by allowing them to focus on their research programs.

8. *Through the miracle of modern technology, we can actually hear Sir John Gurdon talking about his receiving the Nobel Prize– the link is below. But could you perhaps summarize and explain why he was awarded the Nobel Prize and his relationship to "stem cells."*

There are two types of stem cells: the somatic type (adult), and the embryonic type. In general, these stem cells have two important properties: first, they are undifferentiated, and second, they are pluripotent.

Let's consider the undifferentiation property of stem cells first. It merely means that a stem cell has no specialized function or structure to it. In this sense, a stem cell is said to be in a primitive state. The second property, pluripotency, means that the stem cell has the potential to become specialized, by differentiating into new types of cells and picking up new and specialized cellular functions. The stem cells are vastly crucial for these and other reasons. The stem cells can be used to generate badly needed specialized cells for use chemotherapeutically. They can also be quite beneficial for learning about life's fundamental processes and for medical applications.

In the natural world, stem cells are the starter cells for the development of organisms. An egg that's fertilized by sperm are at first primitive types of stem cells, undifferentiated but pluripotent, and they begin the painstaking process of forming a new mature organism by invoking the various cellular, tissue, and organ specializations. The fertilized stem cell has a nucleus with its specialization information already embedded, a condition known as nuclear programming.

In short, Dr. Gurdon discovered that if he could transfer a nucleus from a cell to another cell that has had its own nucleus removed, he could reprogram the newly injected unfertilized cell to undergo differentiation, but for a completely different developmental program! Furthermore, he found that his protocol of nuclear transplantation resulted in animal progeny being genetically identical, and in so doing, he cloned higher organisms!

Dr. Gurdon's Nobel Prize-winning work at Oxford was done as follows. First, he took out the nucleus from the frog eggs, and in their place, he put in other nuclei that had been taken from growing tadpole gut cells, i.e., mature somatic cells. Then, the graduate student Gurdon let the transplanted frog eggs grow and develop. The result was an experimental production of new frogs, all of whom were genetically identical. He had, in fact, created a clone of frogs!

With the accompanying work of co-Nobel Laureate from Kyoto University, Dr. Shinya Yamanaka, who showed that he and Dr. Kazutoshi Takahashi could actually convert adult somatic cells into embryonic-behaving stem cells, complete with their undifferentiated states, it made Dr. Gurdon's own pioneering work even more meaningful from a biomedical science standpoint. This new type of stem cell and the accompanying conversion system that had been developed by Drs. Yamanaka and Takahashi have been called induced pluripotent stem cells, or iPS cells. They reprogrammed adult somatic cells, which had already been differentiated, into iPS cells by artificially introducing several genes that encode individual proteins called transcription factors, such as c-Myc, Klf4, Oct4, and Sox2. These transcription factors were produced in the injected cells, and they worked to mediate the induction of the pluripotent state, making primitive stem cells out of adult cells. This new work eliminated the ethical concerns raised by many and made the work of Dr. Gurdon even more relevant.

The nuclear transfer technique of Dr. Gurdon's might be applied to introduce essential reprogramming machinery in order to replace lost somatic cells or tissue in medical patients. Dr. Yamanaka's work makes this approach significantly feasible. In theory, a patient with a medical disease might have hope. First, cells from the patient can be removed, converted into stem cells, fixed with Gurdon's nuclear transfer method, allowed to differentiate with the correct cell type, and then re-introduced back into the patient.

The approach might even be useful in replacing the conventional approach of organ and tissue transplantation! In this case, the grafts would actually be the patient's own corrected cells, and, thus, a detrimental immune response and transplant rejection would be circumvented.

Another promising approach may be to use these systems of Drs. Gurdon and Yamanaka to learn about the cellular mechanism of a given medical disease. Then, potential medicines can be developed and screened for prospective therapies.

9. What have I neglected to ask about this Nobel Prize winner?

In an interview with Dr. Gurdon after the receipt of the Nobel, he conveyed the story about how he found out he was to get the coveted award. Before the official Nobel Prize announcement was made, there had been already rumors that he had gotten it. He conveyed the story that, at first, he received a phone call in the middle of the night from a reporter asking him how he felt about getting the Nobel Prize. When he told the reporter that he hadn't heard about it, the surprised reporter replied that, well, he'd call back later.

The next phone call came from a Swedish person informing him officially of the Nobel award; Dr. Gurdon thought it might be a hoax! After all, there had been rumors flying about.

That day, however, Dr. Gurdon was not to be thoroughly convinced about the Nobel until he went to the laboratory where it was looked-up on the Internet at the Nobel Prize web site. Only then, were he and his laboratory personnel convinced that day.

A great multitude of students, postdocs, and colleagues have all attested to Dr. Gurdon's amicability. Such is the esteem for Dr. Gurdon that a large group of biomedical investigators published a multiple article volume in the journal *Differentiation*, with each article dedicated to this great scientist, the science, and to the kindheartedness of an immensely pleasant human being. In the series of papers in the particular volume, many a grateful scientist communicated a high degree of gratitude to Sir Gurdon for having been given a chance by him to prove themselves scientifically when perhaps they might have felt less than deserving. The tribute is poignant.

For future study and in-depth reference:

https://www.nobelprize.org/prizes/medicine/2012/gurdon/lecture/
Sir John B. Gurdon - Nobel Lecture: The Egg and the Nucleus: A Battle for Supremacy - NobelPrize.org

www.nobelprize.org

Chapter 12

LEROY HOOD – DNA SEQUENCING

1. *One name that seems to be synonymous with the Human Genome Project is Leroy Hood. Where was he born and where did he go to school?*

Dr. Leroy (Lee) Hood was born in the city of Missoula, Montana, in the U.S., on the 10th day in the month of October, in the year 1938, to parents Myrtle Evylan Wadsworth and Thomas Edward Hood. Hood's father, an alcoholic, was an engineer working for Mountain States Telephone Company, and his mother held a bachelor's degree in home economics.

Hood would later say that his tenacity was due to his mother's upbringing, encouraging Hood and his three younger siblings, Doral,

Myron, and Glen, to stand up to their challenges, to do their very best, never to quit when times became difficult, and to figure out their own solutions to their problems. The Hood family, because of his father's occupation, often moved, and as a child, Hood was consequently raised in several Montana-based cities like Ramsey and Butte, finally settling in the city of Shelby, MT.

Hood first attended Prescott elementary school in Missoula, and all three Hood children were known to have academically excelled in school. The young Hood learned to play the piano and clarinet. Later in high school at Shelby, Hood played sports, especially football in which at some point in his high school career, the team took the state championship, with Hood as its quarterback. Hood flourished academically in high school, even becoming class president and being voted Best-all-Around in his class yearbook.

He later attributed his successes to several of his teachers. One such teacher was Mr. Cliff Olson, Hood's teacher in science. Olson encouraged Hood and his doubtful parents to apply for admittance to the California Institute of Technology, commonly called Caltech. The Hood family had been leaning more towards Carleton College or Montana State University. Another high school teacher of note, Ms. Corlie Dunster, provided needed advice about the rigors of Caltech, which Hood appreciated only later on. Hood graduated from his Shelby-based high school as its valedictorian, in 1956.

Hood was accepted into Caltech with a scholarship funded by the General Motors Foundation despite not having had a course in calculus while in high school. Hood majored in Biology. He later speculated that his interest in human biology stemmed from his youngest brother, Glen, who had been born with Down syndrome. After much debate between his parents, Glen had been institutionalized. The experience had an influence on Hood's choice of major at Caltech. Additionally, two Caltech faculty played a role in Hood's choice of major. Drs. James Bonner, a biochemist who studied plants, and Ray Owen, a professor of immunology, both scientists of whom shared their enthusiasm for the biological sciences with their students.

At the time, Caltech was already famous for its students and faculty. Prominent scientists who were associated with Caltech included Drs.

Richard Feynman, Murray Gell-Mann, Linus Pauling, Thomas Hunt Morgan, Max Delbrück, and George Beadle.

A biographer has noted that at Caltech, Hood studied many long hours, taking courses such as Chemistry, Physics, and Math, in addition to his Biology courses. The foundation was to solidify his later entry into the arena of molecular biology. Hood also managed to join the Glee Club, play college football, and even do volunteer work giving guest lectures to high school students at the local YMCA. During his junior year, he took a trip abroad participating in a European tour with his brother, Myron, and his roommate, Eric Adelberger, who would become Hood's life-long friend and physics professor in later years. In June of 1960, Hood took his undergraduate degree, his B.S. in Biology, with high academic honors.

After his college graduation, Hood moved to Baltimore, Maryland, in the U.S. to attend medical school at the prestigious Johns Hopkins School of Medicine, having turned down Harvard Medical School. An influential professor in medical school was a microbiologist, Dr. William Wood, Jr., who imparted the importance of the immune system upon his students. However, Hood became more interested in biomedical research, rather than in clinical medicine. Interestingly, Hood had been intrigued by technology, after having spent some research time in a laboratory at Johns Hopkins devoted to the study of neurophysiology, with its sophisticated equipment for measuring nerve conduction. Dr. Leroy Hood took his M.D. degree from Johns Hopkins in 1964.

Next, Dr. Hood moved back to Caltech to enter graduate school for the pursuit of the Ph.D. Living back in Pasadena, CA, Dr. Hood studied in the laboratory of newly minted faculty member Dr. William J. Dreyer, who would later become a world-famous immunologist, having formulated a ground-breaking notion for somatic recombination of genes involved in encoding antibodies. In 1963, Dr. Hood would become prof. Dreyer's first Ph.D. student.

It was about this time, the 14th of December, in 1963, that Dr. Hood married his longtime girlfriend, Valerie Logan, who was a secondary school teacher.

Studying again at Caltech in the Dreyer laboratory as a graduate student, Dr. Hood was to recount in later years that he was given the sound advice of conducting research at the leading edge of science and, if possible, try inventing a new technological system. Prof. Dreyer had adopted a hands-off approach to his lab management policies, a policy that Dr. Hood would later adopt as well when he later became the head of his own laboratory.

Dr. Hood's first project for his graduate thesis involved an essential problem regarding antibodies, called at the time as the Bence-Jones proteins. The proteins were strongly believed to be mostly responsible for conferring an immune-based protection from pathogens and cancer. The problem involved determining how the antibody managed to harbor vast diversity to recognize antigens and how it somehow maintained a consistency in neutralizing and destroying these antigens.

New ideas were emerging about these antibodies, the Bence-Jones proteins, and their ability to consistently destroy an incredibly diverse array of pathogens. One idea held that the diversity and constancy of antibodies was performed by the joining together of separate genes, one gene of which accounted for the diversity, called a variable region, and the other gene, called a constant region, accounting for the constancy in effecting antigen destruction. The hypothesis became known as the somatic recombination mechanism.

Towards this, Dr. Hood needed to isolate the proteins and determine their amino acid sequences. Though the protein isolation work was labor-intensive, Dr. Hood had managed somehow to purify a sparse few milligrams of the Bence-Jones antibody proteins.

Then, a life-changing incident occurred for Dr. Hood regarding the Bence-Jones project. His graduate thesis advisor, Dr. Dreyer, walked into the laboratory and announced that Dr. Hood was taken off of the project.

Prof. Dreyer felt that, as a graduate student, the somatic recombination hypothesis was too risky for him to examine. It was a controversial idea. There were two huge problems with the somatic recombination hypothesis. First, it violated the so-called "one-gene leads to one protein" notion of Drs. George Beadle and Edward Tatum. It was a Nobel Prize-winning notion, after all. Second, the somatic recombination idea went totally against the widespread belief that in all somatic cells of an organism, the DNA should be the same; that is, the DNA is unchanged in non-sex cells.

An established postdoctoral fellow, Dr. J. Claude Bennett, who was working in Dr. Bennett's laboratory, was given the project. Together, Drs. Bennett and Dreyer set out to test the so-called Dreyer-Bennett hypothesis of somatic recombination leading to antibody diversity. The new work was published in 1965, leaving out Dr. Hood as a co-author.

Although, on the one hand, Dr. Hood never really forgave Dr. Dreyer for the slight, it nevertheless spared Dr. Hood from the onslaught that was to come to Drs. Bennett and Dreyer—the work was widely and quite harshly criticized from all scientific circles. Yet, despite being spared from the forefront of the controversy, Dr. Hood regretted the omission for many years.

Dr. Hood's new graduate thesis work was relegated to the protein purification of the Bence-Jones proteins and in simply providing further supporting evidence for the somatic recombination model of antibody diversity, a hypothesis that was initially formulated by Drs. Bennett and Dreyer. Thus, when Dr. Hood completed his Ph.D. project, the significance of the findings had been somewhat diluted. Consequently, he had neglected to write up the final version of his thesis for a while, leaving instead for a new post, in 1967, as a senior investigator, at the National Institutes of Health (NIH), in order to satisfy a public service activity required by the draft board *in lieu* of serving time in the ongoing Vietnam War. Nevertheless, at NIH, Dr. Hood managed to find the time to complete the thesis write-up and defend it, officially taking his Ph.D. from Caltech in 1968.

2. *Apparently, he did not work alone – but he and his co-workers developed a type of DNA gene sequencer and synthesizer – what exactly is this, and why is it important?*

Both machines invoked automation. The DNA gene sequencer (sometimes called a DNA sequenator) was designed to determine the nucleotide sequences along a DNA chain for the purpose of knowing what gene products, i.e., proteins, the genes encoded. The DNA sequences could then be compared, and the evolution and relationships of groups of organisms could be examined more closely. The DNA synthesizer machine was invented for the purpose of making stretches of DNA of desired sequences, which may be used, for example, to make DNA probes, for diagnostics, cloning, or mutagenesis. The making of DNA with known and desired nucleotide sequences allowed biomedical scientists to progress in their individual fields of study.

To sequence or synthesize DNA by conventional means, it necessitated hands-on, labor-intensive laboratory work. Every aspect of each task had to be performed by hand. The toil was slow, cumbersome, and tedious. The automation in the machines provided the everyday laboratory work that had been required to sequence or synthesize DNA. The automation could replace the laborious effort. Dr. Hood's involvement in the human genome project entailed determining the entire nucleotide sequences for human chromosome numbers 14 and 15. The complete human genome was sequenced by two independent groups, publishing in separate papers, in 2003.

One of the key figures who participated in the development of an automated DNA sequencer included Mike Hunkapiller, who in 1978 had been a postdoctoral fellow in Dr. Hood's laboratory at Caltech, where he (Hood) had already been a faculty and investigator. Hunkapiller had already proven his acumen in the development of the protein sequencer. He had had expertise both in chemistry and engineering, skills which would aid significantly in enhancing automation of DNA sequencing.

Another key figure was Mike's brother, Tim Hunkapiller, who joined the Hood laboratory at Caltech as a graduate student, also in 1978. Shortly after his arrival at Pasadena, Tim Hunkapiller had formulated an innovative idea. His brainstorm took the form of a modification of the Frederick Sanger method for DNA sequencing. Dr. Sanger's original technique involved detecting the DNA fragments using radioactively labeled nucleotides. Tim Hunkapiller's idea was instead to use fluorescently-labeled nucleotides to accomplish the needed DNA fragment detection. The Hunkapiller brothers worked together to realize Tim's idea. The new modification permitted the sequencing to be performed with more than one sample at a time.

A new prominent figure in the push to automate DNA sequencing in Dr. Hood's laboratory was Dr. Lloyd Smith, who had taken his Ph.D. from Stanford, CA, in the area of biophysics and had expertise in computer programing, optics of lasers, and physical chemistry. These elements would all be needed to design the automated DNA sequencer in an efficacious manner.

Dr. Smith hired a team of personnel devoted to the task of working up the chemistry. The team included Chris Dodd, Peter Hughes, Robert Kaiser, and Jane Sanders. They helped to sort out the fine-tuning needed to get accurate fluorescent signatures for each of the nucleotides along the DNA chain.

An additional person on the Hood team was Kip Connell, who had previously been an engineer at Hewlett-Packard and was at ABI, which had formerly been Applied Biosystems, Inc. Connell had developed a critical optic device for the detection of one remaining fluorescent dye in the DNA sequencer machine.

Unfortunately, when the groundbreaking work was published in June of 1986, Connell was left out of the co-authorship on their seminal *Nature* paper. It was considered a glaring slight. To make matters worse, Dr. Hood never mentioned by name any of the others on the team during a press conference about the discovery. The rift upended the relationship between Hood and the others on his team. It paved the way, thus, for other investigators to take the lead in pursuing automated DNA sequencing.

3. *Then aligned with the above is the protein sequencer and synthesizer– how do all these work together?*

Together, with the DNA synthesizer and the DNA sequencer mentioned above, the protein synthesizer and protein sequencer constitute a quartet of biomedically necessary scientific research instruments. Dr. Hood was influential in contributing to each of these advancements.

The protein synthesizer is also an automated machine that will chemically connect amino acids together to form polypeptide chains of varying lengths. Early on in its history of development, the number of amino acids that could be made was relatively low, but with time, as improvements were incorporated into the early prototypes, the amino acid numbers were enhanced. In more modern times, about 100 amino acids can be chemically connected to each other. Furthermore, new advancements have been made in which chemically-made peptides can be connected to each other to produce even larger polypeptides and complete proteins.

These short peptides could be used for various purposes. For instance, a short synthetic peptide could be used as a probe to recognize and bind a desired protein. Alternatively, new peptides could be made in order to occupy the binding site of a deleterious enzyme and inactivate it for potential therapeutic purposes. Biochemists can also study more closely the catalytic behaviors of synthetic enzymes. Furthermore, biomedical investigators may choose to design new stretches of amino acids along a protein chain in which the newly synthesized chain can fold into a three-dimensional shape that contains certain desired activities. The types of biomedical research projects that could be enhanced by the availability of proteins with desired amino acid sequences seem endless.

A proper context of protein-synthesizing technology is important to consider here. Although investigators may be able to make proteins artificially in which the end-products have about 100 or more amino acids, the laboratory process may take days, if all works well, of course. On the other hand, microbes, e.g., bacteria or yeast, come to mind, have the ability to biosynthesize similarly sized proteins in only a few seconds! Thus, protein chemists still have a long way to go in order to catch up with our microbial friends.

The protein sequencer, also known as a sequenator, permitted biomedical scientists, such as protein biochemists and even cell biologists or molecular biologists, to determine the sequences of amino acids along a protein chain. With about 20 well-known amino acids in our existing repertoire and the varying degrees of chain lengths, the sequences and types of proteins can become extremely diverse.

New technologies for determining protein sequences of amino acids that were developed prior to automation relied on brute force chemical and biochemical methods. The work was laborious, and the lengths of the amino acids were relatively short, and perhaps only a handful of amino acids could be sequenced. Early on in its history of development, perhaps as many as 20 amino acids could be sequenced.

Automation permitted more amino acids to be sequenced along a given polypeptide chain. Additionally, much less protein was needed to conduct the automated analyses, compared with earlier conventional methods. Today, about 100 amino acids can be directly sequenced with newer technologies, such as mass spectrometry.

With their new protein sequenator in hand, Dr. Hood and his colleagues were able to show early on, in 1980, how proteins from various species of organisms could be studied, from mice to humans. One of the first proteins they sequenced was interferon, a short protein known to fight viral infections and cancer. Knowledge of the amino acid sequence was then used to elucidate the genetic element, i.e., the gene that was responsible for encoding the interferon protein. Molecular biologists could then use the gene to produce large quantities of interferon in biotechnology labs and to purify the artificially made proteins.

A more efficient method of deducing protein sequences, however, relies first on determining the DNA sequences of the gene that encodes the proteins. This is where DNA sequenators can significantly help in the effort. The ability to determine DNA sequences has been tremendously enhanced by many orders of magnitude. In fact, biomedical scientists have moved from determining DNA sequences for individual genes to those of entire genomes to those of entire collections of genomes (metagenomics) that are found in various niches.

With the aid of a computer, the information gleaned from the DNA sequences of genes and of genomes can be easily used to translate into protein sequences. Whether one gains the protein sequences directly by protein sequencers or indirectly by DNA sequences first, the process can delineate a vast wealth of information.

For example, knowledge of protein sequences can be used to formulate structures of proteins, which can then be used to study the protein functions. We can learn where a protein resides in a cell or a tissue, depending on whether the protein has location-based sequences, i.e., amino acid sequences that specify where a protein is to be delivered. We may learn how a protein has evolved using its sequence and comparing it to those sequences of all other known proteins. Along these lines, if a new protein of unknown function is discovered, then we may use its amino acid sequence to evaluate its evolutionary history, comparing its sequence with those sequences contained within vast protein sequence databases in order to find its function.

Furthermore, by studying the evolutionary relationships of proteins, biomedical investigators may discover specific sequences that are shared with seemingly unrelated proteins. Such shared sequences are considered conserved by evolution, i.e., homologous, shedding light on the potential mechanisms of protein action. We may then test the functions predicted by these shared conserved amino acid sequence motifs. We may even be able to coax the proteins to enhance their functional efficiencies or to conduct new desired functions, such as for disease preventive chemotherapy or biotechnology.

4. Dr. Hood's research seemed to focus on cancer biology– prostate, ovarian, breast, and liver cancer– why these specific areas?

Dr. Hood's interest in cancer stems from his early days as a graduate student, focusing on so-called myeloma cells, which were a form of bone marrow cancer. He had used these cancer cells to isolate the Bence-Jones proteins, also known as a type of antibody. These particular types of cancer cells had been fused with specific antibody-producing cells, called plasma cells, which were derived from B-lymphocytes. The fused cells were now immortal and could be used for studying the antibodies. His interest in immunology is closely related to cancer, as the immune system is a critical defense mechanism in the fight against cancer.

Dr. Hood's determination of the amino acid sequence for several members of the interferon family, in 1980, garnered a significant amount of attention, not only amongst his biomedical scientist colleagues but also amongst members of the press and then potential benefactors. Dr. Hood's fame among the public was an opportunity for him to have an influence on the direction of research. He gave compelling public speeches in which members of the audience were eager entrepreneurs, venture capitalists, and wealthy bankers. He spoke of the remarkable potential for biotechnology, making sure to mention, among other ailments, promising avenues for treating cancer.

In 1983, Dr. Hood, working with Dr. Hunkapiller, used their protein sequenator to find the amino acid sequence for a protein called platelet-derived growth factor (PDGF). They then showed that the PDGF was somehow connected to an oncogene, that is, a cancer-causing gene! The discovery started in a new field of cancer biology, a field that is still a hot topic even to this day.

The advent of DNA sequencing on a massive scale, i.e., high-throughput sequencing, opened a new area of focus, namely, that of genome sequencing and its potential promise for cancer treatments. This is where cancers like those involving the prostate, the ovary, the breast, or of the liver came into play with the putative benefactors. One such benefactor was Michael Milken, a wealthy Wall Street magnate and a past survivor of prostate cancer. In the mid-1990s, Milken and Dr. Hood hit it off, finding that they had common interests and personalities.

The collaboration between benefactor Milken and scientist Dr. Hood, however promising, proved to be contentious. It was short-lived, with only a few publications coming out of the massive effort and with no treatment for prostate cancer discovered after three years of work. The reasons for collaborative derailment are unclear. Perhaps the unmatched application of the business model to a scientific endeavor, however worthy a cause, cancer, resulted in the clash. The business model required set schedules for specific accomplishments, and the scientific arena dealt with the unknown frontiers of science. Another reason that has been put forth is that the consortium itself lacked robust management. Whatever the reasons were, the collaboration was at an end, in 1998.

In the years since the consortium terminated, great strides have been made in all of these areas of cancer biology, cancers of the prostate, the breast, the liver, and the ovary. Dr. Hood's approach, namely, examine the oncogenes encoded in the DNA and their expressed protein products in these and other cancer tissues, was an insightful one. In more modern times, biomedical scientists have gained an understanding regarding the failures of cell cycle growth checkpoints, from both molecular and cellular standpoints. Nevertheless, since cancer includes a vast constellation of specific diseases, depending on the type of cell, tissue, or organ involved, much work remains to be completed before clinicians and researchers can get a handle on these terrible illnesses.

5. What is meant by "prion disease in mice"? And why is this important?

The term prion is derived from their characterization. It is short for proteinaceous infectious agent. Discovered by Dr. Stanley Prusiner, Nobel Laureate, the prions were known to consist primarily, if not wholly, of protein, and they were infectious all on their own, without the help of any sort of nucleic acids, such as RNA or DNA. In mice, the prions caused a form of the disease characterized by a constellation of holes in their brains. The infected brains took the form of a sponge-like consistency. These pathological conditions in mice were vital because they served as useful model systems for study in higher organisms.

Other such higher organisms that were susceptible to the prions included cows (mad cow), deer, and humans. It was found that in these and other types of hosts, the prion proteins would fold-up in an improper manner, causing them to produce more abnormal prions and somehow result in the holes called plaques within their brains.

Dr. Hood's involvement, starting in the early 1980s, was that he and his colleagues used the protein sequenator to elucidate the entire amino acid sequence of the prion protein, which had been purified first. Dr. Prusiner's laboratory collaborated with that of Dr. Hood's, and together they published the new work.

They then used the protein sequence to search for the corresponding gene DNA, and they cloned the relevant gene. They found that the prion gene was present in the genomes of their hosts. Next, they determined that the pathological version of the prion protein, called scrapie, was distinct from the regular version of the same protein. Surprisingly, they found that the sequences were virtually identical! The primary difference was that the scrapie and the healthy protein were structurally dissimilar.

They even managed to examine how sugars would bind to the prion proteins, a biochemical process called glycosylation. They learned which amino acids of the prion protein were attached to by the sugars. They purified prion proteins from a variety of animal hosts, and they used antibodies to delineate the structural differences between the regular cellular versions from the abnormal scrapie versions. Using traditional biochemical methodology, they learned of new proteins that were making bonds with the prion proteins. These types of studies went into the 1990s. At some point, Dr. Hood grew weary of the work. He was a type of scientist who was continually coming up with new ideas about disparate fields of study, and he did not wish to become fastened with prion biology for the remainder of his career. While the progress of the prion work was fascinating, if not groundbreaking, he felt the need to move onto other areas of study.

6. *Now, he apparently worked with "hematopoietic stem cells." Can you describe these and why they are important?*

The so-called hematopoietic stem cells are of tremendous importance. One of the biggest reasons for their relevance is because they are pluripotent. That is, they have the potential to develop into functionally specialized cells.

For example, they may give rise to brain cells, or liver, or kidney, whatever cell one desires or needs. Much work is still being conducted in this area to take stem cells and coax them to become heart cells, bone cells, pancreatic cells, etc.

Dr. Hood started his work with pluripotent hematopoietic stem cells in the early 2000s. They searched for genes that were expressed in specialized adult mice cells and compared with those expressed in the stem cells. They wanted to know the gene expression programs involved in the cellular development of a stem cell to a more specialized neuronal cell. They then cloned the genes that had shown expression during their cellular developments. One of the critical organs that Dr. Hood's laboratory and those of his collaborators focused on was the kidney. They examined how the hematopoietic stem cells differentiated into kidney cells while delineating the genes and their corresponding proteins that were responsible for the differentiation.

The work proved to be fruitful throughout the 2000s. The hematopoietic stem cell studies were focused on cancer. In so doing, a new field of study emerged—systems biology. Dr. Hood has been credited with starting the new branch of biomedical sciences.

The new discipline, systems biology, seeks to integrate the various components inherent in living organisms with each other. Basically, biomedical scientists want to know how organs, tissues, pathways, genes, and molecules, etc. are connected to each other. It represents a holistic view, as opposed to a reductionist approach in which individual components are separated from the rest of the body's systems for study. The methodological approaches include bioinformatics, mathematics, molecular biology, biochemistry, physiology, and cell biology. Stems cells, with their undifferentiated states with no specialization to them and their great potential to develop into differentiated, specialized states (pluripotency), can be at the very center of the systems biology field.

Recently, in 2018, pluripotent hematopoietic stem cells were used to produce cells that secreted the hormone insulin. The new pancreatic cells were then cultured and implanted into diabetic mice, and their diabetes condition was alleviated. The mice had reacquired normal levels of blood glucose! The field of stem cell biology may, in the future, show even more promising avenues for the treatment of biomedical diseases.

7. Blood proteins and nanotechnology– how are these interlinked?

The nanotechnology discipline emerged from the systems biology field, in which the seemingly disparate components that constitute a living being are connected to each other via molecular interactions. It can also be used for the purpose of detection of elements involved in connecting the various cellular and molecular systems. Another application of nanotechnology is to visualize pathological states within the context of healthy tissue. The nanotechnology field also seeks to provide targeted treatment of diseases by focusing on the precise components that are involved in the illnesses and providing a nano-based therapy delivery scheme.

As your question above alludes, nanotechnology can be used to measure levels of specific proteins in the blood. Such approaches have been referred to as sensor systems. The sensors may take the form of probes consisting of elements (e.g., DNA, proteins, antibodies, etc.) which specifically bind the desired proteins and which are connected to nano-sized wires that are strewn across a glass slide. A sample of blood will be passed through the glass slide containing the probe with the nanowires. If the desired blood protein is detected by the probe, the nanowire sends an electrical signal, thus announcing the presence of the desired protein.

The announcement of the desired protein's presence can take the form of an image. The probe that's attached to a nano-based cantilever will alter its orientation. The altered cantilever can be visualized, and the signal will be sent to the observer.

Nanotechnology can be used to highlight cancer within the context of healthy animal tissue, lighting up the cancerous tissue within the host. Nanocrystals called quantum dots that are made up of detectable metals like cadmium, or even mercury will fluoresce distinctly, depending on whether a cancer-specific molecule, like an anti-cancer antibody, thus, allowing visualization of cancerous tissue inside an intact animal host.

Lastly, nanotechnology can be used to deliver specific chemotherapy in a targeted fashion. Individual nano-sized containers harboring a therapeutic agent can be connected to individual probes that are specific to the tumor, or to the pathological tissue within a host. The delivery system will specifically recognize the target and bind to it and release the therapeutic agent.

8. *Apparently, Dr. Hood was also interested in Diabetes – specifically Type 1. For the uninitiated – what is the difference between Type 1 and Type 2, and what did Dr. Hood find in his research?*

As you indicated, there are two main categories of diabetes, Type 1 and Type 2. Type 1 diabetes is also called insulin-dependent diabetes mellitus (IDDM). It often manifests itself in children. It is autoimmune in nature. Auto-antigens may include insulin itself or other seemingly unrelated proteins, such as glutamate decarboxylase or peripherin, for example. Type 2 diabetes is also called adult-onset or non-insulin-dependent diabetes mellitus (NIDDM). Type 2 is often correlated with obesity, diet, or genetic inheritance. Recently, type 2 was associated with inflammation due to infection with the bacterium *Staphylococcus aureus*.

Dr. Hood's involvement with diabetes started in the early 1990s. The research group examined the repertoire of so-called beta chains along the T-lymphocyte receptors in patients with type 1 IDDM, and disappointingly found no differences between these patients and individuals without the IDDM. Next, in 2002, Dr. Hood participated in a large consortium in which they examined type 1 diabetics for the presence of specific genes believed to place individuals at risk for diabetes and for the presence of specific autoantibodies to autoantigens. The findings revealed certain molecular genetic markers for type 1 diabetes. Expanding on these genetic markers, the group focused on an immune system component, the major histocompatibility complex (MHC) in mice, known as human leukocyte antigen (HLA) in humans, and one of its autoantigen targets called the inositol triphosphate receptor gene, publishing the work in 2006. More recent work has focused on particular metabolite markers in the human gut microbiome that are somehow linked to diabetes. As of this writing, work in this critical area is still actively pursued.

9. What have I neglected to ask about this fascinating scientist?

Dr. Hood has proposed a vision for the future of medical practices, namely that of P4 medicine. The four Ps include medicine that (1) makes predictions, (2) advocates prevention, (3) invokes personalized medicine, and proposes (4) participatory practices amongst patients and physicians alike. Towards this effort, he has helped to establish an entire institute devoted to the implementation of the P4 mode of practicing this type of medicine.

Interestingly, while Dr. Hood, at over 80 years old, has garnered numerous awards and accolades for his significant biomedical science contributions, such as the preamble to the Nobel, the Albert Lasker Award, to date, the coveted Nobel has, nevertheless, eluded him.

For more information go to:

https://www.youtube.com/watch?v=ZRHcTlCZXrE
https://www.youtube.com/watch?v=j5HLDQwj_V0
https://www.youtube.com/watch?v=HlQcH3zgoVs

Chapter 13

Tim Hunt – Cell Division and Cell Cycle

1. *First of all, Sir Tim Hunt (Knighted in England) was born in England–what do we know about his early life?*

Sir Dr. Richard Timothy (Tim) Hunt was born on the 19th day of February, in the year 1943, in a small residential town of Neston on the peninsula called Wirral, located in the county of Chesire, near the famous city of Liverpool, England. Dr. Hunt's parents were Katherine (Kit) Eva Rowland and Richard William Hunt. After the death of his father, and unbeknownst to Hunt, he learned that his father possibly had a particular role within the intelligence world of England, working at the World Service radio of the BBC, although the precise nature of this intelligence role is mostly unknown. Whatever role Hunt's father played in this intelligence world, the secret was taken with him to the grave when he died, as he had no doubt signed the Official Secrets Act.

His father, starting in the year 1945, was based in Oxford, England, where he was a handler of Western manuscripts at Bodleian library, a collection known to be of great importance for medieval literature.

The kid Hunt was raised early on with a governess, who taught him Latin at his home, and the experience represents one of his earliest educational memories. Another early memory is of Hunt carting a pram (a baby stroller) towards a coal depot, watching large delivery vehicles getting stuck along the road during the snowy winter of 1947 and 1948.

2. *Like the Beatles, he hailed from Liverpool– what do we know about his early life?*

Liverpool was known at the time as a working-class industrial-based town. Hunt, in later years, recalled the food rationing that was pervasive during post-war (World War II) England. Prior to their move to Oxford, Hunt's father had taken a lecturer (professor) position at Liverpool, England, until 1945, when Hunt was about two-years-old.

Hunt further recalled that when he was young, his father's fellow faculty lecturers at the University of Liverpool, many of whom had expertise similar to that of his father's, i.e., studies pertaining to medieval-based manuscripts, a discipline called paleography. Hunt related how generous his father's colleagues were, providing food supplies that were in short supply during the post-war rationing of England. Since many of these generous medievalist lecturers were from the U.S., Hunt's initial impressions of Americans was a most favorable one. It quite likely influenced his later decision to move to the U.S.

3. *In England, for an excellent education– you go to Oxford. What transpired during his time there?*

The first educational institution he recalled attending as a child, until the age of eight, was known as Oxford High School for Girls, where he stayed at the Infants Department on a daily basis. Next, he attended Dragon School, a preparatory boarding school, where he was taught Greek, Latin, English, math, history, and science. Regarding his science education, years later, he pointed out the instruction of an excellent teacher, Gerd Sommerhoff, who strongly influenced Hunt's long-held interest in Biology.

Another area of interest was in cricket, but he recollected that he was not good at playing this sport. He also remembered that his grades in both math and history were less than stellar. Hunt attended these schools at Oxford until the age of 14.

4. *He attended Magdalen College (I believe it is pronounced "maudlin"), and what did he study there?*

In 1953, at the age of 14 years, Hunt moved to Magdalen College School, also located in Oxford, England. The school focused a tremendous amount of its curriculum on the sciences, such as chemistry, a course taught by an inspiring teacher named "Colonel Simmons." In his laboratory-based courses, the students were given a certain degree of independence, and consequently, there were the occasional laboratory fires resulting from the flammable chemicals.

He enjoyed the school, developing further his interest in the biological sciences. One educational experience was spent apparently dissecting his brother's dead rabbit, a situation that was actually warmly welcomed as it provided respite from the endless dogfish dissections. He also thoroughly enjoyed the evening guest seminars given by investigators who were also university faculty, as well as the so-called Christmas lectures, given at the museum at Oxford.

At Magdalen College School, Hunt flourished. He fondly recollected great treasures to be held there, such as the famous shrunken heads collection displayed at the Pitt Rivers Museum at Oxford. There were dinosaur bone displays that held a fascination for him. He remembered with delight the fascinating guest lectures on topics pertaining to the discovery of the famous Krebs Cycle and to evolution, the latter of which was given as a tribute on the 100-year anniversary of the publication of the *Origin of the Species* by Charles Darwin. He remembered Nobel Laureate Dr. George Beadle having spent a year at Oxford as a guest investigator as asking him to provide a description of his *Neurospora* work that led to "one-gene codes for one-enzyme" hypothesis.

5. On to Cambridge – and what is termed "Clare College" – what was his time like there?

At the age of 18, Hunt moved to the University of Cambridge in Cambridge, England, where he attended Clare College, a school believed to be as prestigious as those in Oxford. At Clare College, Hunt majored in the Natural Sciences, emphasizing in the burgeoning field of Biochemistry. He recalled one of his teachers, Dr. Sydney Brenner, who was to be a key figure in the establishment of molecular biology as a bona fide field of investigation. Hunt recollected that Prof. Brenner's lectures were off-limits to the biochemists! Nevertheless, Hunt would continue to concentrate on Biochemistry and graduate with his undergraduate degree (B.A.) from Cambridge University in 1964.

Next, Hunt stayed on at the Biochemistry Department at Clare College, in Cambridge, for graduate school. His graduate advisor was Dr. Asher Korner. Hunt's choice of prof. Korner, as a supervisor for his thesis project, was a fortuitous one, as Dr. Korner's policy was total freedom in choosing a project, as long as it dealt with the synthesis of DNA, RNA, or protein.

Hunt decided on studying protein synthesis, also known as translation, as his Ph.D. thesis project. Towards this, Hunt focused on the synthesis of the blood protein called hemoglobin. He wondered whether the heme component of the hemoglobin protein was incorporated into the mature protein early or late in the translational process. Hunt also became interested in whether the ribosomes, i.e., protein-making factories, formed a crowed line of ribosomes along the mRNA transcript during translation even if the requisite iron was left out of the hemoglobin-making equation. He found that the ribosomes did not collect in a jam on the transcript; instead, the ribosomes stayed evenly spaced along the mRNA molecule during hemoglobin synthesis.

The findings were good enough for a doctoral project, and he successfully defended his graduate thesis. Dr. Hunt received his Ph.D. in 1968, from the University of Cambridge, at Clare College.

6. *The New York-based College of Medicine at Albert Einstein University is a vast research Institute. Apparently, he worked there with someone named Irving London, working on hemoglobin. First, why is hemoglobin essential, and how does it fit into the big scheme of things?*

The hemoglobin protein is essential for providing needed oxygen molecules (O_2) to all of our living cells in the body so that it can remain alive. As humans are considered strictly aerobic, i.e., oxygen is an absolute requirement for life, the hemoglobin molecules in our red blood cells serve this essential life-role by providing this vital substance to the body.

Virtually all mammals on Earth require oxygen molecules for life. Without oxygen, our cells, tissues, and organs would start to die within a few short minutes. Thus, knowledge of the structure and synthesis of hemoglobin is crucial for our understanding of oxygen binding and transport to the living cells.

Hunt had met Dr. Irvin London in 1966 during a scientific conference about hemoglobin in Thessaloniki, Greece. Dr. London was chair of the Medicine Department and an investigator who was housed at the Albert Einstein College of Medicine in New York. Dr. London had been interested in the genetics of hemoglobin, and he had developed a so-called reticulate experimental system for studying hemoglobin. Hunt related a story about how he had invited himself to spend a summer in Dr. London's laboratory, hoping to learn about the reticulocytes, which are immature red blood cells, and its associated program for measuring the synthesis of proteins, a process called translation. The "invitation" was accepted, and Hunt spent the summer of 1966 in New York, residing in a non-air-conditioned dormitory and spending most of his time in the air-conditioned laboratory of Dr. London's.

During that fateful summer, in 1966, Dr. London had invited Hunt to return as a postdoctoral fellow once he had completed his Ph.D. with Dr. Korner at Cambridge. Thus, with his newly minted Ph.D. in hand in 1968, Dr. Hunt moved to New York. At the Albert Einstein College of Medicine, Dr. Hunt participated in investigative projects dealing with the regulation of hemoglobin protein synthesis and working in the London lab with Drs.

Nechama and Edward Kosower, they found that translation was prevented by oxidized glutathione (denoted as GSSG) in lysates of reticulocytes. Dr. Hunt recalled that the result brought him great joy because it was an idea that he had come about by himself. He also learned that the ion of calcium, Ca^{2+}, was a necessary requirement for an enzyme called a micrococcal nuclease and that this nuclease did not affect the rate of protein synthesis in the reticulocyte system if the Ca^{2+} was absent from the mixture. Working with Dr. Ellie Ehrenfeld and the nuclease as a digestor of RNA, it was discovered that double-stranded RNA molecules derived from poliovirus also inhibited the synthesis of proteins in Dr. London's cell-free reticulocyte lysate system.

Dr. Hunt stayed at the Albert Einstein College of Medicine, in Dr. London's laboratory, until late 1970, when he returned to Cambridge, where he continued to study the conditions for controlling the process of translation.

7. *I have seen sickle cells, but what do we mean by immature cells? And why are they important?*

I believe you are referring to the reticulocytes that Dr. Hunt and others were using for their experiments. The reticulocytes are immature red blood cells, and they make a suitable biological system for measuring protein synthesis. Their protein synthesis machinery was considered most efficient for measuring the effects of agents that could regulate the activities of translational machinery.

Furthermore, if the reticulocytes were used as a starting point, then these immature cells could be broken up into a so-called cell-free extract material called a lysate. The reticulocyte cell-free system exhibited a high rate of translational activity if certain experimental conditions were met, and translation could, thus, be readily measured.

Thus, Dr. Hunt and other investigators could focus on studying the rates of hemoglobin protein synthesis. The was this laboratory technique, the cell-free lysates of reticulocytes, that Dr. Hunt used to find out that poliovirus double-stranded RNA was potently inhibiting translation.

8. Woods Hole, Massachusetts and mitosis (which we all study in high school biology) – but refresh our memories as to mitosis and meiosis and what was going on in Woods Hole?

While the cell-free reticulocyte system had a perfectly suitable protocol for examining the regulation of translation, Dr. Hunt found out about a better system. It involved using fertilized eggs from sea urchins. The new system was introduced to Dr. Hunt at a scientific conference in 1966, in which Dr. Henry Borsook, who was at Caltech in California, gave a seminar about this novel system that he had developed earlier in the 1950s. Dr. Borsook had elaborated that his sea urchin egg system was perfectly suitable for examining protein synthesis.

Years later, after Dr. Borsook's seminar, when Dr. Hunt had been at Cambridge, sea urchins, and their eggs, however, were not entirely available for biomedical studies. Thus, Dr. Hunt bided his time when he could get his hands on the desirable sea urchin eggs. The opportunity provided itself in 1977 when Dr. Hunt was offered the chance to assist in the teaching of a summer course offered at the Marine Biological Laboratory (MBL), located in the small town of Woods Hole, Massachusetts. The course was on the topic of embryology, but more importantly, the waters around Woods Hole were teeming with sea urchins and their eggs!

Thus, Dr. Hunt co-taught the embryology course, and in his free time collecting as many sea urchin eggs as he possibly could. With the sea urchin eggs in hand, he returned home to Cambridge to conduct protein synthesis studies. Unfortunately, the efforts with the sea urchin eggs failed to demonstrate a productive translational activity. It had been a terribly disappointing result.

The MBL at Wood Hole had its limitations at the time of Dr. Hunt's first visit. The facilities were not terribly conducive to biochemical or molecular biological studies. The laboratories were mostly empty of essential equipment, such as deep freezers, for sample storage, or electrophoretic gel apparatuses, etc. The sea urchins had a terribly short fertilized-egg season with which to play around within the sparse laboratories. The next summer of 1978 was, thus, spent at home in Cambridge.

The vast array of excellent summer courses, however, and the exciting research being conducted at Woods Hole every summer with their daily seminars given by top-notch investigators in their fields, not to mention the allure of the nearby sea (beaches?), were all too tempting for Dr. Hunt to resist staying away for long. He returned to the MBL at Woods Hole in the summer of 1979, hoping to hone his skills learning cell and molecular and developmental biology. This time he brought the necessary laboratory supplies with him, and he made arrangements for a deep freezer to be available for his samples. While the progress with protein synthesis in sea urchin eggs was slow, Dr. Hunt did manage to discover a protein kinase, which was an important finding.

Another more critical development occurred for Dr. Hunt at the MBL during that summer of 1979 in Woods Hole. He attended a delightful seminar given by Dr. John Gerhart, in which Dr. Hunt first learned about the nuances of the cell cycle and its known mechanisms for control. Dr. Gerhart told of his troubles trying to purify a cell cycle-related protein, called maturation promoting factor, MPF. The seminar inspired Dr. Hunt to consider a biochemical approach to the study of the cell cycle. Dr. Hunt speculated that there might possibly be an enzyme that could catalyze the process of mitosis, working at the level of control with the cell cycle.

The insight made Dr. Hunt return to Woods Hole for subsequent summers. He became a fixture in the famous Physiology Course at the MBL. It was during the summer of 1982, however, that Dr. Hunt would make his Nobel Prize-winning discovery at Woods Hole.

9. *The Nobel Prize – was apparently shared with two others – what did the three of them basically discover?*

Dr. Hunt shared the Nobel Prize in Physiology or Medicine in 2001 with co-Laureates Drs. Leland (Lee) Hartwell and Sir Paul Nurse.

Dr. Hartwell's primary contributions towards the Nobel involved his interests in the control of the cell cycle during the development of an organism. He discovered numerous genes and their corresponding proteins that are involved in this control process, such as the famous checkpoint protein, CDC28, which is necessary for directing the beginning stages of the cell cycle. He further showed that when DNA becomes damaged in any way, the cell cycle checkpoints come into play to halt its further progression.

Dr. Nurse's main contributions regarding the Nobel concerned his discovery of the famous *cdc2* gene in the yeast microbe called *Schizosaccharomyces pombe*. The *cdc2* genetic element was discovered to regulate the progression of the cell cycle from the so-called G1 phase to the DNA-synthesizing S phase and from the G2 phase into the mitotic phase. Furthermore, Dr. Nurse was instrumental in discovering the human version of the gene, now called *cdK1*, which encodes the Cdk1 protein. The human protein is also known as a so-called cyclin-dependent kinase enzyme.

Dr. Hunt earned his Nobel Prize for having discovered one of the most famous proteins that cell cycle biologists and biomedical scientists have ever known, namely, that of the protein called cyclin. The experimental work was performed at the MBL during the summer of 1982.

The aim of Dr. Hunt's 1982 work in Woods Hole was to examine whether any interesting patterns of protein synthesis could be discerned in fertilized sea urchin eggs during their cellular growth, a process called mitosis, which invokes the cell cycle. Dr. Hunt's famous experimentation is briefly described below.

The investigational method involved first adding radioactively labeled amino acid called methionine to sterile seawater harboring fertilized sea urchin eggs. Periodically, at different time points, samples of the radioactive methionine-eggs mixture were removed, and the resultant protein levels were measured. The data were startling, if not puzzling.

With time, during cell division, the measured protein levels increased, and then surprisingly, at some point later in time, the protein levels simply went away! Dr. Hunt spent an afternoon trying to make sense of these results. Insight into the problem occurred that night at the weekly Friday Evening Lecture.

At the MBL, the Friday Evening Lectures have been a long-held tradition in which virtually the entire town of Woods Hole congregates in the grand auditorium of Lillie Hall to enjoy an excellent keynote lecture, followed by wine and cheese for students and, importantly, a unique chance to interact with the speaker and with fellow colleagues.

During the wine and cheese session that evening, Dr. Hunt learned from Dr. John Gerhart that Drs. Mike Wu and Marc Kirschner had, too, observed a new appearance of MPF protein activity was necessary for meiosis to start a new round of cell division between meiosis I and meiosis II. They had also found that if protein synthesis was inhibited, then the MPF failed to materialize itself again. These findings predicted that protein was degraded at first and that new protein synthesis was essential for the next stage involved in the cell cycle to manifest itself.

At this point, Dr. Hunt formulated his Nobel-Prize-winning hypothesis. He predicted the existence of cyclin.

Furthermore, he postulated that the presence and absence of cyclin had something to do with the behavior that MPF was exhibiting. Dr. Hunt observed cyclin to oscillate in its appearance and disappearance! Next, they examined other species, and cyclin did its oscillations in, for example, clams, just as well.

In 1986, Dr. Hunt's laboratory cloned the gene that encoded the cyclin sub-unit B. The cloning of the cyclin A gene followed soon afterward. The cyclins have been a prime focus of study in many disparate fields, including biomedical science, ever since.

10. His later work in London focused on what makes cells go cancerous, or what makes cells go crazy– or am I off on this underlying causal factor in cancer? (I think the scientific term is "proliferate uncontrollably"? What did he find?

Dr. Hunt's discovery of the cyclins had direct relevance to cancer. The cyclins are critical to the growth of cells. Thus, he began to focus on cancer biology research in the early 1990s when he had moved to the Cancer Research UK London Research Institute, known then as the Imperial Cancer Research Fund. Tumor cells like cancer may "proliferate uncontrollably" in that such cells fail to stop growing when they should have otherwise. Normal healthy cells actually *do* stop growing when they are supposed to, while tumors, unfortunately, do not.

One of his first forays into cancer biology involved the study of a healthy version of a cell cycle control gene, a proto-oncogene called *c-mos*, which encodes a protein kinase enzyme. Dr. Hunt's laboratory found that the C-Mos protein phosphorylates another essential protein called mitogen-activated protein (MAP) kinase, which in turn participates in a protein cascade system that regulates the cell cycle progression. The work led to the discovery of another critical protein called p38, which is a homologous member of the MAP kinase superfamily of related proteins. Dr. Hunt was also involved in the discovery of the so-called MO15 kinase protein, which in turn participates in the activation of mutated versions of Cdk2 and Cdc2 cell cycle control proteins. Thus, Dr. Hunt's cancer biology work has dealt primarily with faulty cell cycle checkpoints, and specific breakdowns in the various steps within the cell cycle may lead to uncontrolled cell growth, causing tumorigenesis.

11. What have I neglected to ask about Sir Tim Hunt of Oxford?

Dr. Hunt had recalled in later years that while he much enjoyed teaching his courses in Cell Biology and Biochemistry at Oxford, he nevertheless found that the process of *learning* was much more of an enjoyable task. At

Oxford and at the MBL, he incorporated teaching with learning new aspects to the cell cycle, as well.

He wrote in a supplemental postscript to his Nobel speech that he felt rather fortunate to have met so many bright and talented investigators during the course of his career, especially at Oxford but also at the MBL in Woods Hole. In his speech, he had given credit to many investigators, such as Drs. Joan Ruderman and Andrew Murray. This is an experience to which I personally can relate. When I had been a fellow of the American Society for Cell Biology (ASCB) at the MBL during the summer of 1991, I had the great fortune of meeting Drs. Ruderman and Murray, and I found both investigators to be extraordinarily brilliant and amicable.

For additional information go to:

https://m.youtube.com/watch?v=4fP3i3BO5HA
https://m.youtube.com/watch?v=vgScAdoZ9w4
https://m.youtube.com/watch?v=I1I-UIyu0jU

Chapter 14

ANDREW HUXLEY – NERVE IMPULSES

1. *Another great scientist from Great Britain apparently came from a great family. When and where was Sir Andrew Huxley born, and can you on tell us about his family of origin?*

Sir Andrew Fielding Huxley's grandfather, considered the family patriarch, was none other than the famous zoologist and biologist, Professor Thomas Henry Huxley. The prominent Huxley family apparently starts with

Thomas, who was born in 1825. He was an influential educational policymaker in England at the time. He wrote a famous book titled *Evidence as to Man's Place in Nature*, in 1863. It was a treatise that was devoted to the scientifically-based support of evolution, a controversial topic of the era. Thomas Huxley spawned a vast family with many well-esteemed relatives, including his famous grandson Andrew F. Huxley.

Sir Dr. Andrew F. Huxley was born on the 22nd day of November in the year 1917 in the Hampstead area of London, England, to parents Rosalind Bruce and Leonard Huxley. Rosalind Huxley had been the second wife of Leonard as his first wife, Julia Arnold Huxley, had died because of cancer in 1908. Andrew was the youngest and last child of Leonard and Rosalind.

Dr. Andrew Huxley was granted the Nobel Prize in Physiology or Medicine in 1963 with Sir Alan Lloyd Hodgkin. Together, these investigators elucidated the flow of sodium and potassium ions across the neuronal membrane during the action potential conduction of nerve impulse function; the field has been referred to electrophysiology. Dr. Huxley was also famous for his studies on muscle contraction and physiology.

2. *Sir Andrew had a most invigorating and exciting and enthusiastic childhood. What do we know about it?*

Growing up within a prosperous family in Hamstead, London, young Andrew Huxley had recalled a happy childhood. The household was filled with intellectual pursuits, such as literature, science, and engineering. One of young Andrew's earliest memories is that of meeting his great-grandparents, probably those on his mother's side of the family. He recalled that his great-grandfather had given him a toy wheelbarrow.

The Huxley household has been described as filled with mechanical devices, namely, with microscopes being among these. Huxley children not only used their microscopes, but they also built them. His mother, Rosalind Huxley, who was agile with her hands and a rather practical human being, had bestowed upon her children the gift of a lathe, of which the children presumably also put to use. The Huxley brothers spent many hours designing equipment and then testing them; such mechanical apparatuses included simple objects, like a wooden candle, as well as more complicated devices, such as an operational internal combustion engine!

These sorts of childhood experiences were to be of great benefit for Dr. Huxley in adulthood when he worked with more complicated laboratory machinery as an investigator. His early childhood experience with the microscope would also become a tremendous advantage for him later on in his scientific career.

In later years, Sir Huxley had reminisced about his childhood and early home-schooling with a governess, who had actually been engaged by the Huxley family to treat his brother who had had the measles. So the governess served two purposes: healthcare and home-based teaching.

Attendance at elementary school began in 1925, at a junior branch for children of the University College School, located in Hampstead. After approximately five years, Huxley went to Westminster School, in 1930, which was situated in another location of London, in a more central district. His academic performance at Westminster School was so excellent that Huxley had been bestowed the prestigious King's Scholarship. An influential teacher at Westminster had been J.F. Rudwick. For the remainder of his life, he would be entirely grateful to many of his teachers. He graduated from the school at Westminster at the age of 17.

3. *Cambridge and its spires and research facilities. Huxley attended there – and what did he study?*

After high school graduation at Westminster School, in 1935, Huxley moved to Trinity College, located in Cambridge, England, where he concentrated his studies on the Natural Sciences. Prior to this major, Huxley had had every intention of becoming an engineer or studying one of the physical sciences; however, he changed his academic focus to the Natural Sciences after having enrolled in an elective course in physiology, a subject devoted to the study of the physical and chemical functions (activities) of living systems. The choice of physiology had been a fortuitous one, as he been encouraged by his good friend B. Delisle Burns to take the life-changing course. The Physiology Department was filled with many inspiring teachers, such as William A.H. Rushton, Francis J.W. Roughton, and 1932 Nobel Laureate Dr. Edgar D. Adrian. Huxley took his undergraduate degree, his B.A., from Trinity College, Cambridge, in 1938.

Huxley stayed on at Trinity College, Cambridge, to pursue a graduate degree in medicine, focusing on anatomy and undergoing the associated clinical training, when World War II broke out. The new war interrupted this particular mode of his education. Instead, Huxley focused his attention on war-related work, such as gunnery research.

In the month of August, in 1939, Huxley was recruited by one of his professors and advisor, Dr. Alan Lloyd Hodgkin, to pursue studies in the electrical behavior of the giant squid axon at the Marine Biological Laboratory at Plymouth, Massachusetts, in the U.S. Huxley earned his M.A. degree in 1941. In later years, the Hodgkin-Huxley duo had worked together also at the Marine Biological Laboratory at Woods Hole, Massachusetts, in the U.S.

In 1941 Huxley took a research fellowship at Trinity in Cambridge, and in 1946, he started teaching at the Physiology Department, where he stayed until 1960 when he moved to University College in London. It is here at the University College in London, where he performed his Nobel Prize-winning research, collaborating with Sir Dr. Alan Hodgkin, who was at the University of Cambridge. Dr. Huxley became professor emeritus in 1983.

4. *We use our muscles all the time – day in and day out – but never really give them much thought as to how they work, and how the brain tells them what to do. What did Huxley contribute to this realm?*

Interestingly, Sir Andrew F. Huxley was utterly unrelated to his namesake, Prof. Hugh Esmor Huxley, a biophysicist who did groundbreaking work on muscle contraction physiology in 1953. Apparently, and coincidentally, Dr. A.F. Huxley, working with Dr. Rolf Neidergerke, and Dr. H.E. Huxley, working with Jean Hanson, simultaneously postulated the famous sliding-filament theory for the contraction of skeletal muscle.

Both of these independent investigative groups studied muscle contracting using various forms of microscopy. The sliding filament theory involved myofibrils and an interconnected system of cross-bridges. On the one hand, the E.F. Huxley—J. Hanson team used the electron microscope in which they examined transverse sections on glass slides of muscle tissues, as well as the phase-contrast microscopy of detached myofibrils. On the other hand, the A.F. Huxley—R. Neidergerke's research team used the so-called interference microscopy technique of isolated but intact muscle fibrous tissue.

H.E. Huxley further studied the ATP energy requirements for the contraction, positing that ATP was hydrolyzed by the myosin component of the actin-myosin complexes during contraction. Dr. H.E. Huxley also generated elegant-looking electron microscopic photographs (micrographs) of skeletal muscle, clearly indicating cross-bridges between thick myosin-containing filaments and thin actin-containing filaments. The myosin-actin connections came to be known as active sites or cross-bridges.

Dr. A.F. Huxley also studied the muscle contraction phenomenon more closely, starting in the mid-1950s. He merged two independent muscle phenomena, namely, a cyclic nature between muscle tension and heat emittance and an independent system of muscle force generators, by postulating an active kinetic-based behavioral component. While the kinetic theory failed to account for physiological nature, key features nonetheless emerged, which still hold true. They included, among other elements, an elastic factor during attachment that occurs during muscle contraction.

Dr. A.F. Huxley's research team also examined the muscle tension dynamics between overlapping thick and thin muscle filaments and their various lengths of the contractions. In the mid-1960s, his laboratory invoked a so-called servo mechanism, in an effort to explain how the muscle fibers maintained a constant sarcomere length during their contractions. The work highlighted how the changes in muscle tension during nerve stimulation were proportional to the amount of overlapping thick and thin filaments.

In the early 1970s, both Huxley teams merged in their investigative treatments of the myosin-actin bridge interactions. The mechanism seemed to involve a tilting behavior for the myosin heads as an elastic motion took place during muscle contractions. The myosin tilting phenomenon was supported by later X-ray crystallographic studies of the myosin and actin protein structures, in which a hinge section was discovered in the myosin protein; presumably, the hinge permitted myosin tilting. This mechanical motion of myosin in which ATP energy is utilized to conduct its tilting behavior during muscle contraction has led to the notion of the myosin, a protein, acting like an energized motor. Many of these and other muscle studies that were conducted by Dr. A.F. Huxley are still relevant in modern times.

5. *World War II apparently interfered with his studies– but he apparently contributed much while under attack and dodging bullets. What happened?*

In 1935, Dr. Andrew Huxley moved to Cambridge to become a lecturer in the natural sciences at Trinity College. While there, he altered his focus from the physical sciences to study medicine. Then, he concentrated his efforts on conducting basic research in 1939 as a result of having met Dr. Alan Hodgkin, a tutor who was then studying nerve action potentials in the giant axons of squids. Drs. Huxley and Hodgkin traveled to the Plymouth-based Marine Biological Station in Massachusetts, in the U.S. After stimulating a giant axon with an electrical pulse, Drs. Huxley and Hodgkin had observed the full membrane potential, recording it from start to finish. They were the first investigators to accomplish this feat. They were the first to actually measure a full action potential in the giant axons of squids, and in their experiments, they observed an overshoot phenomenon.

They recorded an overshoot of about +40 millivolts and then a drop in the recordings below the resting membrane potential just prior to a slow leveling back to eventually reach the original resting membrane potential level.

The unexpected electrical overshoot was a mystery.

Just as they were getting good results in terms of measuring a full action potential in the squids' giant axons and in getting a handle on the overshoot phenomenon, World War II interrupted their progress. The basic electrophysiological research program was, thus, abandoned.

The war work performed by Dr. Huxley involved gunnery operation research. He started first working for the so-called British Anti-aircraft Command (BAC). At the BAC, he worked on controlling anti-aircraft gunnery using the newly invented radar technology to do so. Next, Dr. Huxley moved to serve with the Admiralty in order to work on the new Navy-based gunnery technology being developed at the time. He was to conduct this sort of war work for the duration of the conflict until 1945.

Interestingly, Dr. Huxley also participated as a guinea pig for the war. He participated as a human subject for a research project conducted by Drs. Robert McCance and Elsie Widdowson, who had been interested in the physiological consequences of food rationing by counting calories of various foodstuffs consumed before and during the war.

The war effort proved to be a rather beneficial experience for Dr. Huxley. During the war, he honed his mathematical and engineering proficiencies, which were to prove quite helpful in his electrophysiological work after the war had ended.

6. Action potentials and muscle contractions– we hear about these in science all the time–what were Huxley's contributions?

Prior to the onset of the Second World War, Dr. Huxley and his advisor Dr. Hodgkin had succeeded in measuring a full-blown action potential inside of the giant neurons of the longfin inshore squid, a sea-faring organism that they scientifically called at the time *Loligo forbesi* (now called *Doryteuthis pealeii* in modern times), which had possessed the most prominently sized neurons ever known. The giant neurons of the squid made it possible for investigators to examine their electrical activities experimentally.

Their first breakthrough occurred shortly before the onset of the Second World War when Drs. Huxley and Hodgkin managed for the first time in history to measure a full action potential in the giant neurons of their squids. They stabbed the squid giant neuron with micro-sized glass pipettes that were filled with a solution of concentrated salts. An electrical wire inside of the glass micropipette served as an electrode. As the pipette was inserted into the inside of the giant neuron of the squid, the equipment would record a resting membrane potential between –40 to –90 millivolts. They followed the action potential from the beginning to its end. The result was a profound and unprecedented recording of an entire action potential, an electrical pulse, in a living neuron, for the first time in scientific history.

Drs. Huxley and Hodgkin quickly wrote a short manuscript describing their historical findings, and they published it in a two-page article in *Nature*, in 1939. They further described their famous positive overshoot but did not elaborate on it. Instead, the work was stopped in its tracks due to the outbreak of World War II.

It was not until 1946, after the war, that they started to regain an explanatory handle on the positive overshoot phenomenon. Dr. Hodgkin and his assistant Bernard Katz had postulated that the overshoot discovered by Dr. Huxley, back in the summer of 1939, was due to changes in the conductance of sodium ions across the membrane, which turned out to be selectively permeable to the sodium ions.

Drs. Huxley and Hodgkin used a then newly invented technique called the voltage-clamp method, developed by Drs. Ken Cole and Howard Curtis, and using their knowledge of mathematics, Drs. Huxley and Hodgkin then developed a rather elaborate set of equations for describing the behavior of the action potential, first publishing their analyses in 1952. The explanation became known as the so-called Hodgkin-Huxley model, and it is still in vogue today.

The Hodgkin-Huxley model predicted the thresholds for generating an action potential upon stimulation. Their model also described the changes in the permeability of ions across the membrane during the course of the action potential. The model predicted the presence of molecular gates in the neuronal membranes and of gating mechanisms within these gates for opening and closing the ion passages. The Hodgkin-Huxley model described how specific membrane-bound channels for sodium and potassium ions opened and closed during the propagation of an action potential along a giant neuron of the squid. Their model predicted ion conductances and allowed for descriptions of their conductance behaviors. It was a remarkably accurate discovery!

In 1952, Dr. Huxley turned his studies to the field of muscle physiology of frogs. He was able to demonstrate muscular activity in terms of brute force mechanical contractions after stimulation of the muscle surface with an electrical charge. He noticed alterations in the muscle striation patterns, indicating muscle movements.

In 1954, Dr. Huxley turned his attention to the actual contraction of the muscles. Along with several other scientific investigators, Dr. Huxley independently formulated the so-called sliding filament hypothesis to explain the muscle contraction mechanism. In one crucially elegant experiment, published by Dr. Huxley in 1966, he showed a correlation between muscle tension that was generated in a separate muscle fiber and the overlap in the sliding filament itself. The work had a direct implication in support of the cross-bridge hypothesis in that the sliding filaments made contacts using actin and myosin.

In 1957, he showed that during the sliding filament process, cross-bridging was under the control of calcium ion and ATP. He demonstrated that at rest, the insides of muscle cells had an adequate concentration of ATP but low amounts of intracellular calcium ions. However, during the course of the muscle contraction, cross-bridge formation manifested itself during the sliding of the associated filaments, and that the calcium played a role in initiating the process. With respect to the ATP involvement, Dr. Huxley found that hydrolysis of the ATP energy occurred later in the cross-bridge process after dissociation of the actin and myosin from each other.

The physiological studies of muscle by Dr. Huxley has gained a tremendous amount of attention in many of today's writings, both in the scientific journals as well as in physiology textbooks. One written tribute denotes Dr. Huxley's contributions to this realm constituted an evaluation of the "mechanical engineering of living beings."

7. *"Ionic mechanisms of the nerve cell" was the research for which he won the Nobel Prize – why was he so deserving?*

Dr. Huxley studied the giant axons of squids. He and Dr. Hodgkin invoked the voltage-clamp method to evaluate the ionic mechanisms of the squid nerves. The electrical activities of the squid neurons involved changes in the levels of ions across the neuronal membranes, and as ions moved across the membrane, they brought with them an electrical current. These ion-based currents moved across the membrane as the action potentials were generated along the squid nerves. The resting membrane potential could be artificially set to a specific voltage by the voltage clamping technique. Once the voltage value was set, they could then evaluate the changes in the resulting ion permeabilities through their new voltages as a function of time. They focused on two positively-charged ions, sodium (Na^+) and potassium (K^+). The behaviors of these ion movements across the voltage-clamped nerve membranes were evaluated in terms of their ion conductances. They evaluated the Na^+ and K^+ conductances separately, isolating their individual contributions to the action potential.

Dr. Huxley applied mathematics to the ion conductance data. He deduced that during the action potential, a membrane depolarization resulted first in a Na^+ movement across the membrane into the neuron at a high rate producing an active initial Na^+ conductance. He found that as the Na^+ conduction dissipated, a slower outward movement of K^+ manifested itself, reaching a lower peak than that of Na^+, but eventually, both ion conductances would return to base-line clamped levels, complete with their overshoot phenomenon. The entire ionic mechanism that played out during an action potential would be over in less than 4 milliseconds!

Their ionic mechanism became popularly known as the ionic hypothesis, in which Na^+ was thought to be the prime culprit responsible for the overshoot. They reasoned that Na^+ entered the neuronal cells. The Na^+ involvement was not enough to explain the entirety of the overshoot. When they included K^+, it helped to explain the overshoot phenomenon more thoroughly. The K^+ was believed to exit from the neuronal cells. These principles were some of the primary bases for the Nobel.

8. *He was during his lifetime the Editor of the Journal of Physiology and the Journal of Molecular Biology. Most people in the field recognize the Nobel Prize as the highest honor – but in a sense – to be the Editor of two of the most prestigious journals of the time HAS to be commented upon. Your thoughts?*

Dr. Huxley became an editor of the prestigious *Journal of Molecular Biology*. He had been recruited to do so personally by Sir John Kendrew, who had helped to found the new journal in 1959. It is likely that Dr. Huxley was invited to be an editor because of his research that dealt not only with electrophysiology but also because of his discoveries pertaining to the physiology of muscle contraction. Molecular biologists became eager to elucidate each of the molecular players involved in both of the areas.

In 1950, Dr. Huxley had been appointed to the editorial board of the *Journal of Physiology*. He served in this capacity until 1957 when he was then appointed to the journal's committee between the years 1957 and 1961 and during the years between 1970 and 1974. Indeed, *J. Physiology*, sponsored by The Physiological Society, is considered by many physiologists to be the gold standard for publishing their research findings. When Dr. Huxley died on the 30th day of May, in 2012, at the age of 94 years, the prestigious journal dedicated an obituary in his honor in that same year: DOI: 10.1113/jphysiol.2012.238923. It was a warm tribute to a great and highly revered biomedical scientist and physiologist.

9. *Sir Andrew Huxley died May 30, 2012, a year before another famous Huxley died. I am referring to Rick Huxley, the bass player of the Dave Clark Five, who died approximately one year later on Feb 11, 2013. We just needed to mention some other Huxley's in closing – Aldous Huxley – and were there other famous Huxley individuals?*

Indeed, what a prominent family the Huxleys were!

Leonard (Andrew's father) and Julia Huxley had had four offspring. The oldest was Sir Julian Sorell Huxley, an evolutionary biologist who dabbled in eugenics, the now-defunct notion of improving the characteristics of human heredity through selective breeding, an infamous movement that was immersed in white supremacy. The second oldest was Aldous Leonard Huxley, who was a philosopher and writer of the famous book titled *Brave New World*. The third sibling, Noel Trevenen Huxley, died of suicide at the age of 25. The fourth child, Margaret Arnold Huxley, lived to be 82 years old.

Andrew's grandfather Thomas Henry Huxley was also a contemporary of Charles Darwin and champion of Darwin's theory of evolution. Andrew's father, Leonard, had been a well-respected writer, editor, and educator. Andrew's brother, David Bruce Huxley, had a daughter, Angela, who married Charles Darwin's grandson, Sir Charles Galton Darwin, a noted physicist.

For further study:

https://www.youtube.com/watch?v=WdL-81i3Qg4
https://www.youtube.com/watch?v=jKFLtxQqu6w

Chapter 15

ERNEST EVERETT JUST – CELL SURFACE AND DEVELOPMENTAL BIOLOGY

1. *Ernest Everett Just had somewhat of a difficult childhood. Can you start with his date of birth and then talk about the various adverse childhood experiences that he encountered?*

Dr. Ernest Everett Just was a preeminent embryologist but primarily forgotten to history by many modern biologists. The story of Dr. Just's life and science represents a definitive account of adversity but especially in overcoming such adversity. Recently, Dr. Just became known as the *Black Apollo of Science* as a result of the publication in 1983 of the award-winning biography of a similar title.

Dr. Just was born on the second week, the 14th day, of the month of August in the year 1883 to parents Mary Mathews Cooper and Charles Fraser Just, Jr., in the sprawling aristocratic city of Charleston, South Carolina, in the U.S.

His grandfather, Charles Just, Sr., born in the year 1805, had been a slave of George Just, who was a German immigrant. Charles became free after the American Civil War had eventually come to an end in 1865. Charles Just, Sr., had become a pillar of the community in Charleston, S.C.

Just's parents Mary and Charles, Jr., were married on the 19th of September in 1878. The Just's first offspring had been stillborn, but the couple had nevertheless continued to have children afterward. The child Ernest was the third oldest of five siblings, but the oldest two children had, unfortunately, died earlier of infectious disease; one sibling had died from the effects of cholera and the other from diphtheria, leaving Ernest to become the eldest of three children, in the Just family.

In 1886 during the last day of August, an unprecedented earthquake destroyed the city of Charleston and nearby areas. It had been widely believed that the end of the world was at hand. The Just family lost their home and almost all of their possessions. After recovering from the fright of an impending doom that did not arrive, and the shock of the disastrous incident, the family got to work rebuilding what they had lost.

The Just family was poor, as his father had also been paying for the welfare of another family, with several children. The Just household of which Ernest was a member had been remortgaged in order to generate funds for the treatment of illnesses that the second family had been experiencing. The effort was to no avail as two of the children, Vivian and Joseph Just, both passed away from their infections, and meanwhile, both of the Just families were now even deeper in new debt.

At the age of 4 years, in 1887, Just's father had died of alcoholism, leaving no money (only debt) and, furthermore, leaving his mother alone to care for Ernest, Hunter, and Inez, the three surviving young Just children.

Within a few months, Charles, Sr., Just's grandfather, passed away, as well, leaving additional debt that needed payment to an increasing number of creditors. It had been hoped that an endowment might be forthcoming after Charles Just Sr., had passed away, but alas no funds transpired; instead, more debt had arrived to make matters worse. Very quickly, the debts accumulated, even after putting their home up for sale—the $200 received from the house sale did not meet the debts owed to the creditors.

The surviving members of the Just family soon became penniless, and they consequently moved to James Island, where it was thought that work for Mary, Just's mother, might be found. Having found a job there for 97 cents a day and which required heavy labor working in phosphate mines, Mary managed to save enough to purchase a substantial new property, and like her grandfather-in-law, eventually became a well-respected and model community leader. In fact, a new town, Maryville, was established and named after her.

2. *Ernest Everett Just stands out for one specific reason in our studies of scientists. What would you say that is?*

I think that Dr. Just's studies pertaining to the changes that occur on the surfaces of fertilized animal cells during the process of fertilization and embryonic development represent critical advances in the history of the natural and biological sciences. His body of scientific work significantly enhanced our understanding of the evolutionary relationships regarding the relevant fields of ecology and of cellular development. His work has present-day relevance also in the cell cycle, cancer, and in the necessary field of cell biology.

Towards this, I believe that the prime legacy that he has left behind for the rest of us are at hand within his extensive writings, both in the scientific journals with over 70 scientific articles and in his two books, one of which is titled *The Biology of the Cell Surface*, and the other being a technical methods-based book.

This legacy has led directly to substantial new scientific inquiries, significantly expanding the field of cell biology, many new developments of which are still in progress to this day. Although not routinely mentioned by name, Dr. Just's seminal discoveries are included in good modern textbooks of basic Biology as well as in Developmental Biology and in Embryology.

3. *Back during his time period, there were various schools that had various names – but few continue to exist today.*

One of the first schools that Just attended had been founded by his mother, Mary Mathews Just. She had sold her James Island property to invest in the new school. Mrs. Just had observed a real need for African American children and education. This particular population was found to be lacking in opportunities towards attendance at good educational institutions. In fact, the town had no school whatsoever, and Mary was eager to fill the void.

The new scholastic establishment was called the Frederick Deming, Jr. Industrial School. The school had been the first such school of its kind, established in 1893 when Just was 10-years old. Unfortunately, in 1899, the school had caught fire and burned to the ground. The structure had been completely destroyed. It had been a devastating incident, with Just's younger sister having been severely burned during the conflagration.

In 1896, at 13 years of age, Just enrolled in the so-called Colored Normal Industrial Agricultural and Mechanical College, located in the town of Orangeburg, in South Carolina. It had been a precursor to the South Carolina State College. At this school, Just focused on training geared for teachers, taking courses in math, reading, spelling, English grammar, history, geography, and physiology. Just took his teaching licensure in 1899, at the age of 15 years, a year earlier than anticipated.

After working briefly in a restaurant in New York, Just was awarded a scholarship to attend Kimball Union Academy, located in a town called Meriden, in New Hampshire, starting in 1900. His mother had learned about the institution via a magazine advertisement. Just's arrival at the school had been quite a change in culture, as he was the only African American to attend it at the time. In fact, when he graduated from Kimbal Union in 1903, there was only one other African American student enrolled. In 1901, his mother passed away. On commencement day, in honor of his outstanding academic performance, he gave a speech that was later published in the school newspaper.

In 1903, newly graduated Just had moved to Hanover, New Hampshire, to attend the prestigious Dartmouth College. He had again encountered a culture-shock, so to speak, just as he had back at Kimbal. His first semester at Dartmouth was a disaster, earning deficient grades in most of his courses. He had to retake his exams the following spring to earn passing grades.

He then concentrated his studies in Biology while minoring in history and Greek. His choice of Biology as a major was influenced by his professor in the course, Dr. William Patten. Having found his favorite topic, he flourished in all of his Biology courses. He had been especially proud of having received the prestigious Rufus Choate scholarship two years in a row. In 1907, he took his undergraduate degree with all of Dartmouth's highest honors, *magna cum laude,* including entry into the Phi Beta Kappa, while being the top award-winning student in his class, and ranking number 10 out of 182 graduates. No one that year had earned the coveted *summa cum laude*. Sadly, he was not chosen to be a commencement speaker that year.

With no apparent prospects for teaching at whites-only colleges or universities in the U.S., Just took a teaching post at one of the best historically-black institutions in the U.S., Howard University, located in Washington, D.C. He taught a plethora of courses ranging from Literature, Rhetoric, Narration & Description, and Exposition, but in 1909, he switched to Biology when a new Science facility had been built. In 1910, he was appointed as assistant professor of biology. Anxious to continue his education, however, Just took the advice of his old biology professor at Dartmouth and contacted Prof. Frank Rattray Lillie, who was chair of the Zoology Department at the University of Chicago, and director of the Marine Biological Laboratory, in Woods Hole, Massachusetts. Worried about Just not gaining acceptance as an African American graduate student, Prof. Lillie suggested that Just spend a summer in Woods Hole, taking graduate courses there, in 1911. He was officially enrolled at the University of Chicago *in absentia,* conducting his Ph.D. thesis project in Woods Hole.

At the MBL, Just flourished. He had had an unprecedented opportunity to meet with some of the most prominent scientific investigators of the time, many scientists of whom spent each summer in Woods Hole, teaching and conducting research. He learned directly from their example. On the 12th day of June, in 1912, Just married his first wife, Ethel Highwarden Just. The Just couple would eventually have three children, Margaret, Highwarden, and Maribel.

In 1911, Just made his first significant scientific discovery, making it a basis for his first publication in the journal called the *Biological Bulletin*, in 1912. He found that during cell cleavage that transpires after fertilization, the site of sperm entry into the egg cell defined the location where the fertilized egg will initiate the line of cleavage. In short, he had corrected the largely incorrect notion that the cleavage line was determined by the so-called median line. It was his first project, and turned out to be a tremendously significant discovery! The work was to be included in his Ph.D. thesis write-up in addition to other work involving the breeding and swarming habits of the clam worms *Nereis limbata* and *Platynereis megalops*. Thus, with a suitable amount of original work being performed, Just was ready for the defense. In 1916, Dr. Just took his Ph.D. degree in the areas of physiology and zoology from the University of Chicago, taking high honors, *magna cum laude*.

Dr. Just had begun teaching again at the historically black institution Howard University, returning in 1916. He made his way through the ranks at Howard, eventually becoming a full professor and then chair of the Biology department and later chair of the new Zoology department. It was an appointment he was to keep until his untimely death on the 27th day of October of 1941 from pancreatic cancer.

4. *Just apparently contracted typhoid. Can you first tell us what typhoid is, the symptoms and treatment, and what happened to Just as a result?*

One incident that was to have profound effects upon Just for the rest of his life was his bout with the notorious typhoid fever that occurred shortly after their move to the Island of James. The illness was prolonged, and it caused Just, who was about 5-years old, to miss six weeks of school and to forget how to read and write; these skills had previously been acquired by Just with an acumen. The recovery, however, was a prolonged one, and he had to learn to read and write over again.

His mother had been incredulous about his newfound reading and writing inabilities, and it caused a severe rift between them for the duration of the prolonged illness. So distraught was Just about the incident that when he eventually did recover his abilities to read and write again, he kept his re-acquired aptitude a secret from his mother for several months.

At about the time of Just's illness with the typhoid fever, approximately 1888, evidence that microbes can indeed cause illnesses had been published that same year by Dr. Robert Koch. However, it was not entirely known that the typhoid fever had a microbial cause. While the *Salmonella enterica* Typhi bacterium had been discovered to grow in culture in 1880 by Dr. Carl Ebert, its association with typhoid fever was not then established. It was not yet clear what caused typhoid fever. The microbe-illness association was not confirmed until the work of Drs. Daniel Salmon and Theobald Smith, who isolated the relevant bacterium from swine with the so-called hog cholera.

The typhoid fever ailment is brought about by infection with a bacterium called *Salmonella enterica*, of the serovar called Typhi. In clinical terms, the illness is referred to as a type of salmonellosis, and in modern times the term typhoid fever is called enteric fever. The disease is started by acquiring the *Salmonella* bacteria after consuming food or water that's contaminated with these microbes. Often the primary mode of bacterial transmission between patients is via the fecal-oral route.

After an incubation period of 10 to 14 days, which is the time needed for the *Salmonella* bacteria to reach the organs like the liver or the spleen, the symptoms manifest themselves. Symptoms and signs of typhoid fever include a gradual fever, plus a headache, muscle aches and pain (called myalgia), feelings of uneasiness or discomfort (malaise), and loss of appetite for food (anorexia). After approximately one week, gastrointestinal tract disorders appear.

Modern treatment includes antibiotics like cephalosporin, chloramphenicol, a fluoroquinolone (like ciprofloxacin), or trimethoprim-sulfamethoxazole. Preventative measures include a vaccine and proper handling and preparation of eggs and poultry products.

5. *His book "The Biology of the Cell Surface" seems to be a summative review of his work. Why is his work on the cell surface so important, and how does his work contribute to our work today?*

Dr. Just's definitive book *The Biology of the Cell Surface* was his magnum opus and a significant success in scientific circles. It was his second book, and it was published in 1939 as an elegant-looking, leather-bound volume, dedicated to his mother. He had sent a complimentary copy of his book to the MBL library, and it is believed that that historic copy now sits in the rare book room of the library, which in present times holds 3 copies of the book, including an accessible eBook version: https://archive.org/details/biologyofcellsur00just

Dr. Just had started writing his famous book in February of 1934 while in Naples, Italy, and he had finished it in February of 1939. The book was immediately cited amongst many of the relevant textbooks of the day. In some cases, the book is cited even to this day. Early critics, while generally appreciating its content, nevertheless criticized some of his inaccuracies, such as his apparent rejection of Thomas Hunt Morgan's notion of organismal development involving a genetic aspect. Instead, Dr. Just had invoked his notion of a cytoplasm-centered hypothesis called "genetic restriction" as an explanation of how an organism undergoes development. While largely inaccurate on a general level, his cytoplasm-based hypothesis nevertheless has certain aspects of accuracy, namely, in the way that cells will undergo so-called epigenetic processes for gene expression modification in the cytoplasm!

The book addressed many of his critics who had previously criticized many of his published works. It had been a total vindication of his lifetime's investigative scientific work. Thus, the book is relevant today on a purely scientific basis. His scientific contributions dealt with many aspects that are still *apropos* in modern times, such as cell fertilization, developmental biology, ecology, systems biology, epigenetics, and embryology. Dr. Just's writing is beautiful, and the book takes on not only a biological approach but a philosophical one as well. It is considered by today's historians of the biological sciences to be a true classic.

6. *Dr. Just apparently worked for many years in Italy. What did he work on, and how was his work received there?*

Dr. Just's first foray to Europe began in 1929 when he traveled to the Stazione Zoologica, located in Naples, Italy, in order to pursue his research program on cellular fertilization. He discovered that with mature sea-urchin eggs of the genus called *Echinus*, tiny protrusions were noticed on their cell surfaces prior to their completion of competency for fertilization. On the other hand, Dr. Just found that when such eggs were ready for fertilization to occur, their surfaces were rather smooth, and their so-called ectoplasm, a historical term, meaning cytoplasm or the structured layers underneath the surface of the cell in today's parlance, had a rather homogenous appearance.

He then astutely noticed that after fertilization, the eggs of the so-called parchment tubeworm called *Chaetopterus* had dramatic observable changes in their ectoplasm in which the cellular contents appeared to migrate to their animal poles and covered their vegetal poles. He noticed that prior to fertilization, the spermatozoa entered the competent cell via its vegetal pole.

Also, at Naples, he studied a related sea-urchin of the genus called *Arbacia*. He studied their mitotic behavior observing the first cellular cleavage of the fertilized egg into two daughter cells. He noted their two opposing centrospheres, which consist of cytoplasmic-based ectoplasm layers surrounding the centrioles of the centrosomes, which were associated with their asters. Dr. Just recorded the growth properties of the centrospheres and the asters, and he noted the shapes of the eggs, the migrating patterns of the ectoplasm, and the activity of the so-called hyaline plasma-layers as the nuclei of the cell as it underwent mitosis.

Dr. Just was very well received and well-liked at Naples and throughout the rest of Europe. He had achieved a tremendous amount of respect for his research studies. Interestingly, in Europe, his everyday life was made relatively stress-free. For example, when he traveled throughout the bulk of Europe, he did not have to plan ahead in terms of hotel and food accommodations. That is to say, Dr. Just needed not to fear staying at or dining in whites-only establishments in Europe, as such places were rather scarce in their existence.

This had been a stark contrast to the treatment he received in the U.S., where racism was rampant and openly practiced. In the U.S., African Americans needed to plan their entire travel itineraries extremely carefully, lest they encounter a hostile food or hotel establishment—for whites only! It took energy and time for living a daily life, and travel planning was a task that required painstakingly careful attention. In contrast, Caucasians in the U.S. needed not to worry as such about *their* travel plans.

Even at the famous MBL in Woods Hole, a white student-waiter who was from the Deep South had vociferous reservations openly at the thought of having to serve Just his meals! The waiter did not want to wait on an African American; the southerner said it "felt wrong." Such racist behavior was put to a sudden halt by a one "Miss Belle" Downing, who was in charge of the MBL cafeteria and in the seating arrangements. She refused to alter her seating arrangements and stood firm about it. She had, for many years, purposefully sat faculty and students from all walks of life with each other in order to facilitate the meeting of disparate minds and to open up productive discussions. It also facilitated an air of people just getting to know each other better. Dr. Just responded to the racist waiter by asking him what he was interested in studying and even invited him to his laboratory to learn about his (Just's) research program. Apparently, after getting to know

Dr. Just the white waiter's reluctance to serve him and his apparent racism and prejudice subsided.

In the U.S. as an African American, Dr. Just had been denied access to research grants and professorships at most of the colleges and universities. Instead, he was relegated to becoming a faculty only at historically black colleges and universities; in fact, he was strongly encouraged to do so by his mentors who feared for Dr. Just and his possible encounters with racism, and his mentors knew all about the racism he had had to deal with. Worse, he had had a falling out with the president of Howard University. Taken together, with these different circumstances in mind, Dr. Just had little reservations in going to Italy.

7. *World War II devastated millions, and Just was no exception. What happened to him, and what was the result?*

During World War II, in August of 1940, Dr. Just was arrested in France by the Nazis!

The dramatic saga of Dr. Just and his brand new second wife, Hedwig Schnetzler Just, in Nazi-Germany-occupied France during the war started back in the summer of 1939. Dr. Just had previously divorced Ethel in April of 1939, and he married Hedwig on August 11th of the same year. Hedwig was his laboratory assistant, a citizen of Germany, and white. The second marriage of Dr. Just to a white woman would have most certainly been met with shock and disdain by a majority of Americans in the day. In fact, meanwhile back in the U.S., there had been rumors that Dr. Just had been having love affairs with white women in Europe. Fortunately, for Dr. Just, he was in Europe.

He had, however, other problems!

These problems were significant, and they consisted, namely, of the rise of Hitler, plus his white-nationalist and pro-fascist Nazi Party, into the German government!

Before the Nazi problem had risen its head upon Dr. Just, he had been quite busy in 1939 working at the famous Biologique Station, in the small town of Roscoff, France, where the European political problems, such as the acute ones between France and Germany, did not manifest themselves in Roscoff. He had also amassed a great deal of scientific data and had carefully recorded his data for all of his projects. Dr. Just had been in the midst of his data collection and in his writing of a lengthy technical paper dealing with the philosophical aspects of Biology as he had envisioned them when a fateful letter addressed specifically to him had arrived.

In October of 1939, the letter, which was from the official but German-occupied French government, stated that foreigners were no longer welcome at the Biologique Station and that Dr. Just needed to move out of his current housing in Roscoff.

Shortly afterward, Dr. Just received another letter, this time from the head of the Biologique Station, which amounted to a rather longwinded apology for the inconvenience. His new unwelcome status, however, did not change.

Initially, the newlyweds, Ernest and Hedwig, who was now pregnant, tried very hard to make the best of the rather precarious situation. They tried to leave Nazi-occupied France. It seemed that everything they tried, and everywhere they went, the Justs encountered mass confusion, as no one exactly knew what was going on or what was yet to come. To make the matter worse in trying to leave France, they faced widespread panic, a bureaucratic nightmare, excessively long lines for getting the paperwork completed, and delays in getting the needed approvals for traveling abroad.

Then, in early August of 1940, Dr. Just was taken prisoner by the German Nazis. He was sent to a Nazi internment camp, perhaps at Chateaulin, France. It had been a severe disappointment, especially for Hedwig. Her father, fortunately, had particular contacts with members of the Nazi Party through his membership on a board of directors for a Germany-based company, Brown, Boveri Co., which was associated with Dr. Just's father-in-law, a German citizen. Hedwig's father made a few calls, and an officer was dispatched to France in order to secure the release of Dr. Just from the prison camp. The effort worked.

The Justs, however, were still stuck in France! The German Nazis were already in charge of France in 1940! Meanwhile, Dr. Just's American friends and colleagues had not heard anything about his status and were worried. They entreated the Red Cross and the State Department in Washington, D.C., to make inquiries of the new French government regarding Dr. Just.

By this time, however, the Justs had finally managed to obtain apparent approval for the travel abroad and actually left France for Spain, and then on to Portugal. In Lisbon, they purchased two one-way tickets to Washington, D.C., U.S., on the S.S. Excambion.

However, *another* last-minute problem had emerged.

The ship's captain of the S.S. Excambion refused passage onboard for Mrs. Hedwig Just. The captain was leery of Hedwig, who by this time was visibly pregnant, and the captain had feared she might possibly have untreatable complications trying to deliver a baby while on board. The Justs managed to coax if not cajole the captain into relenting on his stance, and they thus sailed to the U.S., where Dr. Just's daughter Margaret and news reporters were there to meet the new Justs.

The Justs had actually escaped from the Nazis!

Shortly after their arrival from war-torn Europe to the U.S., in 1940, Hedwig Just would give birth to a daughter named Elisabeth.

Incidentally, because of the confusion involved in making good his escape from the Nazis, all of his scientific records, data accumulated from his research in France, had been mistakenly left behind! Back in the U.S., Dr. Just had to write what were to be his last scientific publications from memory!

8. Apparently, water can move into and out of the cell structure. Why is this important?

In his 1939 classic book *The Biology of the Cell Surface*, Dr. Just devoted an entire chapter dedicated to the topic of water. He wrote about the importance of water in general for life. He acknowledged that living cells contained water. He speculated whether the substances within living cells were dissolved in water or existed in colloidal suspensions. He wistfully wondered whether water surrounded cellular substances or if these substances surrounded the cellular water. Did both circumstances exist? Dr. Just was clearly a curious writer and scientist.

Turning to the topic of water movement in and out of cells, Dr. Just had written about his experiments and made the following conclusions based on his results. First, he perceived that water left cells as individual droplets. Further, as the water did so, it must somehow have passed through the membrane barrier of the cell, probably through little "canals" embedded in the cellular membranes. Third, the developing yolks of the fertilized eggs must also take up water.

During this latter process, the yolk water-uptake, Dr. Just speculated that the protein and lipid mixture inherent in the yolk disintegrated, releasing the lysed lipid into the cytoplasm of the cells. Thus, as water leaves the yolk, it also leaves the cell, permitting then the lipid to re-enter the yolk. Dr. Just referred to these water movements as yolk hydration and dehydration, and the yolk lipid correspondingly moved in the directions opposite from those of the water. Dr. Just had also determined that other sub-cellular structures must permit water movement, as well, structures like the nucleus itself or certain yet undiscovered elements of the cellular cytoplasm.

Dr. Just had further deduced that the solute concentration in the laboratory of the seawater used, whether hypotonic, hypertonic, or isotonic, had something to do with the water movement in and out of cells. Towards these, he considered the nature of the membrane that enclosed the cells. Much of his treatment was speculative, as it was uncertain at the time, the mid-1930s, what formed the actual molecular basis of the biological membrane. On this score, Dr. Just astutely accurate, writing that the cellular membrane was composed of a mixture of lipid and protein and that movement of substances across the membrane was semi-permeable, meaning that membrane-crossing transport was allowed for some substances but not for others.

Dr. Just concluded that water moved in and out of cells in order to maintain a specific water concentration at a constant level inside of the cells. He felt that water passage across the cellular membrane was a normal physiological process of living cells. Based on this conclusion, Dr. Just went on to logically reckon that substances besides water must also occur in precise amounts and that the rates of solute transport must occur appropriately in order to maintain their constant solute concentrations on the insides of cells.

Given what we know today regarding the nature of the biological membrane and of the transport of water and solutes across the membrane barrier, it is remarkable that Dr. Just was startlingly accurate. Indeed, transport of water and solutes across the cell membrane is still a widely studied field in the biomedical sciences.

9. *In terms of being an African American, Just seemed to succeed "against all the odds" as they say. What do you see as his legacy?*

Indeed, overcoming the incredible odds that were stacked against him is most certainly one of his non-science legacies. In short, he overcame racism to no small extent. He lived in a time of overtly practiced legal racism and prejudice. He circumvented all of it.

Dr. Just's life story may be considered an inspirational one from the standpoint of example. He possessed a strength, determination, a real passion for learning, a steadfast refusal to give up, and genius.

He overcame tremendous hardship in his youth, and he later became astonishingly successful in garnering a most productive higher education to the level of the coveted doctorate and used his education most effectively in the pursuit of his passion. He possessed a tremendous excitement for science. He worked tirelessly in his quest to understand how his beloved sea creatures made more of themselves and lived in the sea!

Those who read about Dr. Just and his example will surely benefit from knowing his life and science. I surmise his life will provide ample inspiration for all walks of life for many generations to come!

10. What have I neglected to ask?

While Dr. Just's relationship with his mentor and great scientist Dr. Frank Lillie, for whom a prominent building holding the grand auditorium is named after at the MBL, was primarily a collegial one, the same cannot be said for Dr. Just's relationship with another great Woods Hole scientist, Dr. Jacques Loeb, for whom another MBL building is named.

The rift between Drs. Just and Loeb was a serious and long-lasting one. It had to do with a criticism that Dr. Just had regarding the experimental technique for formulating Dr. Loeb's so-called lysin hypothesis of the artificial parthenogenesis mode of fertilization. Dr. Lillie's early experiments had already placed a certain but tacit skepticism of Dr. Loeb's experimental parthenogenesis. Likewise, Dr. Just had felt that the parthenogenesis involved elements intrinsic to the eggs themselves, a phenomenon he coined called "independent irritability" in which the egg, with its underlying ectoplasm, was postulated to innately harbor a full capacity for its own development, an idea in stark contrast to that of Dr. Loeb. The rift came to a head when Dr. Just not only published the criticism in increasingly forceful terms but also mentioned it in a public seminar given by Dr. Just at a scientific conference. Immediately, two sides emerged: a pro-Just/Lillie versus a pro-Loeb side. The schism had its supporters on each side. The correct one, i.e., Dr. Just's understanding, ultimately emerged, but it was an extremely awkward situation, to say the least.

In the time-period between Dr. Just's early death at the age of 58 in 1941 and the publication of a famous biography about him in 1983, Dr. Just had been essentially all but forgotten. The book reminded historians and scientists alike about the remarkable life story of Dr. Just and about his significant scientific contributions.

In 1996, Dr. Ernest Everett Just was commemorated with a portrait on the cover of a U.S. postage stamp.

In 2009, a special issue of the *Molecular Reproduction and Development* journal had been devoted to Dr. Just and his scientific discoveries, most of which are still relevant today. In 2012, The University of Chicago Biosciences division established a lecture series called the

Annual E.E. Just Lecture, and in the Erman Biology Center, an oil portrait of Dr. Just resides in the E.E. Just Room. Remarkably, perhaps regrettably, no laboratory building at the MBL in Woods Hole has yet been named after Dr. Just.

For more information go to:

https://www.youtube.com/watch?v=I0EBEUdLoW4
https://www.youtube.com/watch?v=_gLHLcxLOnQ
https://www.youtube.com/watch?v=dvgr8HW_rXs

Chapter 16

KARL LANDSTEINER – ABO BLOOD GROUPS

1. *Who was Karl Landsteiner? And what did he discover about ABO blood groups?*

Nobel Laureate Dr. Karl Otto Landsteiner was a famous immunologist and biomedical scientist. His worldwide fame arises from his milestone discovery of the so-called ABO blood types, a blood classification scheme.

His discovery revolutionized the course of human medicine because it permitted physicians for the first time in history to conduct safe, life-giving blood transfusions, based on his ABO system.

Prior to Dr. Landsteiner's groundbreaking discovery that there were different blood groups, medical transfusion of blood between individuals was fraught with potential disaster. The blood-transfused patient might succumb to a dramatically fatal outcome, and, worse, the types of outcomes (death versus survival) from the transfusions were unpredictable. Dr. Landsteiner's discovery that human blood consisted of three (and later 4) different types changed the course of medical history and ushered in a new era of clinical medicine. Thanks to Dr. Landsteiner's pioneering work, it became possible to determine the blood types of a patient and of a blood donor before the transfusion would take place. This allowed properly matched blood types to be identified beforehand. Thus, it permitted clinicians to provide blood to their patients in a safe manner.

In his experiments during the late 19th century and early portions of the 20th century, Dr. Landsteiner collected samples of blood from many individuals, including his own blood and those of his colleagues. Next, he purified the red blood cells, separating them from the white blood cells and clotting factors, a substance he called serum. Then, he mixed each of the red blood cell samples with each of the various sera samples, examining the mixtures for the occurrence of clotting, a process now called agglutination. Some mixtures of blood and sera "clotted" (agglutinated) and others did not show this agglutination.

After analyzing the various blood clotting data, Dr. Landsteiner devised the ABO system. He proposed that the various types of blood harbored what he called the agglutinogens, now known as antigens. He said that type A blood had A antigens, whereas type B blood had so-called B antigens. He also proposed that the agglutinating sera had antibodies, like anti-A and anti-B antibodies. If the blood harbored neither A nor B antigens, he referred to the blood as type C, later called type O. Shortly thereafter, he found a fourth blood group, called type AB. In November of 1901, Dr. Landsteiner published his findings in a scientific journal called *Viennese Weekly Journal of Medicine*.

More recently, the ABO system has been revised such that the antigens are now considered the ABH system to reflect the molecular nature of the blood antigens better. These blood antigens are found on the surfaces of the red blood cells. Surprisingly, blood antigens are mainly sugars! The sugary blood antigens consist of molecules like galactose, fucose, *N*-glucosamine, *N*-acetylgalactosamine, plus, a platform of lipid or protein.

Type O individuals (i.e., those lacking both A and B blood antigens) nevertheless harbor H antigens on their red blood cell surfaces. In fact, all humans, independent of blood type, have antigen H on their red blood cell surfaces.

2. *Where was he born and where did he go to school?*

An only child, Karl Landsteiner was born on the 14th day of the month of June, in the year 1868, to parents Leopold and Fanny Hess Landsteiner, in the small town of Baden Bei Wein, in the province of Lower Austria, Vienna. When the child Karl was only 6 or 7 years old, his father, a noted journalist, and lawyer died suddenly of a heart attack at 56 years of age, leaving his wife to care for the young child. Mother and child were known to have had a close relationship for the rest of her life, and when Fanny Landsteiner herself passed away, in 1908, her devoted son was known to have displayed her funeral death mask in his bedroom for the rest of his life.

He was recognized at an early age as being intelligent. Young Karl attended State grammar school in Linz and then at Wasagasse Austrian Imperial high school in Vienna, graduating in 1885 with honors. He subsequently enrolled in medical school at 17 years of age and graduated with his M.D. degree in 1891 from the University of Vienna Medical School. During his tenure in medical school, Karl and his mother Fanny converted to Catholicism from Judaism, in 1890, hoping to escape persecution by the rising anti-Semites of Vienna. Landsteiner managed to keep his Jewish heritage a secret and went through great lengths to maintain the secret, even expensive litigation, in 1937, to avoid exposure. He lost the lawsuit, however, and his inclusion into a Jewish-based encyclopedia was published.

Having fully developed an interest in chemistry while in medical school, Dr. Landsteiner continued post-graduate study in the research laboratory of an inspirational teacher, Prof. Ernst Ludwig, in an effort to further his interest in conducting investigative research, as opposed to clinical medicine. Dr. Landsteiner's first publication entails work performed in Dr. Ludwig's laboratory.

Dr. Landsteiner's post-graduate pursuits were extensive, gaining advanced training from various investigators, such as Drs. Arthur Hantzsch and Roland Scholl, both of whom were from Zurich, Switzerland, plus, Nobel Laureate Prof. Emil Fischer, from Wurzburg, Germany, Dr. Eugen von Bamberger, from Munich, Germany, and Prof. Eduard Albert, from Vienna, Austria. In Dr. Fischer's laboratory, Dr. Landsteiner synthesized a compound called glycolaldehyde.

Dr. Landsteiner started a research assistant post, in 1896, at the laboratory of Dr. Max von Gruber, a prominent scientist who was housed at the Institute for Hygiene at Vienna General Hospital in Austria. Prof. Gruber was famous for having earlier pioneered the discovery of a serology-based laboratory test for the presence of typhoid fever. It is here in Dr. Gruber's lab where Dr. Landsteiner learned the basics of immunology and, importantly, of serology, the science of blood serum.

Dr. Landsteiner's discovery of the ABO blood system, in 1901, occurred after he entered the laboratory, in 1897, of Anthony (Anton) Weichselbaum, who was then director of the Institute for Pathological Anatomy. In 1903, Dr. Landsteiner took his Ph.D. degree studying pathology and histology of the parenchyma.

3. *Today we are very careful about blood transfusions because Landsteiner linked human blood transfusions to shock (often resulting in death) jaundice and a number of other conditions. Tell us about this?*

Great care must be taken to ensure that blood transfusion recipients receive the correct blood types. God forbid, if a patient receives an incorrect blood type, then a severe, perhaps fatal consequence can occur as a result of the incompatible blood transfusion. Providing to a patient a blood transfusion that is of the incorrect blood type (an incompatible blood transfusion) will generate a serve immune response called a transfusion reaction. The particular kind of immune response that occurs is called a Type II hypersensitivity reaction. The magnitude of this response can be profound, possibly inducing strong physiological responses such as jaundice and shock that you mentioned. The outcome might possibly lead to death.

During a transfusion reaction, an antibody that is specific for a particular blood antigen will bind to that antigen, forming an antibody-antigen complex on the surface of a red blood cell. This so-called immune complex (antibody-antigen) will then initiate a physiological mechanism called complement. The activation of the complement system, in turn, stimulates the insertion of giant membrane attack complexes into the membranes of the red blood cell target, resulting in lysis of the blood!

Another blood rejection mechanism that's stimulated by an antibody-antigen complex on the red blood cell surface is called antibody-dependent cell-mediated cytotoxicity (ADCC). The incompatible blood transfusion triggers the ADCC system to recruit another specialized type of cell, called natural killer (NK) cells, which have specialized proteins on their surfaces called the Fc receptors that bind to the Fc portion of the antibody. The Fc part of the antibody-forming part of the immune complex on the wrong blood then is bound by the Fc receptor of the NK cells. The NK cell binding to the red blood cell of the incorrect type will then release mediators that destroy the red blood cells!

4. *He was awarded the Nobel Prize for his classification of blood types: A, B, AB, and O. Can you tell us about each?*

The type A blood has so-called A antigens on their red blood cell membrane surfaces. The A antigens can be recognized by anti-A antibodies. Such individuals can safely receive blood from individuals who also are type A, or type O (as type O does not have the A or B antigens). Type A people, however, can make anti-B antibodies. These type A individuals can, nevertheless, donate blood to those who are type A or AB.

The type B blood has B antigens on their red blood cell surfaces. The B antigens are recognized by anti-B antibodies. Individuals of type B blood can safely receive type B or O blood. Type B individuals make anti-A antibodies. Type B people can donate blood to those who are type B or AB.

The AB-type blood has both antigens A and B on the surfaces of their red blood cells. The A and B antigens can be recognized by anti-A and anti-B antibodies, respectively. Individuals with type AB blood do not make anti-A and anti-B antibodies and can, thus, safely receive transfusions from types A, B, AB, and O. Thus, type AB persons are considered so-called "universal recipients" of blood. However, type AB people can donate blood only to similarly typed individuals with type AB blood, because they have the A and B antigens.

The type O blood has neither A nor B antigens. (Though they do harbor the H antigens. All individuals harbor the H antigen on their red blood cells.) Neither anti-A nor anti-B antibodies will recognize type O blood, as the A and B antigens are missing. Type O individuals will produce both anti-A and anti-B antibodies. Thus, type O people can receive only type O blood. However, an individual who is type O is considered a "universal donor" because they lack the A and B antigens. Thus, type O people can donate blood to those who are A, B, AB, and O.

5. *Now we often hear about the Rh factor. What does this mean in this regard?*

In 1940, Dr. Landsteiner discovered the Rh factor system. It represents another very important blood group classification system. Before its discovery, however, clinicians who used the ABO system to cross-match blood donors to their recipients still encountered transfusion incompatibilities. These transfused blood rejections had to do with the Rh factors!

A person will either have or lack the Rh factor antigen, and such individuals are referred to simply as Rh-positive (Rh+) or Rh-negative (Rh-), respectively. The term Rh originates from the *Rhesus* monkey (Rh for *Rhesus*) because about 85% of humans share the Rhesus factor with the *Rhesus* monkeys. The Rhesus antigen resides in the membrane of the red blood cell and transports glucose and anions across the membrane. In modern times, the Rhesus factor is also called the D antigen.

The ABO and Rh blood classification schemes are intertwined. For example, the blood of certain individuals may be A-positive (A+) or A-negative, (A-). Likewise, others may be B+, AB+, and O+, or A-, AB-, or O-, depending on whether they have or lack the Rh antigen on their red blood cell surfaces.

Although the Rh factor incompatibility rejections during mismatched transfusions are relatively minor compared to those with ABO incompatibilities, the Rh factors nevertheless play a prominent role in a drastically more considerable life-threatening situation.

Rh factor mismatches can cause a terribly serious condition called hemolytic disease of the newborn. It's a dreadful disease involving the Rh blood antigen incompatibility. The consequence involves incompatible blood types between a mother and fetus. During a mother's second pregnancy, if a fetus inherits an Rh+ blood type from the father, and the mother is Rh factor minus (Rh-), the mother can develop antibodies that are directed against the Rh+ fetus itself and attempt to destroy it! The baby may be stillborn. However, the pregnant mother can take RhoGAM, a preventative medicine consisting of helpful anti-Rh antibodies. These antibodies will find any incompatible blood and clear them from the system before immune cells are activated, and memory cells are made for the next encounter. Thus, during the mother's next pregnancy, she will not make the dreaded anti-Rh antibodies, resulting in the protection of the fetus from a potentially disastrous consequence.

6. Apparently, he was known for his meticulous scientific work– can you elaborate?

One can certainly envisage the great need for a meticulous nature when conducting scientific experiments in the field of biomedical sciences because such studies can directly have profound impacts on the general health of human beings across the world. While scientists, in general, have to be rather meticulous in their work in order to collect reliable data that's repeatable and accurate, many biographical and scientific sources, especially in a description by the Nobel Commission, attest to this particular character trait about Dr. Landsteiner as being quite profound.

In the case of Dr. Landsteiner, the accuracy of the blood grouping data was enormously important. Lives literally depended on getting the particular blood categories absolutely correct. The meticulous work of Dr. Landsteiner is evident if one examines the work that was involved during the ABO blood type system discovery. He collected many blood samples, keeping careful notes about whose blood was whose. He even collected his own blood! He prepared sera from each of the blood samples, as well as having isolated the red blood cell samples and keeping them separated from the sera samples. He mixed different blood samples with different sera and carefully (meticulously) observed whether an agglutination reaction occurred.

The work had to be repeated and in much the same way as before. Minor variations in the methodology or the laboratory protocols might mean enormous and confounding differences in outcomes. Furthermore, great care had to be taken to ensure that no contamination occurred between samples.

One account reports that Dr. Landsteiner was viewed by colleagues as an enormously critical investigator and educator. His laboratory personnel was made to repeat each of their most important findings while he stood over them observing their methods. He painstakingly checked and verified all of their data.

Others were more critical of Dr. Landsteiner. Another narrative describes him as having been a "stubborn tyrant" as a fellow colleague. More often than not, he was characterized as being rather a pessimistic and skeptical old crab!

Having a meticulous nature is exceedingly important in science, and the biomedical sciences are no exception. Great scientific investigators, regardless of their specific scientific discipline, will want to know the truth. Without question, meticulously conducting experiments will aid in ensuring that accuracy is maintained and that eventually, the truth is uncovered. Other investigators will repeat important findings and confirm or revise the conclusions made in earlier biomedical studies. Therefore, invoking a meticulous nature keeps the pace of science moving in positive ways.

7. In a sense, his blood work permeates much of modern medicine today. Is there any real way to assess his contributions to modern medicine?

Historians of medicine and the biomedical sciences have attributed the discoveries of Dr. Landsteiner has having made one of the most important scientific discoveries in the 20 century if not in the entire scientific history of the world. I'm sure these previous recorders of scientific and medical history are not far off the mark.

The ability to save lives based on life-giving blood transfusions changed everything in medicine. Countless millions of lives have been saved. Billions of more lives are slated to be saved on account of Dr. Landsteiner's ABO and Rh factor discoveries.

Dr. Landsteiner's contributions in discovering these blood groups are epic, and they provide a tremendous challenge to those wishing to assess the degree to which the enormity of the impact in modern medicine and biomedical sciences has been made.

8. Plasma– how does this fit into the picture?

Blood is a complex liquid-based tissue that contains cells and fluid. Plasma may be considered the fluid part of blood, i.e., blood without its red blood cells. Plasma is actually a complex liquid-based substance. It consists of water, ions (called electrolytes), certain gases (oxygen and carbon dioxide), nutrients (e.g., sugars), formed elements like white blood cells, and a complex mixture of various proteins.

For example, this fluid plasma part of blood also contains the protein factors that cause clotting. If the plasma is further treated in such a way that these clotting factors are removed, then the remaining substance is called serum. Multiple serum samples are called sera.

Other proteins include antibodies, which are specifically induced by an antigen and will function to protect the body from foreign (non-self) substances, such as tissues, microbial pathogens, and cancer. If an individual is immunized with an antigen, the blood will harbor responsive antibodies, and the material without clotting factors will be referred to as antiserum. There are many types of antisera.

Plasma can also harbor iron-binding proteins, such as transferrin or certain cytochromes. Iron is necessary for maintaining proper oxygen-binding properties of hemoglobin in red blood cells and in ensuring that certain iron-binding enzymes function properly.

Plasma contains an active complement, which is a physiological cascade system of proteins that work to protect the individual from pathogens by lysing bacteria or stimulating inflammation. The complement system serves a useful purpose as an innate immune system-based form of protection.

Plasma harbors certain white blood cells, also referred to as leukocytes. These types of cells also function immunologically. For instance, some leukocytes called B-lymphocytes will develop into plasma cells when antigen is recognized, and these plasma cells then become antibody factories. Such B-cells play an important role in humoral immunity, a sub-category of the adaptive immune response. Other leukocytes such as the T-lymphocytes also function as useful adaptive immunity components during cell-mediated immunity. The leukocytes represent a member of the formed elements of plasma.

Other formed elements of plasma include the erythrocytes, which are stem cells that are underdeveloped, immature forms of red blood cells. The erythrocytes bind to oxygen and carbon dioxide in the blood and transfer these gases throughout.

Another formed element is called the platelet, which is a cell fragment that can play a role in the clotting of blood. Platelets are derived from larger cells called megakaryocytes and harbor bits and pieces of their membranes as part of these formed elements.

9. *What have I neglected to ask?*

Dr. Landsteiner's body of scientific work was not limited to blood grouping. He made other important contributions to the biomedical sciences.

In 1904, he studied a medical condition called paroxysmal hemoglobinuria, in which levels of hemoglobin in the urine are elevated under extremely cold temperatures. He showed that the condition is brought about via an autoimmune reaction in which self-antibodies induce complement. Some reports indicate that this study represents one of the first known of the many autoimmune diseases.

Working with Dr. Erwin Popper in 1908, Dr. Landsteiner was the first to demonstrate that polio is caused by a filterable virus! He and Dr. Popper injected the brains of monkeys with a saline-based suspension of spinal cord and brain tissue from a human child who had died from poliomyelitis. No bacteria were detected in the brains of the injected monkeys, suggesting that the causative agent was a virus. Dr. Landsteiner was a key figure in the finding that polio was caused by poliovirus.

In 1906, he developed a new microscope-based method for examining the causative agent of syphilis, *Treponema pallidum*, as a useful tool for diagnosis. He successfully developed an animal model using monkeys for studying syphilis. He discovered that the mechanism behind the famous Wassermann reaction, a test for syphilis, was based on the agglutination of lipid-specific antibodies. He found that the targets of the Wassermann antibodies were phospholipid in nature.

In 1917, Dr. Landsteiner studied small molecules called haptens, which could not provoke an antibody response on their own but could be made to provoke an immune response, a property called immunogenicity if combined with a larger inert carrier molecule. The combined hapten and carrier together, called a conjugate, constituted the intact antigen. The part of the antigen to which an antibody binds is called an epitope or antigenic determinant. Interestingly, his work showed that the haptens could bind specific antibodies, and he felt that Nobel should have been bestowed to him for his hapten-antibody work.

In 1926, he discovered the MNP blood grouping system, which was used early on forensically in criminal cases and for settling paternity disputes. While not widely used today, this system and the ABO groupings were used to award Dr. Landsteiner the Nobel.

Interestingly, Dr. Landsteiner became good friends with another prestigious scientist, Nobel Laureate Dr. Linus Pauling, discoverer of the famous alpha-helix and proponent of the virtues of vitamin C. The two investigators even collaborated together in which Dr. Pauling contributed a chapter in a revised book originally written by Dr. Landsteiner. The book edition was called "*The Specificity of Serological Reactions.*"

Dr. Landsteiner was known to have played the piano. However, when neighbors complained they couldn't hear the radio, he sold the piano. Dr. Landsteiner's wife, Helene Leopoldine Wlasto Landsteiner, whom he married in 1916, developed cancer of the thyroid later in life. Dr. Landsteiner devoted his time to researching her disease. Unfortunately, he suffered a heart attack and died two days later, on the 26th day of June, in 1943, at the age of 75, leaving behind his wife Helene and his son, Earnest. Helene passed away of her malignant illness a few months later, on Christmas.

For visual learners and future study:

https://www.youtube.com/watch?v=dW8MdFTWQ3A
https://www.youtube.com/watch?v=uyGZnXimBiY
https://www.youtube.com/watch?v=ukwAvHlHYA4

Chapter 17

Rita Levi-Montalcini – Nerve Growth Factor

1. *Professor Varela, an extraordinary person, researcher, scholar and person who investigated both the growth of neurons and the "nerve growth factor" was Rita Levi-Montalcini, who interestingly enough, hailed from Turin Italy, where the legendary "Shroud of Turin" is kept.*

Let's start with her birth– when was she born and tell us something about her parents.

Dr. Rita Levi-Montalcini was born on the 22nd day of the month of April, in the year 1909. As you mentioned, she was born in the famous city of Turin, Italy. Her parents were Adele Montalcini (mother) and Adamo Levi (father). Both of her parents were wealthy Jewish Italians. Dr. Levi-Montalcini's mother has been described as a gifted painter, while her father has been depicted as a brilliant mathematician and electrical engineer. However, in later years, Dr. Levi-Montalcini would describe her father also as an entirely Victorian-minded totalitarian who refused to let her attend high school or even to pursue a career, a situation she grew to resent highly.

Her father was convinced that if the girls in the family, Rita (the youngest), her twin sister (Paolo), and her eldest sister (Anna) were educated or had a career, such pursuits would interfere with their marriages. In contrast, her older and only brother, Gino, was indeed permitted without recourse to acquire an education, and he later became a professor of architecture at the University of Turin. Her mother was supportive of her endeavors and encouraged her to have a conversation with and seek her father's authorization. Thus, possessing a particularly persistent resolve, she actively appealed to her father one evening after dinner. With his reluctant permission now at hand, she was finally given the go-ahead to pursue medicine as a career.

Dr. Levi-Montalcini further noted later that she had then become quite dissatisfied with the treatment of married women as second-class citizens, a situation she had observed her mother having experienced, and Levi-Montalcini, thus, forever vowed never to marry nor sire children. It is a promise to herself that she kept for the remainder of her life. In the interim, she made the astonishing discovery of the nerve growth factors.

2. *Her early education– where did she go to school, and what did she initially study?*

At the time when Levi-Montalcini was of school-age, elementary schools in Turin were separated based on gender, with the girls taught one curriculum in a distinct classroom and boys in another. After completion of primary school, the children were sent to a particular middle school based on their predicted promises for their future. Furthermore, boys were invariably sent to a middle school in which the arts, mathematics, and the sciences were emphasized, and it was a curriculum that prepared them for a future in teaching or in acquiring a higher education at any of their universities.

The school situation for girls was completely different, with art and writing skills being primarily emphasized. None of the mathematics nor the sciences, such as the biological disciplines, were taught to females, and thus, sadly, no preparative educational opportunities were provided for female entry into the universities, even at the high school level. In high school, the curricular situation remained much the same. Based on the example of her older sister and her proclivity for the written works of Swedish 1909 Nobel Laureate Selma Lagerlöf, Levi-Montalcini, as a teenager, was inspired by the influential Lagerlöf to pursue writing as a career. All directions pointed Levi-Montalcini to study literature writing.

This unfortunate educational direction for Levi-Montalcini changed suddenly as the result of the death of Giovanna Bruttata, her lifelong governess.

Bruttata had succumbed to a malignant cancer of the stomach and passed away at the age of 45 years old, only a few months after her diagnosis. The young governess's death had a profound impact on 20-year old Levi-Montalcini. It inspired her to study medicine as a career instead of her initial interest in writing. The only rub was getting the same notion across to her father, in order to acquire his permission. The conversation that occurred in bringing up the contentious issue to the forefront between father and daughter was tense. She broached the topic with her father after dinner one evening, on the advice of her mother. Levi-Montalcini informed him clearly that she had no interest in marriage whatsoever or in even having children; furthermore, she told him, she wished once again to pick up new educational studies, and that the topic of choice was medicine. At first, he objected, stating it was a subject too demanding for her to study and that it was, furthermore, an entirely unsuitable course of study for a woman. The story is told that she stood firm in her conviction that fateful evening, and he grudgingly relented. The requisite permission had been finally secured.

With her father's permission in hand, the preparation for medical school was indeed challenging. At 20 years of age, for the study of medicine, Levi-Montalcini virtually lacked all required prerequisites, such as Greek, mathematics, and Latin. Tutors were hired, and after intensive study of the necessary disciplines, she passed her entrance examination. Interestingly, she had persuaded her cousin, Eugenia Lustig, to attempt the same course of medical school preparation. Both Levi-Montalcini and Lustig entered medical school at the University of Turin. They were two of only 7 females in the entire class of over 300 medical students that year.

Two of her classmates, Renato Dulbecco, who is featured elsewhere in this book, and Salvador Luria, would go on to acquire the Nobel before she did. Dr. Dulbecco received his Nobel in 1975, Dr. Luria in 1969, and Dr. Levi-Montalcini in 1986, at the age of 77 years. One of her medical school professors of histology, the distinguished Dr. Giuseppe Levi, would inspire each of his future Nobel Laureates with his superb teaching skills. In particular, Professor Levi (no relation) would have another positive influence upon the newly minted physician, Dr. Rita Levi-Montalcini, shortly after her obtaining her doctorate.

Dr. Levi-Montalcini took her M.D. degree, specializing in the areas of surgery and medicine, and emphasizing in psychiatry and neurology, in 1936, from the University of Turin Medical School, with its highest honors, *summa cum laude*.

3. *Apparently, her M.D. was in medicine and surgery, and then she went on to study psychiatry and neurology. What is it about her background that led her to study the growth of neurons?*

Dr. Levi-Montalcini began a postgraduate fellowship training post as a research assistant working under the laboratory supervision of the famous professor G. Levi, who was housed in the Faculty of Medicine, the Institute of Anatomy at the University of Turin.

Dr. G. Levi assigned a project for Dr. Levi-Montalcini devoted to the study of brain structure. Her plan was to study how the human brain developed and to understand where each of the growing neurons in the human brain went and how they were formed during spinal cord development. At the time, the project turned out to be virtually an impossible task. The main difficulty was that it had been extremely challenging to get ahold of any human fetuses for brain development studies. In later years, speaking of the episode, Dr. Levi-Montalcini revealed that it would have been an arduous task even for an established investigator and quite impossible for a postgraduate student. Thus, the research project was abandoned.

Therefore, Dr. Levi-Montalcini focused her attention on examining the brain and spinal cord development in chick embryos, a neuro-tissue which was easily accessible. In chick embryos, she examined the developing spinal cord tissue and where the peripheral neurons ended up. Dr. Levi-Montalcini found that many neurons did not take hold if the peripheral neurons had no target to move towards. She had, thus, deduced that the neurons simply degenerated instead of concluding that the failed neurons couldn't undergo differentiation. Her notion ran afoul of the generally accepted idea at the time of the so-called differentiation model of neuronal development. The differentiation model had been postulated by Dr. Victor Hamburger, who had been housed at the Washington University in St. Louis, Missouri, in the U.S. Dr. Hamburger had proposed that the differentiation of individual neurons to acquire their particular mode of specialization was due to external elements that were inherent within their destinations. That is, neuron differentiation during brain and spinal cord development was dependent on their final location.

Sometime following the conclusion of the Second World War, in 1946, Dr. Hamburger had extended a special invitation to Dr. Levi-Montalcini to visit his laboratory and to work together to resolve their scientific dispute whether neuronal development occurred by the degenerative method (Dr. Levi-Montalcini's hypothesis) or by the failure of differentiation to transpire at the neuron's destination (Dr. Victor Hamburger's theory).

With the Levi-Montalcini-Hamburger collaborative experiments fully underway, all evidence pointed directly to the conclusion that the neurons suffered massive die-offs during brain development. The experimental evidence clearly showed that Dr. Levi-Montalcini had been correct all along. They published their new findings in 1946 in the *Journal of Experimental Zoology*.

Next, Drs. Levi-Montalcini and Hamburger found that the neuronal development depended largely upon specific feedback signals provided to the growing neurons to attain their final destinations. Without these feedback signals, the differentiated neurons failed to live at their target destinations.

4. *Mussolini and his henchmen and cohorts obviously interfered with her learning. What happened?*

In 1925, Benito Mussolini had established a fascist-based type of dictatorship for the government of Italy. Mussolini and Hilter had become good friends in the late 1920s and allies in the 1930s, and new laws were consequently passed. Shortly after this, anti-Semitism emerged in Italy. By the time that Dr. Levi-Montalcini had obtained her M.D. degree in 1936, anti-Semitism was in full swing, and human beings of Jewish descent were openly persecuted.

In 1938, Mussolini had passed legislation through the Italian government, his so-called *Manifesto of Race*. Jewish people were banned from holding both professional and academic positions. Dr. Levi-Montalcini was prohibited from landing a laboratory assistant position, or *any* job for that matter, at any Italian university. These developments resulted in severely curtailing Dr. Levi-Montalcini's research progress.

Her research pace managed to resume in full swing once the war was over. In the meantime, she made other arrangements to assemble her own provisional laboratory in her own bedroom of her house! Such dedication to the pursuit of knowledge is virtually unheard of within many areas of scientific investigation.

5. *Apparently, she did research in her very own home! What was she studying under somewhat primitive conditions?*

Because of the new Hitler-Mussolini axis of power had banned persons of Jewish descent from holding academic posts, Dr. Levi-Montalcini had to resign her lab assistant position, in 1938. Undeterred, she converted the bedroom of her house into a makeshift laboratory! In her new "laboratory," Dr. Levi-Montalcini studied chick embryo brain and spinal cord development.

During World War II, in 1941, because American and British allies were regularly proceeding with air-raid bombings of Italy, she would have to stop work and routinely move her laboratory equipment to an underground basement to prevent bombing damage. In 1942, Dr. Levi-Montalcini and her family fled from Turin and went into hiding in nearby hills of Turin, continuing her work in a new make-shift laboratory, conducting her neuronal experiments.

When the Germans invaded Italy, in 1943, she fled to Florence, where she went into hiding for the duration of the war. According to some sources, she continued her studies of chick embryos and their neuronal development by convincing nearby farmers that she needed the chick eggs for her children, but she did have actually have any children at the time, or ever for that matter. In later years, during an interview, she conveyed no regrets about this decision regarding children.

As I mentioned above, she correctly concluded that developing growing neurons died at their final destinations unless some factor provided a feedback signal to stay alive. Without the growth factor, the neurons exhibited massive die-off. Furthermore, the neurons were already differentiated by the time they reached their final destinations.

6. *The war brought death, infectious diseases, and she gave her all at that time in Florence, Italy. What do you think she learned about "human infectious diseases," and how did this impact her later work?*

During the Second World War, after the British and American forces had invaded Europe and made their way to Italy, from where the Germans had retreated back into Germany, Dr. Levi-Montalcini had been hired in August of 1944 as a physician in a war refugee camp in Florence, Italy. The encampment was replete with infectious diseases, and mortality rates were high. It had been a dangerous assignment because both patients and attending physicians had been exposed to the same infectious agents. Thus, she could have succumbed to any of the contagious diseases that she had encountered at the war refugee camp.

Many years after her Nobel Prize-winning discovery of nerve growth factor, Dr. Levi-Montalcini and her collaborators had discovered an interesting fact about it and its relationship to HIV, the human immunodeficiency virus, which is the causative agent of AIDS, the acquired immunodeficiency syndrome. The investigators, in 1999, found that her nerve growth factor protected specific white blood cells called macrophages from the lethal effects of HIV by serving as a so-called autocrine factor. The nerve growth factor was secreted by the infected macrophages, and it somehow worked on the macrophage that secreted the nerve growth factor to provide the protection. Her nerve growth factor helped macrophages survive infection from HIV. The autocrine factor function of the nerve growth factor prevented HIV from mediating its so-called cytopathic effect, that is, the detrimental effects of viral infection upon a host cell.

7. *Keeping it simple – the "chick embryo" seemed to play a significant role in her research. What do you know about "the chick embryo" and why it was used? (In my undergraduate work, we dissected cats and used hamsters and gerbils in those now-famous "Skinner Boxes" or operant conditioning chambers as they were called at that time! Great memories!)*

The chick embryos were used by Dr. Levi-Montalcini to study how the central nervous system was developmentally connected to its peripheral nerves. The chicks provided a readily available source of new neurons for her studies. She had tried to get hold of human embryonic brain and spinal cord tissue for this purpose but was thwarted by a lack of available human embryo neuronal tissue for the purpose because Italy had had a moratorium against human fetal abortions. It had been just as well, anyhow, because the task of learning about human brain development had been a rather formidable experimental task—impossible at the time, one might say.

Her experiments dealing with the chick embryos had been a fortuitous choice. She collected spinal cords from various stages of chick embryo development and prepared microscope slides for each of these neuronal growth stages. She studied the nerve migration patterns for each of the developmental stages in the growing neurons. Dr. Levi-Montalcini could follow their paths along the neuron migrations as the chick embryos developed. Next, she recorded how the ever-increasing neurons reached their final destinations along the spinal column. She then made the astute observation that once the grown neurons reached their targets, they underwent massive die-offs, leaving behind only specific neurons alive at the end of the neuronal outgrowth and development processes. Specific neurons were pruned back, while others were eliminated, and yet other neurons stayed alive and established a viable connection.

Dr. Rita Levi-Montalcini would later record that once she had made these perceptive findings, she celebrated by listening to a favorite cantata by J.S. Bach. She had, indeed, garnered great memories, too!

8. *Nerve growth factor and the growth of neurons– what did she learn– and why is it important?*

Interestingly, Dr. Levi-Montalcini's discovery of nerve growth factor started with the study of cancer. Preliminary data from the laboratory of Dr. Victor Hamburger in which he and his postdoctoral fellow, Dr. Elmer Bueker, observed in 1949 that when a malignant form of a mouse tumor was incubated alongside fresh chick embryos, the cancer had been invaded by sensory neurons! It was as if the diseased tissue was somehow permitting the growth of nervous tissue for the purpose of sensing its own immediate outside microenvironment.

The original purpose of the experiment had been to test the hypothesis that the transplanted tumor tissue could serve as an external limb function in order to permit spinal cord development and sensory nerves. Drs. Hamburger and Bueker had found that the transplanted tumor tissue was easily cultivated within the 3-day old chick embryo host, but the tumorous growth allowed the entry of peripheral neurons and that nearby dorsal root ganglia had been enlarged in size. They had unknowingly interpreted these findings to mean incorrectly that the growing tumors simply provided increasing spaces for the nerve infiltration to occur more readily.

This is where Dr. Levi-Montalcini comes into the picture. She had had an altogether different hypothesis.

First, she repeated the experiments of Drs. Bueker and Hamburger, supplying chick embryos with tumor transplants, and allowing the nerves to grow. Next, she invoked the method of Ramon y Cajal, the so-called silver staining technique, in order to follow the growth of the chick embryo neurons into the living tumor tissue. She had cut thin tissue slices during each of the stages of chick development, following the trail of the growing neurons into the tumor.

While confirming the same sort of data as had been obtained previously by Drs. Hamburger and Bueker, she had astutely found new data. First, Dr. Levi-Montalcini observed that in addition to sensory neuron invasion into the tumors, as had been seen with Drs. Hamburger and Bueker, she noticed that sympathetic neurons had also invaded the cancer! Second, Dr. Levi-

Montalcini observed that the invading neurons had grown with an abnormally high concentration of nerve endings. Third, she noticed that the nerve infiltration into the cancer tissue produced growing neurons with branches occurring at random points along the nerves. Forth, the ever-increasing neurons had no connections, called synapses, between the invading nerves. Lastly, sympathetic ganglia that grew into the tumor were unusually enlarged, considerably large enough to block the veins and obstruct the flow of blood in the chick embryo.

Taken together, Dr. Levi-Montalcini hypothesized correctly that the neuronal growth must be directed by some yet undiscovered diffusible nerve growth factor. This soluble agent must somehow be used as a beacon to direct the nerve growth towards its destination. The hypothesized nerve growth factor must somehow stimulate neuron growth and differentiation. She then extended the hypothesis to state that in healthy chick embryos, average neuronal growth and differentiation were mediated by the same type of putative nerve growth factor.

Unfortunately, her facilities at Washington University, in the U.S., were not suitable for performing the required tissue culturing techniques that would have allowed her to test her new hypothesis. Thus, she paid a collaborative visit to the laboratory of Dr. Carlos Chagas, at the University of Brazil, in Rio de Janeiro. In Dr. Chagas's lab, an excellent tissue culture facility had just been constructed where she could once again invoke the necessary tissue culture techniques that she had learned in Dr. Giuseppe Levi's laboratory years earlier to test her new Nobel Prize-winning hypothesis.

Thus, she boarded a flight to Rio de Janeiro with two laboratory mice in her purse!

The mice had had tumors that were transplanted into them, and they were to be her sources of tumors to then transplant into new chick embryos and to grow in culture. Upon arrival in Rio de Janeiro, Dr. Levi-Montalcini began her experiments. She added the tumor tissue to chick embryo cells in culture, followed the sensory and sympathetic ganglia protruding through the cancer, and measured their sizes. The results were disappointing because the neuronal sizes were the same as in the control groups of chick embryo cultures that had healthy mouse tissue.

Into this scenario in the early 1950s enter two influential biochemists. They were Drs. Stanley Cohen and Arthur Kornberg. Dr. Cohen had joined the group of investigators in Dr. Levi-Montalcini's lab at about the same time as her return from Brazil. Dr. Cohen spoke with Dr. Kornberg about the nature of the nerve growth factor, suggesting that it consisted of some sort of nucleic acid type of molecule like DNA. So Drs. Levi-Montalcini and Cohen turned to snake venom!

If indeed the nerve growth factor was nucleic acid in its constitution, then an enzyme called phosphodiesterase, found within snake venom, would degrade DNA, thus ablating the essence of the nerve growth factor. Adding phosphodiesterase predicted that nerve growth and differentiation would be lost. The experiment was performed by Drs. Levi-Montalcini and Cohen, and they got the exact opposite of the expected results. Their nerve growth and differentiation activities were enhanced by the snake venom DNA-degrading enzyme.

Apparently, the snake venom had, besides the phosphodiesterase, *other* substances, too, like perhaps its own nerve growth factor! The snake venom was, thus, systematically taken apart biochemically until the elusive nerve growth factor revealed itself after an extensive protein purification process. The purified nerve growth protein was studied further, showing that it had a definite molecular weight of 20,000 Daltons and potent nerve stimulating activity! Together, Drs. Levi-Montalcini and Cohen could grow nerves at will, directing the neurons to develop wherever they placed their new protein beacon.

It was the first time in scientific history, in 1952, in which anyone in the world had found such a nerve growth stimulating agent. The discovery was most certainly worthy of the Nobel.

9. *She ultimately was awarded the Nobel Prize, in 1986 I believe–deservedly so–but can you tell us why she was nominated and received this award?*

Drs. Levi-Montalcini and Cohen would share the Nobel in the category of medicine or physiology. The discovery, published in 1956, took the form of a new protein that could stimulate the growth of nervous tissue. In general, the central nervous system tissue cannot grow further once it has reached a particular developmental stage. Thus, the discovery that a protein factor could accomplish the growth of nerves was exciting. The ramifications of their one scientific breakthrough were astonishing.

First, it was thought that the nerve growth factor might somehow be exploited to delay or circumvent senile dementia. Furthermore, it was hoped that the new nerve growth factor would provide some degree of promise towards wound repair of severed spinal cords. While neither of these possibilities were to be fully realized, enormous strides towards their outcomes were undoubtedly made. Current biomedical science studies are still ongoing and making tremendous strides in these realms.

Another biomedical-based area that has been boosted by the discovery of nerve growth factor is cancer biology. In some cases, tumor tissue innervates itself, and it is thought that the prevention of such intrusions of nervous tissue within malignant cancers could somehow reduce or prevent these cancerous occurrences.

The nerve growth factors are thought to be quite relevant in studies pertaining to medical deformities. The use of nerve growth factors might alleviate these types of medical conditions.

Furthermore, the discoveries of the nerve growth factors by Drs. Levi-Montalcini and Cohen have led to subsequent scientific developments towards finding other growth factors for different cells, tissues, and organs. Interestingly, the nerve growth factor itself seems to play a role also in the immune and endocrine systems of the body.

Along these lines, nerve growth factor was later discovered by others to be evolutionarily related to transforming elements, platelet-derived growth factor, interleukins, insulin-like growth factors, T-cell activity-enhancing factors, and B-cell growth factors. Strikingly, the platelet-derived growth factor was discovered to be homologous in protein structure to viral oncogenes, further attesting to the relevance of cancer biology.

10. This is a subjective question, but given that she was born in Italy, lived in Turin and Florence– very Renaissance cities– could this have encouraged her and prompted her to pursue her academic pursuits?

I think you are insightful in your assessment above. As you know, Dr. Levi-Montalcini was born in Turin, and later, as a young scientist, she remained incognito in the nearby foothills of Florence during World War II.

Turin and Florence Italy are famous cities for a plethora of reasons.

Turin (Torino) is located in northern Italy in the Piedmont region and presently serves as its regional capital. It had been established since ancient times and became a part of the Roman Empire around 27 B.C. It was founded in 1563 as the capital of the Duchy of Savoy state, and in 1861 it became the first capital city of the Italian Kingdom. It has been noted to be the epicenter of the Risorgimento political movement towards Italian unification when all regions were combined into the Kingdom of Italy. In 1865, the capital had been moved to Florence. At the time of Dr. Levi-Montalcini, Turin had lost its prime influence after the end of the Second World War. It had had to be rebuilt. Full recovery took almost two decades.

Several notable scientists have also hailed from Turin. Amedeo Carlo Avogadro, born in 1776, formulated his famous number, 6.022×10^{23}, which represents the number of entities in 1.0 mole of any substance, like atoms or molecules, for instance. Dr. Salvador Luria, born in 1912, was a Nobel Laureate for his discoveries of DNA replication and bacteriophage virus genetics. Dr. Luria was the graduate advisor to James Watson, who with Drs. Rosalind Franklin, Maurice Wilkins, and Francis Crick made pioneering discoveries of the DNA structure. Drs. Levi-Montalcini and Luria are the only Nobel Laureates in the sciences to have been born in Turin.

Florence has its ancient history to it, too. It had been established as Fiesole in 200 B.C., and during ancient times, in approximately 59 B.C., Julius Caesar founded Florence as part of the Roman Empire. The city suffered tremendous loss of life during the onset of the Great Mortality, also known as the Black Death, during the medieval times. The Medici family was a prominent power in Florence, starting in the 14th century with Cosimo de Giovanni de' Medici. Today the Medici family is famous for its art displays in a variety of modern museums.

The city of Florence is also famous for its history involving developments in the natural and physical sciences, and architecture, as well as for its popes and artists. Michelangelo Buonarroti was one of the most famous of its artists and sculptors.

Noteworthy scientists who were associated with Florence include the eminent Leonardo da Vinci, a true Renaissance man, and Galileo Galilei, who famously studied physics and astronomy. Also renowned in the Florentine list are Amerigo Vespucci, Paolo dal Pozo Toscanelli, Felice Fontana, and Vincenzo Vivani.

During the time when Dr. Levi-Montalcini was conducting her scientific investigations, Florence had been occupied by the Germans starting in 1943 till its liberation in August of 1944, near the end of World War II. Nazi Germany had come close to destroying the city before they had to flee it during their retreat from the advancing Allies.

For additional study- go to:

https://www.youtube.com/watch?v=3dMQv0xcxQc
https://www.youtube.com/watch?v=WgkAR-vrJpM
https://www.youtube.com/watch?v=scyr_m4eb_M

Chapter 18

CÉSAR MILSTEIN – IMMUNE SYSTEM CONTROL AND MONOCLONAL ANTIBODY PRODUCTION

1. *It seems great scientists come from all over the world and then travel across the globe. César Milstein hailed from Argentina– When and where was he born, and what were his parents like?*

Dr. César Milstein was born on the 8th day of October in the year 1927 in the town of Bahía Blanca, in the country of Argentina to parents Máxima

Vapniarsky and Lázaro Milstein. César's father, Lázaro, was Jewish, and when he was 14 years of age, he emigrated from the Ukraine, Russia, to Argentina. Lázaro Milstein had started out as a poor farmer, who did not get an education, having to learn to write and read Spanish on his own. Lázaro later had many jobs, such as working on a railroad, being a carpenter, working as an assistant in a shop, and as a traveling salesman.

César's mother, Máxima, also Jewish, had been born in Argentina shortly after her parents had immigrated to their new country from Lithuania. Though she had been raised in a poor family, she was recognized early on as a gifted child and eventually became a school teacher. In later years, Dr. Milstein would describe his mother as making many sacrifices on a continual basis so that her three children, all boys (César was the middle child), could gain an education at the university level. His mother was quite successful in this regard in that all of her progeny indeed attended university and received their degrees.

Both parents placed a tremendous value on education.

Máxima was so supportive of César's educational endeavors that she actually typed up his Ph.D. dissertation for him! Lázaro was just as supportive during the educational years in that he regularly offered monetary assistance to César, who refused the offers periodically. When Dr. Milstein took his Ph.D., he dedicated it to his parents. However, after César married his wife, Celia Prilleltensky, in 1953, he graciously accepted Lázaro's generous monetary gift of a down-payment for a new house.

2. "The Jungle Book" and "Microbe Hunters" were books that apparently provided the foundation for Milstein's work. Tell us about his childhood.

Encouraged by his mother to read books instead of playing in the streets with other young children, Milstein discovered Rudyard Kipling's famous adventure story called *Jungle Book.* It apparently fostered his interest in the sciences at the age of eight years. During this timeframe, his new-found interest in science was then further solidified by one of his cousins, a biochemist. She had captivated Milstein's attention by describing in graphic detail her attempts to isolate deadly venom from snakes for the express purpose of someday providing treatment against poisonous snake bites.

At the age of 9, Milstein was given a copy by his mother of the classic book titled *Microbe Hunters* by Paul de Kruif, who described in a most captivating manner the attempts by famous microbiologists to hunt the deadly microbes to study them better. These hunters of microbes could then find new ways for the treatment of the terrifying diseases they caused.

In particular, Milstein was enchanted by the examples of Louis Pasteur, who discovered a rabies vaccine, and of Antoni van Leeuwenhoek, who discovered the presence of tiny living creatures he called animalcules. Reading this beautifully-written book was a game-changer for Milstein. The main consequence that occurred as a result of reading *Microbe Hunters* was a great desire on Milstein's part to dedicate his life to become a scientist who lived the adventurous lifestyle of scientific discovery as described by de Kruif.

3. *Apparently, he did work on the enzyme phosphoglucomutase – and here my memory fails – what exactly is this enzyme, and why is it important?*

The phosphoglucomutase enzyme is known to catalyze the changeover between the molecules called glucose-1-phosphate and glucose-6-phosphate in a reversible manner. Dr. Milstein's work showed that magnesium replaced the chromium in the active center of the enzyme, thus making the catalyst behavior fully productive.

Dr. Milstein's involvement with the phosphoglucomutase enzyme started when he was a graduate student earning his second Ph.D. in the Biochemistry Department housed in the Sir William Dunn School of Biochemistry at the University of Cambridge, a prestigious institution. His new graduate advisor was Dr. Malcom Dixon, a prominent investigator.

Phosphoglucomutase plays an essential role in two crucial metabolic pathways.

The first role of phosphoglucomutase involves the degradation of glycogen, a storage form of carbohydrates, sugars, and the pathway is often referred to as glycogenolysis. In this pathway, conversion of glucose-1-phosphate to glucose-6-phosphate provides a venue for the export of glucose from the liver and for glycolysis in the muscle tissue. The process permits the availability of glucose for energy generation in living cells.

The second role for phosphoglucomutase is in the synthesis of glycogen, which is a process also called glycogenesis. In this particular biosynthetic capacity, the phosphoglucomutase catalyzes the conversion of glucose-6-phosphate back to glucose-1-phosphate, which can then be utilized to make glycogen for storage of the sugar, to be used later if so needed.

Together considered, the phosphoglucomutase enzyme plays instrumental roles in both aspects of glucose metabolism, namely, glycogen degradation and synthesis. The protein will sort of respond to low or high concentrations of glucose by working in one biochemical direction or in the reverse direction, respectively, depending on the glucose levels in the blood.

4. *Fred Sanger appears to be a significant figure in the life and work of César Milstein. What were his contributions?*

Dr. Frederick Sanger was a two-time Nobel Laureate for sequencing amino acid chains of protein in 1958 and nucleotide chains of DNA in 1980. Although he was said to be unassuming, he was considered, in fact, a larger than life character in the department because of his legendary notoriety. He was well-liked and very highly respected among his peers and students, if not an unknowingly influential figure.

An exciting story about the effects of the celebrated Dr. Sanger upon Dr. Milstein has been told. Apparently, in 1958, two weeks after Dr. Milstein's arrival to Cambridge to start his second Ph.D. work, the news story broke that Dr. Sanger was slated to get the Nobel for having determined the amino acid sequence of the insulin protein.

The news broke at the very time that Dr. Milstein had just completed a labor-intensive large-scale preparation of the phosphoglucomutase; it had been his first attempt in the enzyme purification process. However, Dr. Milstein was incubating his enzyme prep in a cold-water bath when he left the experiment unattended in order to make an appearance at a celebratory party given in honor of Sanger's Nobel announcement. The partygoers enjoyed French champagne during the unique occasion.

The Department's celebration of Dr. Sanger's 1958 Nobel, however, turned out to be a disaster for Dr. Milstein, because the neglected phosphoglucomutase enzyme prep was ruined. He was later able to recover his lost protein and continue with his studies of phosphoglucomutase enzyme regulation, but it took enormous effort.

After Dr. Milstein discovered his regulatory activation of the phosphoglucomutase by magnesium dislodgment of heavy-metals from the active site, he opened up a collaboration with the great Dr. Sanger. Their work together began when Dr. Milstein needed to use a pH meter, and Dr. Sanger's laboratory was the only one that actually had such a device. It turned out to be an immensely fortuitous happenstance because their collaboration led to another important discovery.

Drs. Milstein and Sanger elucidated the precise molecular center of the phosphoglucomutase enzyme that conducts its biochemical activity. That is, they determined the actual active location of the phosphoglucomutase protein. It was quite an achievement. The collaborative team published its findings in 1960.

Active centers of enzymes catalyze the biochemical reactions. These active sites bind their substrates, perform their specialized chemical reaction at suitable body temperatures, and then release their resulting products, returning back to their original state to start the catalytically-based biochemical process all over again. These molecular structures, the active centers of enzymes, conduct fantastic chemistry in living beings!

Dr. Sanger would later provide a refuge for the persecuted Milsteins when they had been suffering the turmoil in Argentina. Dr. Sanger had made it possible for Dr. Milstein to return to Cambridge. It was an extremely fortunate turn of events. Dr. Milstein would, for the remainder of his life, be grateful to his scientific mentor, colleague, and friend, Dr. Sanger.

5. *His Ph.D. was from the University of Cambridge – do you know the topic of his dissertation and whom he studied under?*

Dr. Milstein started graduate school once again in 1958 in an endeavor to obtain a second Ph.D. degree. He entered the famous Department of Biochemistry at the University of Cambridge as a graduate student after having already earned his first doctoral degree under the tutelage of prof. Andres Stoppani from the University of Argentina, in Buenos Aries, in 1954.

For his second Ph.D. thesis at Cambridge, Dr. Milstein studied the now-famous phosphoglucomutase enzyme in the laboratory of his new graduate advisor, Dr. Malcom Dixon. He set out to explore the enzyme's requirement for metals — apparently, colleagues of Dr. Milstein, Drs. Edwin Webb and Malcolm Dixon had suggested the project, as it had previously been predicted that phosphoglucomutase activity needed two distinctive metals, chromium and magnesium, in order to function thoroughly.

His studies showed that magnesium displaced heavy metals from the active site of the enzyme. The heavy-metal displacement behavior turned on the protein to fully-active levels. With the new Ph.D. thesis work complete, Dr. Milstein successfully defended the project to his committee and took his second doctorate, in 1961, from Cambridge.

6. *Apparently, events forced him to switch from enzymology to immunology. First, what exactly is enzymology, and why is it important? Give us your summary of immunology– and Milstein's contributions to the field.*

Enzymology is the field of study pertaining to the scientific investigation of enzymes. Enzymes are molecules found in virtually all living beings. They are frequently made up of proteins, which are chains of individual amino acids or are made up of RNA, called ribozymes, which are made up of chains of ribonucleotides. Whether they are protein or RNA in their nature, these enzyme and ribozyme chains will fold up into 3-dimensional structures and can become active.

As active entities, the enzymes will then catalyze a chemical reaction. They will quite frequently do so by binding specifically to a dedicated substrate, which will be a target of the protein, and conduct a biochemical response upon the bound substrate to produce a new product.

The prime advantage of enzymes is their inherent property of having a low energy of activation. This characteristic permits enzymes to conduct their chemical reactions without having to require extremely high temperatures to do so. Another advantageous property of enzymes is that they are unchanged during the biochemical functions that they conduct in converting their substrates to their dedicated products. A third useful property is that the working enzyme can perform its function repeatedly; that is, enzymes can bind their substrate, do their chemistry, release its new product, and start the process all over again by linking to another molecule of the substrate. This enzymatic property is, thus, a catalytic process, and it is quite efficient in its biochemistry.

In addition to working with the famous enzyme phosphoglucomutase, Dr. Milstein had also become interested in another enzyme that was perhaps equally important, if not as famous. He started the new enzymatic work in the early 1960s. The new enzyme is called alkaline phosphatase, and it catalyzes the biochemical removal of phosphates from a variety of proteins. One of the critical aspects of alkaline phosphatase is that in certain cancers, the enzymatic activities can be abnormally elevated. Dr. Milstein's involvement was to study the bacterial form of the enzyme. In short order, he was able to elucidate the precise sequence of amino acids that constituted the enzyme's active site, the location of the protein that conducts its critical function, which in this case, is phosphate removal from the substrate. He published the new alkaline phosphatase studies in 1963 in a scientific journal.

Dr. Milstein's foray into immunology occurred after obtaining his second Ph.D. and his return to Argentina in 1961 to work at the Malbran Institute in Buenos Aires. There, he had inherited a student who was interested in antibodies. This student, and a suggestion by Dr. Fred Sanger, who encouraged Dr. Milstein to examine the active sites of antibodies, were the two main factors that were responsible for switching from enzymology to immunology.

The switch from enzymology to immunology occurred after Dr. Milstein fled Argentina due to their military coup and unstable political turmoil in 1962. It was an untenable situation for many of Argentina's scientists. Dr. Milstein moved back to Cambridge, England, where he worked at the newly established Laboratory of Molecular Biology.

The function of the immune system is to protect an individual from the detrimental effects of microbial pathogens, cancer, and foreign entities, like transplants or other non-self-antigens. The immune system also provides active immunity to antigens after getting rid of or destroying foreign antigens after the first exposure to them.

Immunology can be divided into two general categories: innate immunity and adaptive immunity.

The first category, innate immunity, provides a natural resistance to antigens and involves a series of various barrier types. The multiple barriers can be cellular, physiological, physical, anatomical, or molecular in their natures. Fever and inflammation are good examples of components that fall into the innate immunity category.

There are two main components to adaptive immunity.

The first type of adaptive immunity is called humoral immunity, and it involves white blood cells called plasma cells that are derived from B-lymphocytes (B-cells) and which secrete antigen binding and neutralizing antibodies in response to antigen exposure. The antibodies are good at recognizing foreign antigens and getting rid of them by an assortment of ways. The antibodies could simply neutralize the antigens, or perhaps oxidize them, or even coagulate them. The antibodies might also call in components of innate immunity to help eradicate the antigens.

The second type of adaptive immunity is called cellular-mediated immunity. It involves individual white blood cells called thymus-derived lymphocytes, or T-lymphocytes, or simply T-cells. There are two types of T-cells. The first is called helper T-cells (T_H cells), and the second is called cytotoxic T-cells (T_C cells). The T_H cells help B-cells and T_C cells. The T_C cells will bind to target cells that have encountered and processed antigens and kill these targets.

Dr. Milstein's Nobel-winning contribution to the field of immunology lies in his 1975 collaborative discovery with his postdoctoral fellow Dr. Georges Kohler of a new method for generating desirable antibodies in a pure form, a type of antibody called monoclonal antibodies.

The experimental approach was a rather clever one. They literally fused antibody-making spleen cells with immortal myeloma cancer cells; the cell fusion process produced so-called hybridomas, cells that were hybrids between two completely different cells and were rendered immortal. Any unfused myeloma cells that were incubated in the presence of hypoxanthine would be unable to make DNA because they lacked the enzyme called hypoxanthine-guanine phosphoribosyltransferase. Any unfused spleen cells would be mortal and, thus, die after passaging them for a certain number of times. Therefore, any differentially fused cells, i.e., spleen cells combined with myeloma cells, the antibody-making hybridomas, could make DNA with the added hypoxanthine *and* become immortal, permitting the passaging of new generations of cells potentially forever.

The antibody-making hybridomas were timeless. It was an unprecedented, outstanding achievement.

The implications were profound for many other biomedical investigators. They could perhaps generate antibodies to other antigens of their interest, such as other proteins, cells, cancers, enzymes, even to different antibodies, etc. The possibilities were seemingly endless.

Dr. Milstein made other notable contributions to immunology, as well. His first experiments in the field of immunology were concerned with evaluating the sequence of disulfide-bridges formed within the domains of light chain parts of the antibody. He found that light chains harbored both constant and variable regions. The so-called constant areas did not appear to have a great deal of variability, whereas the variable domains did. He also found disulfide bridges within the heavy chains themselves.

In 1966, he had collaborated with Professor Sydney Brenner, who was housed at the Laboratory of Molecular Biology in Cambridge. Together, they formulated an explanation for the extreme diversity exhibited by antibodies and in their ability to recognize and bind to an enormous variety of antigens. They hypothesized that genes encoding antibodies underwent somatic mutation. In the late 1960s and early 1970s, Dr. Milstein and many collaborators produced experimental evidence for just such a mutational mechanism. It was another fantastic scientific discovery.

7. *Politics and military strife seemed to follow Milstein as well as difficulties– what were some of the things that happened that impacted this great scientist?*

Dr. Milstein and his wife Celia moved to Argentina in 1961. He started work as the director of the molecular biology division and as a professor who continued his enzymology work and who was just beginning to develop an interest in immunology. Celia started her Ph.D. thesis work. The Milsteins were working together, studying disulfide bridges that held polypeptide chains together in a folded manner. It seemed like a perfect start to a promising career for both of the Milsteins.

Unfortunately, they were thrown into the vortex of an unstable political situation brought about by a military coup in Argentina, starting in 1962. First, there was a definite hostility against educated people, especially scientists, in particular. Anti-Semitism reared its ugly head. The unfortunate vortex began with the dismissal of Dr. Milstein's director of the institute, Dr. Ignacio Pirosky, and of four scientists who were in the department. Dissenters and persons of Jewish descent were rounded up and arrested.

Persecution did not end there. Jewish people were falsely accused of communism. To make matters worse, funding for research was cut-off. It became terribly challenging for the Milsteins to continue with their scientific investigations. The state of affairs was simply too much. They had been made to feel unwelcome in their home country. Reluctantly, Dr. Milstein resigned from his post, and the Milsteins fled the then enormously troubled country of Argentina.

Politics and military coups aside, he was almost sacked from his first graduate position. The earlier episode was reported by Milstein in later years. During his first foray into graduate school in 1954, he was seeking his first doctorate in Argentina at the University of Buenos Aires. He was at the time a burgeoning graduate student in the laboratory of biochemistry Professor Andrés Stoppani, and the facilities that were there can best be described as austere. With no funding available for his graduate research, Milstein had to take on a part-time job in another laboratory conducting routine clinical work while also doing his thesis work evaluating an aldehyde dehydrogenase enzyme from yeast cells.

In order to monitor the success of his enzyme preparation and measure its activity, he needed to use a unique piece of equipment called a spectrophotometer, but the Stoppani laboratory did not have one. Thus, Milstein had to carry his large flasks and other necessary materials with him as he walked three blocks to another building that housed the nearest spectrophotometer. He got into rather serious trouble after he broke three of the department's expensive 5-liter glass flasks, and he was almost dismissed from the department due to the costs involved!

8. *In terms of his awards, Milstein, from some small town in Argentina went on to win: The Nobel Prize in 1984, he was elected a Fellow of the Royal Society (FRS) in 1975, he became a fellow of Darwin College, in Cambridge, England from 1980 to 2002, he received the Louisa Gross Horwitz Prize from Columbia University in the City of New York in 1980, he was awarded the Copley Medal in 1989, and later became a Companion of Honor in the year 1995. Summarily, in 1993, the Konex Foundation in Argentina awarded him the Diamond Konex Award. This apparently is one of the most prestigious culture awards given in Argentina. He was acclaimed "the most important scientist in the last decade in his country." What can possibly be added to this list of awards and recognition?*

Indeed, the list of accolades is quite impressive! It is my firm conviction that these honors and others are most undoubtedly well-deserved in the case of Dr. Milstein. His scientific contributions were enormous.

In 1975, when Dr. Milstein received his first prominent scientific recognition, the coveted Fellowship to the Royal Society, his father was in attendance in London at the initiation ceremony. The special occasion befell upon his father Lázaro as a complete shock that his own son was receiving so much favorable attention and such widespread respect for his scientific work. The reverential manner in which the ceremony was held turned out to be much too much for his father, who was overcome with emotion. Sadly, Dr. Milstein's mother, Máxima, had passed away a few years prior to her son's rise to scientific prominence.

Dr. Milstein's father was also to attend personally another award ceremony for his son, this time in Jerusalem, in 1980. This particular award was called the Wolf Prize, and it is bestowed to individuals who make outstanding achievements, such as those within the sciences. The award is usually given by the president of Israel. The story is told that Dr. Milstein's father was so thrilled by the event that he rushed to the stage and kissed his son, to his son's embarrassment. Dr. Milstein related that those in attendance were favorably amused by his father's behavior.

One of my favorites of the accolades is that of the so-called Sir Hans Krebs Medal, which Dr. Milstein received in 1981. It is given to scientists who make outstanding contributions within the fields of Molecular Biology and Biochemistry, and the award is sponsored by the Federation of European Biochemical Societies (FEBS), an exceptional honor. With Dr. Milstein's discoveries in making specific desired antibodies, the breakthrough was deeply felt by molecular biologists and biochemists alike.

By the time Dr. Milstein received the Nobel Prize in Physiology or Medicine in 1984, his father had learned to be somewhat more reserved. As a matter of fact, by this time, the elder Mr. Lázaro Milstein had already become somewhat of a veteran of the television media, having been interviewed about his son on several occasions of note. He had become known as an astute storyteller and was thoroughly liked by his interviewers and audience members alike. He especially enjoyed conveying the story of the poor Jewish immigrants' struggles in foreign countries, and of making a go towards success despite the hardships encountered. These endearing interviews of a proud Mr. Milstein were inspirational to many.

Argentina would later honor Dr. Milstein with his portrait on a mailing stamp in 2005. It was perhaps a sign that the great scientist and his beloved country were reconciled, albeit posthumously because he passed away from cardiovascular disease on the 24th of March in 2002.

9. *In closing, Milstein has said quite appropriately that "Science fulfills its promises when the benefits are shared equally by the very poor of the world." What does this say about the man and his philosophy of science?*

While some sources attribute Dr. Milstein as having written the statement somewhere in print, the quotation you are referring to undoubtedly originates from an award-winning documentary about the Milsteins in their twilight years. The English translation of the film's title is "*A Little Fire: the Story of César Milstein,*" released in 2010. The film is a heart-warming and poignant tribute to such a great biomedical scientist.

He was referring to the fact that he received no monetary compensation from the plethora of new antibodies that were made using his Nobel-winning technique for monoclonal antibody production with the fused hybridomas. There could have been a lot of money he could have made from the antibodies, but he did not patent the invention. The invention was freely available for all to use. The end-result was profound. The price of the antibody could be made cheaply.

He knew how much it cost to produce a given desired antibody, and he was stunned at the prices many new antibody producers were charging. Their prices were outrageous.

Many start-up companies could make use of the latest technology without the prohibitive licensing costs and make antibodies that could be useful in a great variety of venues, biotechnology, medicine, basic research, disease treatment, diagnostics, etc. The possibilities became far-reaching.

The sentiment contained within the famous quote very likely stems from his earlier experiences as a young scientist who had to conduct his own thesis work with limited or no funding available for the job. The experience affected him for the remainder of his scientific life. He made great effort to help those around him, the young, disadvantaged scientists.

Those with a passion for the study of biomedical science are acutely affected because, quite often, such work can be extremely costly. The costs involved in doing the type of work required to produce essential antibodies can be prohibitive. He empathized entirely with the younger generations of scientists who are from poor countries trying to follow their dreams of conducting scientific research for the noble purposes of making their world, and the world of others, a better place.

For additional information go to:

https://m.youtube.com/watch?v=NqM1CY-fFd8
https://m.youtube.com/watch?v=L6K0Z-T0yxU

Chapter 19

ARCHIBALD VIVIAN HILL – CARDIAC PHYSIOLOGY

1. *Professor Varela, as you know, Archibald Vivian Hill was born in Bristol, England, yet his work has received worldwide recognition – and earned him a Nobel Prize. Before we discuss his accomplishments – when and where was he born and what was his early childhood like?*

Indeed, physiologist, biomedical scientist, and Nobel Laureate Archibald V. Hill was born in Bristol, England, on the 26th day of the month of September in the year 1886. His parents were Jonathan and Ada Priscilla Rumney Hill, who were married in 1880. In 1890, the Hill marriage was at an end when A.V. was 3, and his younger sister, Muriel, was about 1 year old. After the break-up, Jonathan, a mahogany timber merchant, never saw his family again.

The remaining Hill family, Ada and her two young children, lived in poverty. In later writings, A.V. Hill attested to his mother's strong sense of determination, resourcefulness, and a strong sense of humor, in the face of financial adversity and the associated hardship in raising two young children as a single-parent. In the succeeding years, Muriel became a biochemist and A.V., a physiologist.

A.V. had had no memory whatsoever about his father. In contrast, Jonathan stayed abreast of A.V.'s scientific progress throughout the years, though they never communicated in any way with each other. A.V. found out about his father's cursory interest only after he passed away in 1924, having learned about his father's far-flung curiosity from an old uncle. Unbeknown to Hill, his father had become aware of his son's Nobel a few months shortly before his death.

A.V. was first homeschooled early on by his mother, who taught him the basics of math, reading, and writing. At the age of 7, Hill progressed from a home-based education to Brean Villa Preparatory School, located in Weston-Super-Mare. At Brean Villa, Hill flourished, acquiring formal knowledge of algebra and geometry, and enjoying extracurricular pursuits such as hiking, hockey, and, curiously, rock-throwing with boys his age.

At the age of 13 years, Hill moved to the town of Tiverton in Devon County, where he was enrolled at Blundell's School, an established boarding school that was famous because of its founder, Peter Blundell, a wealthy 17th-century clothier who intended that children have free access to grammar school. The Hill family also moved to Tiverton, and Hill lived at home while attending Blundell's by day. He excelled in mathematics at Blundell's, and one of his teachers, Mr. Joey M. Thornton, was said to have been an inspiring educator. Hill also participated in sports, such as in running cross country, and was a member of the Debate Team, honing his critical thinking skills as he developed his arguments. It is said that Hill had numerous good friends while attending Blundell's. Hill graduated from Blundell's School in 1905 at the age of 18. It was a school he remembered fondly.

After high school graduation, Hill attended Trinity College in Cambridge, England. He majored in mathematics, wrangling numerous first-class honors as an undergraduate during his Tripos. As a so-called "wrangler" of academic honors, Hill finished his course of mathematics studies sooner than anticipated. While he was quite academically successful in the subject, having been taught by his professors, namely, A.N. Whitehead, plus E.W. Barnes, G.H. Hardy, and R.A. Herman, he nevertheless became somewhat disenchanted, if not bored with their modes of teaching.

Hill's conversion to the subject of physiology in 1906 as his next undergraduate major was due to another faculty, Professor Walter Morley Fletcher, whom Hill had gone to for academic advice. Professor Fletcher then suggested that Hill finish his math Tripos first, but then afterward move on to study physiology under Professor Frederick Gowland Hopkins. Dr. Fletcher had informed Hill of his work with Dr. Hopkins regarding frog muscle physiology and of lactic acid oxidation chemistry during its degradation.

Then, in 1907, Hill started his studies for the Tripos in the Natural Sciences to formally pursue physiology, while also taking new courses in physics and chemistry. At Trinity College, Hill received his bachelor's degree with high honors, having double-majored in Mathematics and Natural Sciences in 1909.

As an undergraduate student at Trinity College, Hill's first attempt at scientific research resulted in the development of a famous equation, in 1909, now called the Langmuir derivation or the Michaelis equation. The project had been suggested by Professor John Newport Langley. Hill examined the molecular kinetic behavior and mode of action of curare and nicotine, which turned out to be one of the first of its kind mathematical description of a receptor-ligand interaction, in frog muscles. Hill had thus developed a so-called saturation equation to describe how the ligand (nicotine or curare) saturated the receptor's binding sites for its ligands. He had referred to these receptors as receptive substances. It was a landmark discovery, still faithfully presented in modern textbooks on physiology. The new development was introduced in Hill's first scientific publication in a journal.

Subsequent work by others showed minor alterations in the shape of the receptor-ligand interactions. In modern times, the Hill plot is known to be sigmoidal in its form as the receptor sites for ligand binding become saturated, as shown in the accompanying figure. The Hill plot involved measuring the relationship between the extents to which the receptors bind ligands as a function of increasing concentration of the ligands.

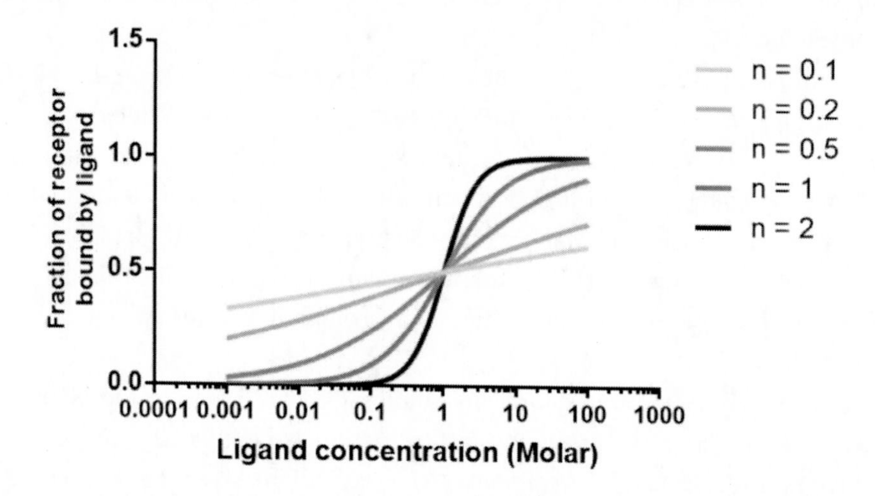

The Hill plot showed how the binding of one ligand to its dedicated receptor converted it to a form that had better ligand-binding properties for a second ligand molecule, a characteristic known as cooperativity. That is, the binding of a ligand made it somehow more natural for the next ligand to bind the same receptor, but with greater ease of binding. To help investigators interpret their cooperative-binding data, they invoked the so-called Hill coefficient, which refers to the extent of the cooperative binding.

Such receptor-ligand relationships could also account for behaviors not only of curare or nicotine and their respective receptors but for other seemingly disparate molecular interactions, as well. For example, cooperative binding has been observed for hemoglobin and molecular oxygen. The same sort of binding cooperativity has been measured for specific DNA-binding proteins, in order to mediate changes in gene expression, such as activation or even repression of gene transcription and translation. In addition, Hill's work had relevance to biochemistry in terms of enzyme kinetics, and his equation was pertinent to the relationships between substrates and enzymes and was deeply related to the famous Michaelis-Menten form of enzyme kinetics. Lastly, this early work of Hill had a direct relevance to the physiology inherent in the so-called neuromuscular junction, and, thus, the studies contributed to our understanding of neuroscience.

Hill then received a physiology fellowship for further study at Trinity, where he stayed an additional four years, working under Drs. Hopkins and Fletcher, as a Trinity College Fellow.

2. Lactic acid in muscle contraction and movement– what is the relationship all about?

As an undergraduate upperclassman, Hill began new formal studies in the field of physiology in 1907, adding a new major consisting of natural sciences. Hill had consequently entered the physiology research laboratory of Dr. Hopkins upon the advice of Dr. Fletcher, who had been sort of an undergraduate mentor to Hill during this time. Before Hill's arrival to the physiology laboratory at Trinity, Hopkins and Fletcher had been interested in the relationship between the production of lactic acid and carbon dioxide in frog muscles during rest and active contractions using a piece of equipment called a calorimeter.

Shortly after graduation in 1910, Hill became a sponsored research Fellow at Trinity College, and he began his studies of lactic acid, still in the Hopkins physiology laboratory. He continued the work of Drs. Fletcher and Hopkins by placing the severed limbs of frogs into the calorimeter device and measuring the quantity of heat released as a function of time upon stimulation of vigorous muscle contraction. Hill recorded that heat reached an early apex at rest but leveled off after a few hours. The heat levels measured by Hill seemed to correspond to the carbon dioxide amounts previously detected by Dr. Fletcher under similar muscle conditions.

Hill then compared the heat and carbon dioxide levels in a variety of frog muscle contraction conditions, such as intense muscular work versus resting activities. Hill found a similar sort of corresponding relationship between heat and carbon dioxide. The data was interpreted to mean that the severe frog muscle contractions exhibited the same type of response metabolically to use up available oxygen. That is, a fast rate of metabolism in the muscle conducted an oxidative process during intense muscle activity. The leveling off of the heat production was interpreted to mean that lactic acid was being produced in the resulting anaerobic condition created by the increased oxygen consumption.

In writing up his results, Hill speculated upon the nature of the substance that produced the lactic acid, the so-called lactic acid precursor. He reasoned that the precursor must be something other than glucose because there was not enough of it to account for the level of lactic acid amounts that were measured.

He further invoked physical chemistry to help him explain the data, referring to the so-called free energy change of the biochemical reactions involved in producing the lactic acid. Hill speculated that when the frog muscles contracted intensely, somehow during the degradation of the precursor source to produce the lactic acid, the energy released and the mechanical work completed must be at an amount that was higher than that energy lost during lactic acid production. Otherwise, the free energy exchange would be a counterproductive process. To accommodate this seemingly counterintuitive process, Hill then concluded that after the operation ended, the lactic acid somehow recharged itself by its oxidation. He then made the astute conclusion that the lactic acid precursor must have an ample energy storage form. We now know this high-energy source as muscle glycogen.

3. *Aerobic and anaerobic– what do these two words mean– and how do they relate to A.V.'s work (apparently everyone called him A.V.)?*

The term aerobic refers to a process, like a chemical or biochemical reaction, that occurs in the presence of oxygen. In contrast, the word anaerobic indicates that a process is happening in the absence of oxygen. Sometimes the process absolutely requires that oxygen be present in order for the reaction to occur. We call this situation strictly or obligately aerobic. Similarly, if the reactive process absolutely requires that there be no oxygen present in order for the process to take place, then it is correspondingly referred to as strictly or obligately anaerobic. It the reaction can take place with or without oxygen, then the task being conducted is called facultatively anaerobic.

In the case of Hill's work at Manchester University in 1920, the terms aerobic and anaerobic relate to the various working conditions of muscles. You'll recall that Hill had studied the heat released during muscle contraction, relaxation, and recovery after an intense muscle workout. He found that the heat generated during frog skeletal muscle contraction and relaxation occurred independently of available oxygen. Hill had observed that the heat produced during muscle and contraction was not affected in any way if it happened in the absence of oxygen. That is, these muscular heat-generating processes were occurring in an anaerobic fashion.

Hill had also had an interesting observation. His laboratory found that under anaerobic conditions, a minute amount of heat had been produced in the early stages of the muscle recovery period after a bout of intense muscle contraction. He termed the phenomenon as a production of "delayed anaerobic heat." After confirming the seemingly strange data with more precisely repeated experiments, the delayed anaerobic heat production remained a stable occurrence. Thus, Hill interpreted his findings to mean that glycolysis was occurring anaerobically and that the heat energy liberated was in the form of ATP breakdown, but that the high-energy phosphate bonds were somehow restored. Hill concluded that muscle contraction used up ATP by hydrolyzing it, thus, breaking the high-energy phosphate bonds and generating the observed heat in the process. Hill further deduced that during the muscle recovery phase, metabolism occurred in the presence of oxygen (aerobically). If true, then it meant that oxygen was used up in hardworking muscles, i.e., during intense muscle contraction activities, and they, thus, had to rely on anaerobic glycolysis metabolism in order to restore the ATP and other sources of high-energy phosphates, such as phosphocreatine, in the muscles.

These findings by Hill strongly suggested that two different pathways were operating during intense muscle contraction and recovery. Hill referred to this anaerobic muscle property as an "oxygen debt." This is where the famous Dr. Otto Meyerhof comes into the picture. Professor Otto Meyerhof had previously demonstrated that during muscle recovery, the lactic acid that was generated during the intense muscle activity was somehow converted back into glycogen in the liver or consumed during oxidative metabolic pathways. The muscle heat and oxygen debt data of Hill corresponded to the production of Meyerhof's lactic acid levels.

Hill had collaborated with Dr. Meyerhof shortly after the end of the First World War. Dr. Meyerhof had been working at the University of Kiel at the time. Together, they pooled their ideas and found a distinctiveness in the pathways involved between muscles working aerobically versus those exercising anaerobically. They discovered two different mechanisms were at play in providing needed energy during intense muscle contraction activity. They termed these separate mechanisms as an anaerobic activity phase and an oxidative recovery phase. The work formed the basis of their bestowment of the Nobel in 1922 in the category of physiology or medicine.

4. *Hill apparently had a good sense of humor about himself and life and said: "Laughter is the best detergent for nonsense." Is there a story behind this?*

Apparently, the full quote, taken from his book titled "*The Ethical Dilemma of Science and Other Writings*," published in 1962, is as follows: "For myself, I confess to a belief that laughter is the best detergent for nonsense, and that serious things can often best be said with a smile." He was referring to matters that he often encountered, which made no sense to him, like Hitler's white nationalist racism, anti-vivisection, persecution of religious beliefs, political views, snobbishness, etc. Towards such entities that he viewed as nonsensical, Hill felt that the most effective counter-response to them was a type of made-up nonsense itself and often in the form of ridicule, of disdain, and of laughter.

Hill was of the opinion that many who held such nonsense-based beliefs quite often stubbornly held onto them and were quite recalcitrant to reason. Thus, Hill thought that arguing with such persons with nonsense beliefs was a futile exercise if one wanted to convert them using the facts and logic. Furthermore, Hill had felt that to engage in serious argument with those whom he felt partook in nonsense beliefs would be to give undue credibility to them.

Another seemingly nonsensical but rather enlightening counter-point made by Hill to such nonsense was the fact that he sardonically seemed grateful to Hitler for sending to him (Hill) so many great scientists who were refugees from Germany and other European countries during World War II. Many of the welcomed scientist refugees had, in fact, worked in Hill's laboratory.

5. The Nobel Prize – what exactly was it given to Hill for?

Hill shared the Nobel Prize in 1922 in physiology or medicine with Professor Otto Fritz Meyerhof. Dr. Meyerhof's contribution towards the Nobel was focused on the anaerobic lactic acid biosynthesis in muscle and the regeneration of glycogen stores in the liver. Dr. Meyerhof is also famous for having elucidated much of the glycolytic pathway called glycolysis. Towards this, Dr. Meyerhof has the distinction, along with Drs. Gustav Embden and Jakub Parnas, of having a central metabolic pathway named after them, the so-called Embden-Meyerhof-Parnas glycolytic pathway.

Hill's contribution to the discoveries for which he would earn the Nobel would encompass those studies examining the relationships between heat production and muscle contraction. Hill had found that heat produced after intense muscle contraction and subsequent relaxation corresponded to Dr. Meyerhof's lactic acid levels. When they combined their disparate discoveries, professors Hill and Meyerhof united them concerning the energy metabolism in muscle.

They discovered that energy requirements for contracting muscle arose from two distinctive pathways. Because of his finding that heat was produced during intense muscle contraction, but not during relaxation, he is known for having discovered a mechanical force during tissue energy metabolism, and Hill's work is, thus, relevant to biophysics. As such, Hill is often viewed in modern times as one of the founding fathers of biophysics.

Interestingly, Hill is also considered a groundbreaking pioneer in the establishment of modern exercise physiology. His heat work regarding muscle contractions led the way to the study of exercise and its associated mechanics, biochemistry, physiology, cell biology, and protein chemistry.

6. *Like a true Brit– he served his country during World War II– what did he do during the war?*

Hill's first foray into war duty involved World War I, and it arose while he was an undergraduate student at Trinity. During his undergraduate years, he had enrolled in a course on officer training. During this instruction, he became an expert marksman. When the Great War had commenced in 1914, Hill became involved first in musketry activities, but later, in 1915, he had focused his efforts towards improving anti-aircraft gunnery.

He formulated a technique for calculating the altitude of aircraft so that the anti-aircraft artillery could better focus their aim. The Hill technique involved using little mirrors to collect data from smoke released by exploding shells and their flight path directions in the air. With such data in hand, one could calculate the proper ranges needed for the accurate aiming of the anti-aircraft guns towards airplanes still in the sky.

The story is told that Hill recruited over a hundred volunteers to help him with the necessary anti-aircraft gunnery calculations. These volunteers were either too young or too elderly to serve combat duty. A few of these

Hill recruits, such as Ralph H. Fowler, an officer who had been previously wounded in battle, and Douglas R. Hartree and E. Arthur Milne, both of whom were too young for combat, and William Hartree (father to Douglas), who was too old to fight and would later be Hill's faithful laboratory assistant publishing 10 papers together, were all members of "Hill's Brigands." The Hill group also calculated the various strategic locations of planes in the sky using the sounds they emitted while in flight. At the end of the Great War, Hill was awarded an Officer of the Order of the British Empire (known as an OBE) medal in 1919 for his military service.

Before the start of World War II, in 1933, Hill became involved in establishing a sanctuary program in England for German and other European refugee scientists who were persecuted by Hitler and Nazi Germans. The program provided support for the refugee investigators by helping them find academic posts in various higher educational institutions in England. Hill worked alongside Lords Ernest Rutherford and William Beveridge to establish the Academic Assistance Council dedicated to this noble purpose. As the political situation in Europe became precarious due to racist programs of Hitler and Mussolini, in 1936, the Council thus developed into the Society for the Protection of Science and Learning. This new sanctuary program against the travails of Nazism was able to assist almost a thousand refugee scientists, about 18 investigators of whom later became Nobel Laureates. During the Second World War, Hill was said to have served on a new committee devoted to the development of radar for the detection of enemy aircraft.

7. *He actually served as a Member of the British Parliament – for five years – what were his accomplishments there?*

Hill had focused his efforts while serving as secretary of the Royal Society towards putting scientists directly into war-work in which such scientists could effectively utilize their formal training. The initiative had arisen out of the failure during World War I to use scientists as such for war work. Working with Sir Lawrence Bragg, they assured that no such failure would transpire during World War II.

As a secretary of the Royal Society, Hill worked closely with the Ministry of Labor to create a list of refugee scientists and their expertise in order to find useful academic posts for each of them. In the early 1940s, Hill became an independent Member of Parliament (MP) at Cambridge University. Interestingly, Hill had been sent to England's embassy in the U.S. to facilitate war work. The story is told that he was authorized for secret-sharing activities with U.S. officials.

There is a story that has been both refuted and nevertheless passed down via the generations of biomedical physiologists who knew Hill. The anecdote is that Hill had kept in his office a saluting Hitler doll, which was meant to be a satirical form of a 'thank you' for having expelled so many great German scientists, some of whom had worked in Hill's own research laboratory in London. Part of this story is legendary and steeped in Hill's famous phrase that "Laughter is the best detergent against nonsense."

8. *Muscle calorimetry, muscle mechanics, and applied exercise physiology seem to summarize his contributions best. Could you summarize these three areas and his contributions and describe their relevance today?*

Muscle calorimetry involves the assessment of heat generated during muscle contraction. Hill used the calorimeter device to measure the heat output by contracting and relaxing frog muscles. Hill was one of the first investigators to conduct these types of physiological studies, and he had to build his own calorimetry equipment in order to do so. The units of the heat measurements took the form of calories.

The muscle calorimetry work was started by Hill in 1911 in a rudimentary manner. He began using the calorimeter for measuring the heat released during muscle contraction. Upon learning of similar heat-muscle data arising from the laboratory of Dr. Karl Burker, Hill stopped his experiments and traveled to Germany to learn how to assemble thermopiles, which were used in conjunction with galvanometers to collect heat data and convert it into a form of electrical data. Hill returned home after his visit and tried to use his newfound technical knowledge and combine it with his calorimeter to measure heat from active neurons, but was not successful.

Next, Hill turned his attention to frog muscles and used a new and improved version of his previously used and rudimentary calorimeter device, referred to later as a micro-calorimeter. The new work was done with his lab assistant and former Hill Brigand member, William Hartree. The work involved preparing frog leg muscle, called a sartorius muscle, with so-called Ringer solution, a sort of liquid buffering salt substance, and inserting a so-called thermopile directly into the muscle tissue. The thermopile heat probe had been connected to a galvanometer, which then converted the heat measurement from the thermopile into an electrical signal that could thus be recorded. By combining the thermopiles and galvanometer with his micro-calorimeter device, Hill was able to measure the heat released over time. By tweaking his apparatus set-up, Hill was later able to measure the heat involved during a single twitch of a frog muscle! The temperature change recorded was a mere 0.003-degrees Celsius! Working with his sister, Muriel Hill, the brother-sister team then applied their muscle calorimetry technology to mammals, publishing the work together as two papers, one in 1913 and the other in 1914.

Muscle mechanics has to do with the muscle contraction, human movement, and the mechanical properties associated with muscle function, such as the physical relationships pertaining to force-length and force-velocities of muscles. Hill's involvement with muscle mechanics began in the early 1920s. He had proposed that there were dynamic relationships between muscle shortening (length) during the time needed for contraction (velocity) and the resulting performance of mechanical work. He measured the effects of load upon the speed of muscle shortening, a process he termed visco-elasticity. The proposed explanation arose from his observation that the contracting muscle fiber appeared more viscous and out of the thinking at the time that muscle mechanics involved a spring-like action, in which muscles were considered analogous to an extended mechanical spring that shortened during its contraction. Taking the velocity of contraction data into account, Hill deduced that an internal viscosity system was at play, functioning to diminish some of the elastic properties.

Unfortunately, Hill's visco-elasticity explanation was off base. In 1923, Dr. Wallace O. Fenn had discovered that during muscle shortening, more heat was released than that seen in so-called isometric conditions, i.e., when the muscle length was kept the same even in the presence of increased muscle tension. The heat result was known as the Fenn effect, and it convincingly went against Hill's viscoelastic hypothesis.

Taking Fenn's new heat data into consideration, Hill then proposed a further explanation in 1938. He postulated that skeletal muscles had two different mechanical systems. The first system, called a contractile component, played a functional role during muscle contraction in which the contractile element shortens the muscle when stimulated to do so. The second system, called a series elastic component, played a prominent role in permitting elongation of the muscle fiber that's had a new tension applied to it.

Applying a mathematical treatment to the new heat and the two-component theories, Hill then proposed one of his famous equations in order to explain the biological-mechanical work of muscle fibers:

$$(\text{Force} + a)\,(\text{Velocity} + b) = (\text{Force}_{\text{max}} + a)\,b$$

The term Force refers to the load that a muscle fiber has to carry while doing its work. The constant, a, refers to the heat temperature associated with contractile shortening of the muscle and is expressed in units of Celsius per centimeter. Velocity is the rate of the muscle shortening its length as a function of time during its contraction and is expressed in units of centimeters per second. The constant, b, represents the change in the rate of the total energy as a function of the decrease in the weight of the load lifted by the muscle, and it is expressed in units of energy per gram.

The new Hill equation was published in late 1938 in the *Proceedings of the Royal Society of London*. The work has been scrutinized by physiologists ever since and has withstood the test of time. In modern times, this Hill equation is presented in good muscle physiology textbooks. At the time of his discovery, the Hill equation permitted physiologists who were interested in muscle mechanics to elucidate mechanical differences between quickly and slowly contracting muscles by developing so-called Power-Force curves in order to deduce the maximum power. The mathematical approach developed by Hill could be applied to individual muscle fibers in solution, as well as to intact muscle tissues, or even to entire living organisms!

In terms of applied exercise physiology, A.V. Hill is affectionately considered by those in the field as a founding father of the modern discipline. As an accomplished athlete himself, Hill's involvement in the area started in 1922 as a fascination with athletic training. He had been interested at the time about the notion of exercise in terms of intense muscle activity and recovery involving the production of lactic acid, the subsequent reduction of the lactic acid in the presence of oxygen levels, plus the association of ATP and phosphocreatine levels during athletic training. Hill had also studied these processes in the absence of oxygen, i.e., under anaerobic conditions. He had considered the relationship between energy production and anaerobic metabolism during exercise and recovery of muscle work as sort of a "acquire oxygen now, pay for it afterward" type of arrangement.

Hill had conducted a series of elegant exercise physiology experiments in which he measured the volume of oxygen uptake during athletic performance. In these classic physiological experiments, he and his colleagues used themselves as test subjects. They collected oxygen uptake volumes using collection devices strapped to their backs as they ran around an 85-meter running track while also keeping time and turning on and off specific oxygen valves at the appropriate times!

The Hill team measured the amounts of oxygen and carbon dioxide during the test runs. After analyzing the data, they formulated the famous maximum oxygen intake value that an athlete might acquire during exercise training. They were able to calculate the relationship between maximum oxygen intakes with differences in running velocities around the track. The running exercise experiments demonstrated the presence of a maximum level of oxygen intake during intense athletic training. These classic experiments of Hill were later applied to cardiac muscle training and the effects of the lungs with remarkably similar results, attesting to the validity of the physiological approach towards the study of exercise biomedicine.

Exercise physiologists have applied Hill's pioneering oxygen data to trace the uptake and expenditure during athletic training within various alveolar tissues of the lung and even within the capillaries and intracellular mitochondria! The common theme was that the oxygen-carrying capacity lost some of its effectiveness along the oxygen uptake route.

Lastly, Hill was able to formulate an overview of the conditions that constitute the maximum efficiency of athletic training from a physiological standpoint. An excellent athletic training program showed a profile with high oxygen uptake, a high peak of oxygen debt, and a low requirement for oxygen. Muscle contraction efficiency corresponded to the proper usage of oxygen during training. The oxygen costs were studied during various types of exercise programs, and Hill discovered that walking quickly required more energy than jogging, if the speeds of both were similar. These data have withstood the experimental scrutiny by Hill and many others and has passed the test of time.

9. *What have I neglected to ask?*

In 1913, at the young age of 27 years, Archibald Vivian Hill had married Margaret Neville Keynes (b. 1885). In later years, in 1970, as he wrote his *Autobiographical Sketch*, Hill related that marrying Margaret was the smartest thing he had ever done. Together the Hills had four children, David (b. 1915), Janet (b. 1918), Maurice (b. 1919), and Polly, the eldest (b. 1914). Margaret passed away in 1974, and Hill died in 1977 at the age of 90.

In 2015, the Hill family house located at 16 Bishopswood, in the neighborhood called Highgate, in London, England, was recognized as a historical site because of the many refugees who were welcomed and were provided with sanctuary there during World War II. The Hill family had lived in this same home for over 44 years, starting in 1923, until his retirement in 1967. In order to commemorate the historical Hill house, the existing structure was bestowed with the English Heritage Blue plaque.

For those who prefer YouTube- here is a link about this great scientist:

https://www.youtube.com/watch?v=_eU4-ZnuU0c

Chapter 20

FRANCIS ROUS – VIRUSES AND CANCER

1. *The name Francis Peyton Rous seems to be synonymous with viruses and cancer. Where was he born and where did he study initially?*

Dr. Peyton Rous was an American pathologist, virologist, and biomedical scientist who was the first investigator to show, in 1911, that cancer was caused by a virus. For this work, he was awarded the Nobel Prize in 1966 in medicine or physiology. His discovery greatly contributed to the advancements of certain biomedical fields such as cell biology, molecular biology, pathology, virology, and tumor biology.

Dr. Rous was born on the 5th day of October, in the year 1879, in Baltimore, Maryland, U.S., to parents Charles Rous and Frances Anderson Wood. In 1890, when Rous was 11 years old, Charles passed away suddenly, leaving Frances widowed with three children, Francis Peyton being the oldest of the three. The widow, now of meager means, chose to live in Baltimore, Maryland, for the benefit of the education for her young children. She, thus, placed them in the Baltimore public school system.

As a child, he was an aspiring naturalist with an enduring interest in botany. One story pertaining to these interests was that young Rous had participated in a flower classifying contest, with a new microscope as first prize, but had run afoul of the prize committee with his non-classical nomenclature for a fern, losing the contest.

He graduated high school in Baltimore, earning scholarships to pay for his tuition partially. To help pay for his higher education as an undergraduate student at Johns Hopkins, in Baltimore, Maryland, he took a job as a writer for a local newspaper, the *Baltimore Sun*, in which he wrote about flowers, on a monthly basis. He took his B.A. undergraduate degree, in 1900, from the University at Johns Hopkins, concentrating in the natural sciences.

Next, he enrolled in medical school at Johns Hopkins. Unfortunately, during his second year of medical school, he had acquired a serious infection while conducting an autopsy, and the infection developed into a tubercular inflammatory condition involving an axillary gland. The infected tissue was removed surgically, but convalescence required a significantly prolonged duration for a full recovery. Rous returned to medical school afterward and took courses with prominent medical faculty, such as the famous Dr. William Osler, who was well known for having refined medical school curricula. Rous took his medical doctorate degree, an M.D., in 1905.

As an intern at Johns Hopkins, Dr. Rous made the realization that practicing medicine as a physician was not for him, and he subsequently switched to a research mode, focusing on pathology as his discipline of choice. Thus, he pursued advanced studies, in 1907, as a post-graduate assistant in the laboratory of Prof. Alfred S. Warthin, who was situated in Ann Arbor, Michigan. He then studied pathology for a year in the laboratory of Prof. Christian Georg Schmorl, in Dresden, Germany. During this interim,

Dr. Rous had acquired a case of tuberculosis, taking more time for recovery in the Adirondacks, as presumably prescribed by his doctors. In 1909, against the advice of several of his colleagues, however, Dr. Rous moved to the research laboratory of Prof. Simon Flexner at the Rockefeller Institute in New York, where he focused on studying cancer biology. Dr. Rous continued to work at the Rockefeller Institute for the remainder of his life.

2. *There seems to be a relationship between certain forms of cancer and certain viruses. How did he initially learn about this?*

In 1911, Dr. Rous was the very first scientific investigator to show that a virus can cause cancer. His work on this front soon began after his arrival at the Rockefeller Institute. A regional farmer came to the Institute with a Plymouth Rock hen that had had a rather large, irregularly-shaped globular-like mass on its breast. Dr. Rous biopsied the breast mass by excising it from the chicken and then examined the specimen under the microscope. Based on its visual properties in the scope, Dr. Rous confirmed the diagnosis that the chicken's breast mass was a so-called spindle cell sarcoma, a type of breast cancer of the chicken.

Next, Dr. Rous took the chicken breast sarcoma tissue and minced the cancerous cells apart from each other, making a tumor "soup." He then injected the minced sarcoma cell soup into several healthy chickens, all of whom were without any previous signs of tumors. Soon after, a spindle cell sarcoma, which is a type of cancer, emerged in various locations throughout one of the injected chickens. The new tumors grew rapidly and soon killed the chicken.

He was able to transfer solid sarcoma tissue from chicken to chicken, each new bird growing breast cancer with every passage of tumor material. It was briefly noticed that the tumors grew more aggressively with each succeeding passage, from chicken to chicken. The results had been the first recorded instance of a so-called transmission of solid chicken tumors between chickens, and Dr. Rous published the work in 1910.

Next, Dr. Rous hypothesized that the transmissibility of the sarcomas between chicken could be accomplished without the need for intact cancer cells. Thus, Dr. Rous excised sarcoma tissue from chickens with breast cancer, just as he had before, except that this time he broke open the sarcoma cells, thus, gaining access to the internal cellular contents, the cytoplasm, of the sarcoma cells. Next, he applied the cytoplasmic contents of the sarcoma, now called cell-free material, and passed it through a specialized bacteria-catching filter, called the Berkefeld ultrafilter. The filter's tiny pores permit agents that are smaller than most of the bacteria to go through the filter, and agents like, perhaps, viruses could pass through the filter.

The cytoplasmic sarcoma-based material that went through the tiny pores of the filter was now referred to as a "cell-free filtrate." It was composed of internal cellular material from the insides of the tumor cells. No intact tumor cells were present—it was cell-free! Next, Dr. Rous injected the so-called cell-free filtrate from the chicken sarcoma into new healthy chickens. The injected chickens grew tumors without tumor cells!

Dr. Rous published the shocking new work in 1911.

Interestingly, a similar type of cell-free filtrate result had previously been observed with bird leukemia, in 1908, by Drs. Ellerman and Bang, but at the time, it was not realized by anyone that leukemia was also a disease of cancer. However, the idea that a virus might cause cancer was not new. The notion for a viral-causation of cancer had first been proposed by Dr. Amedee Borrel, in 1903.

Dr. Rous's papers, however, were the first to provide evidence in favor of the hypothesis that a solid tumor could be caused by a virus. We now know that many microbes can cause cancer.

3. *It seems imperative that science look at causality– and whether cancer is caused by some bacteria in the air or some virus– why is this important?*

Amongst the well-known causes of cancer, such as inheritability and exposure to mutagens, another causative agent for cancer involves a group of assorted microbes.

With respect to the genetic versus the mutagenic causations, the implicated human genes may overlap. For example, the tumor-suppressing genes, such as *p53*, *BRCA1*, etc. can be affected in which mutagenic variations account for enhanced tumorigenesis and which may, in turn, lead to carcinogenesis, if a "second mutational hit" occurs. Regarding the environmentally influenced carcinogens, many of these types of cancer cases are actually preventable. For example, avoidance of smoking (most important), plus proper dieting, obesity control, consistent exercise, moderate alcohol intake, protection from radiation and ultra-violet light exposures, minimization of exposure to occupational carcinogens, and prevention of exposure to oncogenic microbes, all can play important roles in reducing chances of cancer in humans.

Regarding microbial causes of cancer, there are various bacteria, viruses, and others, which are known to have influential roles.

Certain species of bacteria are thought to be associated with cancer. One well-studied example is the Gram-negative and twisted helical-shaped *Helicobacter pylori* bacterium, which not only causes stomach ulcers but is known to be associated with an enhanced propensity for gastric carcinoma, also known as stomach cancer. Additionally, a pathogenic version of *Escherichia coli*, a Gram-negative bacterium and new strain called NC101, is linked to colorectal cancer, also known as colon cancer. Another Gram-negative bacterium that is apparently connected to colon cancer is called *Bacteroides fragilis*, by using a toxin called BFT (for *Bacteroides fragilis* toxin) to do so. A Gram-positive bacterium called *Enterococcus faecalis* has been strongly implicated in adenocarcinoma, a cancer of glandular tissue like the pancreas or the colon.

With respect to the viruses, there are two main classes of viruses, in general, that are known to be carcinogenic. The first of these tumorigenic classes are DNA viruses. There are several families of these DNA oncogenic viruses. One such DNA virus family is called the Hepadnaviridae. An individual oncogenic member of this viral family includes the notorious Hepatitis B virus, a known causer of liver cancer, called hepatocellular carcinoma.

A second DNA family of viruses is called Herpesviridae. Oncogenic members of this family include the Epstein-Barr virus, which can cause Burkitt's lymphoma, a cancer of a certain type of white blood cell called the B-lymphocytes. Another DNA virus member of the Herpesviridae family is called human herpesvirus (HHV), and one prime example is the HHV-8 strain, which is known to cause Kaposi's sarcoma, a form of cancer of the skin and lymph nodes. A third DNA virus group is called the Papillomaviridae family. While there are hundreds of members in this family, a certain few are serious causes of the vast majority of the human cervical and uterine cancers, such as human papillomavirus strains 16 (HPV-16) and 18 (HPV-18).

The second class of tumor-causing viruses is RNA viruses. Under this umbrella of viral microbes associated with cancer, there are several RNA virus families. The first RNA virus family is called the Flaviviridae family. An important oncogenic member within this family includes the Hepatitis C virus, another causative microbial agent of liver cancer, again, called the hepatocellular carcinoma. A second RNA family of oncogenic viruses is called Retroviridae. Two important members of this viral family are the human T-cell leukemia virus type I (HTLV-1), which causes adult T-cell leukemia and lymphoma, and the human immunodeficiency virus (HIV), which is associated indirectly by suppressing the immune system and allowing human herpes strain number 8 to cause Kaposi's sarcoma. A third member of the Retroviridae family is the Rous sarcoma virus, known to cause chicken sarcoma.

4. What is a Rous sarcoma virus? (See below)

The Rous sarcoma itself refers to the chicken-based breast cancer that Dr. Rous originally studied. These tumors are characterized by an uncontrollable growth of the chicken breast cells.

The microbe that causes the sarcoma, the Rous sarcoma virus, is an RNA-based retrovirus. The virus has an internal single-stranded (+)-sense RNA molecule for its genome, with a surrounding capsid protein for protection, and which is, in turn, covered by a lipid-based envelope. The Rous sarcoma virus transforms normal cells into tumorigenic tissue. The oncogenic mechanism for this transformation takes place as soon as the virus infects the normal target cell.

Once the RNA is in place, inside the cell, a viral enzyme called reverse transcriptase uses it as a template to make a double-stranded version of the viral DNA molecule! The Rous sarcoma virus inserts its DNA version of the genome into the nucleus of the normal host cell!

Then, incredibly, the viral DNA version insidiously inserts itself into the genome of the chicken breast cell! The viral DNA insertion brings along with it a brand new gene that's not known to the chicken. The inserted gene is called *v-Src* (pronounced "vee-sark"), and it's better known as one of several oncogenes, that is, genes that cause cancer. These and other oncogenes are cancer-causing genes in the sense that they code for proteins that make cells grow uncontrollably. The Src protein was discovered to be a tyrosine kinase, an enzyme that phosphorylates tyrosine amino acids and serves to transform cells. Thus, modulation of the Src system results in enhanced and uncontrollable growth properties in cells, producing tumors. This breakthrough led to the discovery of numerous other oncogenes.

5. *Apparently, it took the scientific community about 40 years– to truly acknowledge and recognize his work. What were the issues here? (Some say this was the longest "incubation period" for a Nobel Prize.)*

Dr. Rous's works were published in 1910 and 1911. He showed that cancer was transmissible and that a filterable cell-free extract produced chicken sarcomas. Dr. Rous himself was somewhat leery at first of the very idea that a virus could cause cancer, as is evident by the fact that in his two papers, he did not mention the term "virus." Instead, he was careful to refer to the cancer-causing virus as a "filterable agent" or a "cell-free filtrate." At the time, such wording could tacitly be taken as "code" for the virus. Such terminology had been used to justify the discovery of bacteriophages, i.e., viruses that infected bacteria.

The careful wording by Dr. Rous, however, did not fool many of the investigators at the time, and it did not discourage his critics, either. Such naysayers invoked the doctrine of Virchow, who had clearly stated that cancer had its cause from the insides of cancer cells, not from the outside! Therefore, they mistakenly thought that microbes (they were outside the cell!) could not cause cancer.

Thus, disbelief was widespread, and Rous was taken to task. First, his critics charged that Rous' "sarcomas" were not actually cancers. That is, they believed that Dr. Rous's tumors were not tumors! The unbelievers pointed to his methods. Perhaps, they said, Dr. Rous has made terrible errors in his techniques! They suggested that maybe his filtrates had no viruses but some other yet undiscovered sarcoma-causing carcinogen? They even suggested that perhaps Dr. Rous' chicken sarcoma viruses were laboratory mutants!

Whatever the case, his detractors were absolutely sure that the cancer cause was not viral. Scientific disbelief in the idea that cancer could be caused by a virus was strong, publically-professed in scientific conferences, and, as you pointed out, long-lasting, with such stern skepticism languishing well into the late 1950s!

6. Warts and rabbits – how do they figure into the picture?

Because Dr. Rous had so brazenly implicated that viruses might have a causative effect on cancer, he was met with widespread skepticism, which was enough to discourage him from pursuing the matter for decades effectively. The warts and rabbits that you referred to were the other factors that encouraged Dr. Rous to re-examine the matter.

Several of Dr. Rous' contemporaries, led by Dr. Richard Shope, had discovered the tumor-causing papillomaviruses, which he had observed to cause rabbit warts. They had prepared tissue extracts from the warts of certain cottontail rabbits, filtered the extracts, and then applied the material to test rabbits. They recorded the observation of newly formed warts on the test rabbits!

Encouraged by these promising studies, in 1935, Dr. Rous, working with Joseph Beard, then proceeded to demonstrate a potential for causing tumors on rabbit skin after chronic infection with the so-called cottontail rabbit papillomavirus. This particular virus was DNA-based, as opposed to the RNA-based Rous sarcoma virus. The DNA work, however, ultimately led to the discovery, in the 1960s, of the human papillomaviruses as a cause of human cancer. Thus, the idea that viruses could cause cancer was finally gaining widespread acceptance.

7. *What have I neglected to ask?*

In 1915, when Dr. Rous was 36 years old, he married Marion Eckford de Kay, and the couple had three children together, all girls. Family life in the Rous household has been described as a happy one, with plenty of yearly vacations, each often lasting two months. Gardening and fishing were hobbies that occupied Dr. Rous and family. Vacations were, however, also working ones, in which Dr. Rous was known to take along manuscripts for review as he was a devoted editor of the prestigious *Journal of Experimental Medicine*.

One biographer has noted that Dr. Rous frequently experienced serious bouts of insomnia. Thus, a common practice he adopted was to keep a notepad handy on his bedside table along with a specialized pencil that had a light-fixture attached to it, in order to jot down any research ideas he might think up during the middle of his countless sleepless nights.

He officially retired in 1945 but continued to work at Rockefeller University, spending close to 60 years total there. It is recorded that well into his twilight years, he regularly walked to and from the laboratory, a full 15 blocks from home, each day! On the 16th day of February, in the year 1970, Dr. Peyton Rous passed away, at the age of 90, of abdominal cancer.

For additional study and review:

https://www.youtube.com/watch?v=aAkJk0RHIpY
https://www.youtube.com/watch?v=VJUf9nsleB0

Chapter 21

MICHAEL SHEETZ – EXTRA-CELLULAR BIOLOGICAL MATRIX

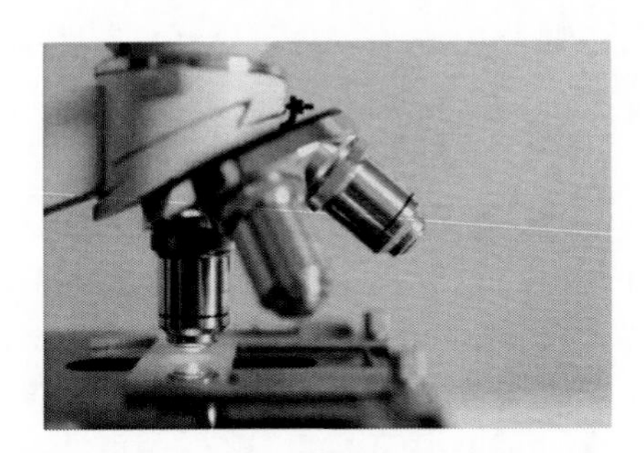

1. *Professor Varela, we have to recognize one of the most influential medical researchers– currently teaching at the University of Texas in Galveston–Michael Sheetz. But we need some background–where was he born and educated?*

Dr. Michael Patrick Sheetz is a world-renowned biochemist and cell biologist who is best known for his remarkable pioneering investigations in biomechanics and mechanobiology. In particular, he is an expert in the extracellular matrix machinery of the cell, especially in motor-based motility of cells and of organelles, especially those involving kinesin. Dr. Sheetz has been credited as a co-discoverer of kinesin. He is also an expert in the cell division-engaging protein called dynein, plus muscle cell biology involving actin and myosin and of the membrane-cytoskeleton adhesion system. One of his famous discoveries has to do with the use of so-called "optical tweezers" to manipulate and measure the forces associated with cell movement and the activity of proteins like kinesin. His body of scientific research relates directly to the biomedical sciences.

Dr. Sheetz was born on the 11th day of December in the year 1946. He took his undergraduate degree in 1968 at a private liberal arts-based institution called Albion College, which is located in the town of Albion, Michigan, in the U.S. He took his Ph.D. degree in 1972 from the California Institute of Technology, which is in Pasadena, CA, in the U.S.

2. *He pioneered mechanobiology and biomechanics. For the layperson or student– how would you summarize these two areas?*

Mechanobiology is a burgeoning and essential new field that combines the biological sciences with those of physics and engineering. The area is concerned with examining biological systems from a mechanical perspective, such as the physical forces involved in the physiology of growing, developing, and differentiating cells and tissues. As such, mechanobiology focuses on the physical properties that control the biological behavior of living cells and tissues.

One important sub-field of mechanobiology is referred to as mechanotransduction. Here, the cells detect outside stimuli and then respond to such stimulation by converting the external signals into specific physiological processes, which, in turn, conduct a behavioral response in the cells. The method of mechanotransduction involves first a so-called mechanocoupling system. This system transduces mechanical forces into cellular sensory signals via a mechanism that detects the individual messages. Next, a biochemical-based coupling system takes over. Here, the method involves converting the mechanical signal into a biochemistry-based reaction for the purpose of influencing a cellular behavior, such as turning on a gene to produce a specific protein. The mechanotransduction process also involves communicating the message from the cells that detected the signal onto other cells, which can then respond with the desired behavior.

Biomechanics is another vast field of scientific study. It deals with exploring the structure and function of biological systems from a physical-mechanical perspective. The area also explores the movement of biological systems, such as organelles, cells, tissues, and organisms. The discipline focuses on the mechanics of these living systems.

There are many different aspects of biomechanics. One of these points includes kinesiology, which studies movements of the body from physiological, mechanical, and dynamic perspectives. Another element of biomechanics is the control of tissue behavior based on the nervous system. Biomechanics also involves sports medicine, in which orthopedics and therapy are carefully examined. One exciting sub-field is referred to as forensic biomechanics, which includes the investigation of accidents using biomechanical engineering to determine the causes of injuries.

3. *His research focuses on cell motility, motor molecules, and integrin-cytoskeleton interactions. Can you tell us why each of these are important?*

Cell motility refers to the migrations of organelles, cells, and tissues within the body, such as dividing healthy cells, muscle fibers, growing cancer cells, and bacteria. Motor molecules are generally proteins that produce the movements of the organelles, growing live cells, and tissues, and they then function within cellular structures to assemble the cells and tissues in the body. Such motor proteins can use biological energy to generate forces and motions of the cells or living tissue masses within the individual.

The integrin-cytoskeleton refers to the protein called integrin and its association with structures inside of the cell, called the cytoskeleton. The internal cytoskeleton is composed of smaller proteins called filaments and tubules, and they can serve to determine the shape and integrity of cells. The integrin molecules function to connect the cytoskeleton to the extracellular matrix, a substance that resides outside of cells. The integrin-cytoskeleton axis participates in the junctions between neighboring cells as sort of a cellular glue, keeping cells stuck together to form larger masses and tissues. The integrin-cytoskeleton axis also participates in cell growth and helps such cells to survive. These cell components often work by signaling other cells to aid in these functions.

The integrins have many essential functions in cells. For instance, in addition to attaching a live cell to a matrix, the integrins also participate in cell signaling mechanisms to modulate cellular behaviors along these matrices. When matrix parts bind to integrins of cells, they form integrin clusters to initiate assemblages of cell-matrix junctions, further triggering cells to bind other arrays, and then grow and become motile.

Integrins function to connect a cell with another cell, forming so-called cell-cell junctions, which then create larger assemblages of cellular masses. These cell-cell connections respond to mechanical forces by recruiting additional integrins to accommodate the stresses induced by the applied forces. Thus, the integrins that are associated with the cell-matrix junctions can perform the processes involved in mechanotransduction.

Integrin molecules also work in the membranes of cells that are migrating along a substratum to form so-called focal adhesions, upon which the proteins actin and myosin function to accommodate cell crawling. Integrin uses adaptors connected to the actin that is located within the cytoskeleton of the cell to bind the substratum, permitting myosin to serve as a force transmitter so that actin filaments can grow longer bringing a protruding living cell with it. The protrusion formed by the growing actin polymers confers the cell migration along the substratum.

Interestingly, bacteria can exploit integrin on human and animal cells to bind and initiate bacterial entry into such cells by reorienting the actin polymers to do so. This mechanism is called zippering because integrin is used to help zipper actin molecules together in long chains in order to mediate phagocytosis of bacteria. But in this case, the bacterial entry occurs in cells which are not equipped to kill the bacteria, and they can wreak havoc inside such non-phagocytic cells, causing damage and pathogenesis.

4. *How are they linked to cancer?*

Cancer cells often grow at a phenomenal rate, and as quick growers, they need to assemble new structures that permit this rapid pace of growth. For example, they may need cell division machinery, like DNA synthesis, or mitotic mechanisms, in order to mediate the separation of newly made DNA into the freshly made tumor cells. As tumor and cancer cells grow, sometimes the extracellular matrix machinery is re-shaped or even sacrificed to permit their rapid growth rates or to permit metastasis.

Tumor and cancer cells also exhibit a growth behavior that involves cytoskeleton modulation in which their mechanosensory machinery is abnormal. Therefore, such tumor and cancer cells have broken mechanosensory systems that lack the ability to sense neighboring cells or substratum. Whereas healthy cells can detect their neighbors or substrate and thus stop growing as necessary, tumor and cancer cells are under no such mechanosensory control. Tumor masses may then overgrow their micro-environments, possibly leading to malfunction of such cells, tissues, or organs and consequently causing cancerous tumors.

Cancer cells are abnormal in their motility behaviors. For instance, cancers can, on occasion, become motile, breaking off of the larger original tumor mass and migrating to other locations in the body to initiate new tumor masses elsewhere. The term that's used to describe this type of tumor cell mobility and growth is metastasis. A great deal of biomedical science research is focused on these cellular systems as targets for modulation in order to curtail tumor metastasis.

5. *Mechanosensing in myofibrillogenesis – why is this important, and what does it mean?*

In heart muscle cells, called cardiomyocytes, disease can occur in which their extracellular matrix composition is altered, leading to abnormal cross-linking and stiffening of the heart cells' so-called microenvironments. Furthermore, damage from a heart attack and cardiomyopathy, a condition in which the heart has to work with a more significant amount of work in order to pump blood through the circulatory pathway, leads to the formation of scar tissue called cardiac fibrosis. This abnormal condition influences the behavior of the heart muscle cells.

In heart cells, a protein called talin serves as a so-called mechanosensitive adaptor, which senses muscle oscillations and the tensions generated during their contractions. The mechanosensing system can detect differences inherent in healthy cardiac muscle versus cardiac fibrosis.

Myofibrillogenesis refers to the generation of so-called myofibrils of the heart. These myofibrils function to contract and relax during heart contractions for blood pumping. During cardiac muscle cell development, early embryonic cardiomyocytes lack a specific stiffness and thus, lack tension. The talin-based mechanosensory system can even distinguish between these younger muscle cells versus more mature heart cells, based on their inherent stiffness properties.

6. *Apparently, he has been studying how cells differentiate and regenerate tissues or, sadly, metastasize. Why are each of these important?*

The cellular differentiation process involves the conversion of a non-functional primordial stem cell into a specialized cell with a specific biological role to play. Part of the character of stem cells is their immense capacity to differentiate into specialized cells, a property called pluripotency.

Dr. Sheetz and his colleagues studied cellular differentiation in his laboratory, starting in the mid-1990s when they examined developing and growing nerves. They found that integrin played an essential role in the nerve growth cone emergence by interacting with the neuronal cytoskeleton. One exciting finding was their discovery that during axonal growth cone emergence, specific mechanical forces were generated. As these forces came about, individual players were identified in the process. One of these players is called vinculin, which is found in the focal adhesion segments of the cells and which binds to the protein called talin. During the growth cone movement, the talin protein is actually stretched, which then exposes vinculin binding sites for its recruitment to the focal adhesion sites.

The process of regeneration refers to the healing manner of biological systems. Often, the healing process repairs damaged tissue by replacing the wounded tissue with fibrous extracellular matrix material that is not as functionally or structurally as good as the original tissue that it replaced. Dr. Sheetz developed an interest in this area shortly after the turn of the 21st century.

Some of the first investigations included his analysis of myosin assembly and its changes during the closure of epithelial tissue wounds. They developed a technique in which they used lasers to damage cellular layers of kidney cells, and they then measured the activities of actin and myosin. When complexed together, the actin and myosin connections are referred to as actomyosin. The Sheetz team found that the actomyosin machine attached to the tight junctions between the damaged epithelial cells forming a ring made by the myosin portion of the actomyosin during the closing up of the wound. They also strongly implicated the role of another enzyme called Rho-kinase in placing the cellular machine in its proper location and turning it on.

As I mentioned earlier, metastasis involves the breakage of a tiny portion of a larger tumor mass and the movement of these tumor pieces to different locations in the body where they can establish new tumor masses. Often metastasis is the most undesirable outcome for a patient who has a tumor. A metastatic tumor can interfere with the normal functioning of the body and make therapies difficult. Dr. Sheetz began studies of metastasis in the early 2000s. His laboratory focused on the rates of tumor movements and the forces involved in the tumor traction properties. He found that both of these processes worked by distinctive cellular mechanisms.

Next, he focused on the role of integrin. He discovered that integrin moved laterally within the membranes of tumor cells and clustered together during cellular migrations. His team then found out that the clustered integrins prompted actin molecules to assemble together, which then permitted myosin to act upon the actin assembly to mediate the generation of contractile forces.

These newly produced forces, in turn, stimulated the activation of a so-called signal transduction system call Src kinase, which then mediated the cell movement along in new directions. The clustered formation of integrin molecules also played a role in bringing together other players, such as proteins like talin, and paxillin, or even vinculin. Dr. Sheetz's work clearly established the functional importance of integrin in the chemistry and biology of the cell.

7. *"The Cell as a Machine" seems to be one of the most provocative books and essential books of the last 10 years. What do you know about the book?*

Dr. Sheetz published *The Cell as a Machine* in 2018, having co-authored the book with Dr. Hanry Yu, who has held principal investigator positions at the National University of Singapore at Singapore and at the prestigious Massachusetts Institute of Technology, in Cambridge, the U.S.

Their book covers a vast array of topics pertaining to the chemistry and biology of the cell from an energy-transducing, mechanical perspective. That is, Drs. Sheetz and Yu view the cell as a specialized living device, complete with an extensive assortment of biological gadgets for implementing its enormous collection of functions necessary for life.

Living cells are remarkable entities, and as a cellome, marvelous functions can be accomplished by their mind-boggling pieces of machinery. The insides of the cells that belong to the living cellome harbor sub-structures that are considered tiny technologies of their own.

Such sub-cellular apparatuses include those for mediating the various developmental stages of a cell, the multiplication of the cell, its evolution, and the integration of these disparate systems into a collection of sensory mechanisms that regulate its adaptable behaviors. The book also addresses how a cell manages to maintain and energize its mechanical functions and then discusses the players involved in the design of the cellular machine. The authors further survey the various pieces of machinery of the enclosed cell from the standpoint of their molecular structures.

The book covers how a cell senses its outside environment and then communicates this external data to its internal cellular workings in order to make decisions on how to respond appropriately. The publication also includes how cells die and the associated ramifications. Lastly, the authors deal with topics pertaining to the multiple ways in which the cell malfunctions, such as in disease, especially in the case of cancer. The book is beautifully written, and, thus, I believe it is definitively geared to become an enduring classic.

8. *Back in 2012– Sheetz shared the very prestigious Albert Lasker Basic Medical Research Award. First of all, who was Albert Lasker, and what did Sheetz win the award for?*

Indeed, the accolade is widely deemed as a sort of preamble to the Nobel. Approximately 50% of the Albert Lasker Basic Medical Research Award beneficiaries go on to acquire the Nobel, especially in the physiology or medicine category. The Lasker awards are considered an extremely prestigious honor, and it is bestowed to individuals who make outstanding contributions in any one of several fields, such as in biology, clinical medicine, human health, and education. The Lasker Awards were established by Mary Woodward Lasker and Albert Davis Lasker in 1945. Albert Lasker was a successful advertising business person.

Dr. Sheetz gladly shared the honor with colleagues, Drs. James Spudich and Ronald Vale, the latter of whom I had had the great pleasure of meeting briefly at the MBL in the summer of 1991 at Woods Hole, MA. Each of these great investigators has collaborated with each other in a considerable number of scientific projects. Dr. Spudich is well known amongst cell biologists, biochemists, and biomedical scientists for his works dealing with myosin and actin in muscle. Dr. Vale is widely known for his works concerning axon movement and co-discovering kinesin with Dr. Sheetz and others. In fact, Drs. Vale and Sheetz coined the term kinesin. Dr. Vale also determined the crystal structure of the motor domain of kinesin in 1996, publishing the work in *Nature*.

The trio of investigators received their Lasker honors together for having made outstanding scientific discoveries pertaining to motor proteins that make up the internal cytoskeleton, energized cellular machines that transport organellar-based cargoes along microtubules, for the contractile behavior of actin and myosin motors within the muscles and especially for their tremendous contributions towards the mechanisms involved in the movements of cells. Their scientific achievements are exceptionally relevant in the field of cancer biology.

As recipients of the Lasker Award, Dr. Sheetz and his two honorees are in good company. Other Lasker Laureates include many of the investigators we have considered in our book-writing collaborations. Such luminaries include Drs. Tu Youyou (2011), John Gurdon (2009), Barry Marshall (1995), Stanley Prusiner (1994), Nancy Wexler (1993), Leroy Hood (1987), Rita Levi-Montalcini (1986), Joseph Goldstein (1985), César Milstein (1984), Harold Varmus (1982), Frederick Sanger (1979), Rosalyn Yalow (1976), Gobind Khorana (1968), Albert Sabin (1965), Renato Dulbecco (1964), Francis Crick (1960), James Watson (1960), Alfred Hershey (1958), Peyton Rous (1958), Jonas Salk (1956), John F. Enders (1954), Hans Krebs (1953), Selman Waksman (1948), Carl Cori (1946), and Karl Landsteiner (1946), to name a few!

9. *What have I neglected to ask about this scientist who is still active and researching away?*

Indeed, as of this writing, Dr. Sheetz is 75 years old and still a busy biomedical investigator. He recently moved to Galveston, TX, in the U.S., in 2019, to become a full professor at the Medical Branch of the University of Texas at the Molecular MechanoMedicine Program. His position is sponsored as the Robert A. Welch distinguished chair in chemistry. Prior to this, Dr. Sheetz had been at Columbia University in New York, U.S., since 1990. Before Columbia, he had been living in Missouri, where he was at Washington University in St. Louis, having arrived there in 1985. He has also held adjacent positions at the Singapore National University in the

Mechanobiology Institute, starting in 2010, and at Duke University Medical Center in Durham, North Carolina, in the U.S., beginning in the early 1990s.

I had the fortune of having met Dr. Sheetz, however briefly, during the summer of 1991, at the famous Marine Biological Laboratory, located in Woods Hole, Massachusetts, when I was a graduate student participating in summer research as a young ASCB fellow. During our brief conversation, Dr. Sheetz was a totally good-natured person. I believe then that he had previously injured his leg and was hobbling around all summer with crutches and a cast around his leg. It did not seem to slow him down in the least.

I also recall that summer that his MBL seminar was fascinating. Dr. Sheetz spoke about the beautiful molecular machines, like dynein or kinesin, and the translocation of organelles along intracellular protein microtubules within axons. It had been the first time I had heard about the concept of the inner workings of a cell operating like an energized motor machine!

It had also been the very first time that I had ever heard about optical tweezers! He had shown those of us in the audience that day about his amazing images from his microscope of cells or smaller sub-cellular particles that were ensnared within a so-called single-beam optical gradient trap system, or optical tweezers! We watched in amazement how he had managed to manipulate an individual cell in its trap, at will!

10. *"Blown away" are the only words I can use to describe Michael Sheetz's work as documented on Research Gate, which indicates: 464 research works with 38089 citations and 2,514 reads. Is there any single book or article which stands out in your mind?*

Indeed, Dr. Sheetz's written collection of scientific literature is vast. He has delivered an astonishing wealth of biological literature to the field of biomedical science, and in particular, to cell biology as well as the fields he established, biomechanics and mechanobiology.

It is my firm conviction that his remarkable citation record is a tribute to the relevance of his scientific work. It is quite clear that his work is tremendously appreciated by an enormous magnitude of biomedical investigators. In fact, I surmise that the article you referenced above regarding Dr. Sheetz, having been listed in 2013 as a member of the top-twenty most influential biomedical scientists in the world, is a testament to the immense popularity of his written works.

Dr. Sheetz is in an extraordinary *esprit de corps*. In the same top-twenty list, Dr. Sheetz is connected with other great scientists featured in our own books, including the present one. Such scientific luminaries include Drs. Tim Hunt, James Watson, Harold Varmus, Gerald Edelman, Tu Youyou, and the inimitable Sir John B. Gurdon, taking the number one spot on the list.

A few years after his remarkable MBL seminar during the summer of 1991, I had read with wonder his newsworthy publication in my newly delivered issue of *Science* in April of 1993. In the new paper, he revealed how he had trapped the kinesin mechanomotor within the clutches of his optical tweezer apparatus. I was astonished! With a single molecule of the famous kinesin caught in the trap, he had actually measured the forces involved to the pico-Newton level for the mechanical activity of a single motor protein! The mechanical force findings for the individual kinesin motor had direct applications towards the eventual construction of behavioral models for tissue contraction, such as those seen in muscles, developing cells, neuronal axon cone growth, and cancer cell movements.

For interested readers - here is Prof. Michael Sheetz speaking about his research and interests:

https://www.youtube.com/watch?time_continue=27&v=ZB37zi4e0Vs
https://www.youtube.com/watch?v=OkJNpikySh4

Chapter 22

MICHAEL SMITH – SITE-DIRECTED MUTAGENESIS

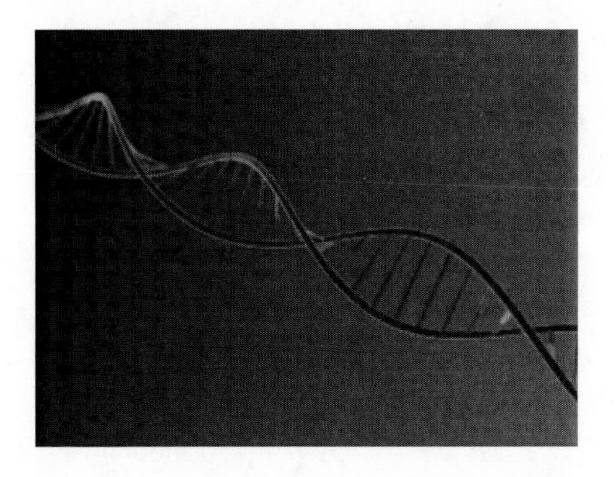

1. *Professor Varela– like a lot of other famous scientists and Nobel Prize winners, Michael Smith came from England– Specifically from Blackpool and Manchester and Cambridge. When exactly was he born and tell us about his early education.*

Dr. Michael Smith is known for having invented the molecular biological technique called site-specific mutagenesis. The method permits investigators to alter the sequences of DNA in just about any way one so desires in order to produce their corresponding mutated proteins.

Dr. Smith was born on the 26th day of the month of April in the year 1932 in the coastal town of Blackpool, nearby to the Irish Sea, in the northwestern part of England. The Smith family was poor. Smith's mother, Mary Agnes, was a bookkeeper, and his father, Rowland, was known to be a gardener.

Starting at the age of five, Michael attended elementary school at the Marton Moss Church of England, located in Blackpool. The school was associated with the St. Nicholas Church of England. At the age of 11 years, Smith qualified for a scholarship to a private school after having scored very well on a qualifying examination.

Thus, he attended Arnold School, a prestigious private institution. At Arnold, Smith found that the institution served up terrible war-rationed meals. He was later to recall that he was not very good at sports while enrolled in Arnold.

During his years there, however, he became a boy scout. It had been a serendipitous occurrence for him. He had been teased mercilessly because of his protruding teeth, and he had been sent, therefore, to a dentist to fix the teeth. While his teeth did not get fixed, his dentist introduced him to a one Mr. Barnes who admitted him into the Boy Scouts, where he flourished. The experience led him to appreciate the great outdoors for the rest of his life.

But it is also at Arnold where Smith became enamored with chemistry, graduating from high school in 1950. He attributed his love of chemistry to his high school chemistry teacher, the inspirational Mr. Sidney Law. Mr. Law later advised Smith to read a good newspaper, such as the local newspaper called the *Manchester Guardian*. Dr. Smith recalled later, after his move to the U.S., that he started up a subscription to the *New Yorker*.

After high school graduation, he was unable to gain admittance to Oxford or Cambridge because of a lack of knowledge preparation in Latin. Smith instead attended the University of Manchester under a scholarship provided by the Blackpool Education Committee. He was enrolled in the university's honors program concentrating in chemistry.

Smith took his undergraduate degree in 1953 from Manchester, having majored in chemistry. He later cited Profs. M.G. Evans and E.R.H. Jones as running a superb honors program in chemistry. While his bachelor's degree was disappointingly not accompanied by its top honors, his academic performance was respectable enough to earn a graduate fellowship supported by the State Scholarship program. The scholarship was prestigious, and it helped his educational studies for the pursuit of a Ph.D. Smith studied chemistry in graduate school under his graduate supervisor, Professor H. Bernard Henbest. In 1956 Dr. Smith took his Ph.D. in chemistry from the University of Manchester.

2. *Smith worked with H. B. Henbest on something called cyclohexane diols and was awarded the Ph.D. in 1956. What exactly are these cyclohexane diols? And what did he find?*

In Professor Henbest's organic chemistry laboratory Smith studied the stereochemistry of cyclohexane diols. The organic molecules of interest were members of the group called cholestane-2:3-diols. His focus was on examining the stability of the oxygen atoms contained within the cyclohexane diol rings, which consisted of six-carbon circles and their diol substituents.

From their starting points, Smith synthesized derivatives of the cyclohexane diol molecules. In particular, he performed chemical reactions involving cyclohexane-1:3-diol mono-arenesulphonate anion molecules using an alkali solution in order to examine their stereochemical properties.

In addition to his Ph.D. thesis, titled "*Studies in the stereochemistry of diols and their derivatives*," Smith published two papers from the graduate work, in 1957, with his graduate advisor, Dr. Henbest, as a co-author. The duo was later to collaborate on several additional projects, publishing them in 1958.

3. *Smith apparently was eager to learn and was not afraid to travel. Apparently, he finally made it to Vancouver Canada– and worked with Gobind Khorana ... to work on the synthesis of biologically essential organophosphates. First, tell us about Gobind and then these organophosphates.*

Prof. Har Gobind Khorana took the 1968 Nobel Prize in Physiology or Medicine for having participated in solving the genetic code. The organophosphates, also known as phosphate esters, can be thought of as esters of phosphoric acid. Of the organophosphates that are known, the most biologically important ones include those composed of DNA, RNA, or ATP. Dr. Khorana had used the so-called phosphodiester method for chemically making short DNA chains, which he called polynucleotides, later called oligonucleotides. Khorana also invoked enzymatic as well as chemical synthesis methods to construct the nucleotide sequence for the entire length of an intact gene!

In September of 1956, with a newly minted Ph.D. in hand, Dr. Smith moved to Vancouver, Canada, to undergo training as a postdoctoral fellow in the laboratory of Dr. Khorana, who was then a young investigator housed at the British Columbia Research Council. Dr. Smith participated in several new research projects. Two of these postdoctoral investigations included developing further improvements in the techniques for the chemical syntheses of ribonucleoside-5'-triphosphate and deoxyribonucleoside-5'-triphosphate compounds. The work was published in a chemistry-based journal in 1958.

Another project that was conducted by Dr. Smith as a postdoc in professor Khorana's Vancouver laboratory was concerned with improving the synthesis methods of the so-called ribonucleoside-3',5'-cyclic phosphate compounds, such as cyclic AMP (cAMP). The new studies were published in 1961. The cAMP compounds would later gain notoriety for their critical cell biological roles in signal transduction systems involving extracellular ligands and their corresponding membrane-bound receptors.

Dr. Smith also studied the formation of phosphodiester bonds, which play essential roles in linking the nucleotides together to form longer DNA chains, such as the oligonucleotides. He was able to build phosphodiester linkages between two uridines and between uridine and adenosine. This work was published in 1962, sometime after his postdoctoral stint had been completed.

Altogether, Dr. Smith spent four years as a postdoctoral fellow in the Khorana laboratory, until about 1960. During this extra training beyond the Ph.D. in Vancouver, Dr. Smith had made acquaintances with other notable investigators, such as Dr. Arthur Kornberg, who had spent the summer of 1956 in Dr. Khorana's lab building DNA. Dr. Kornberg would garner a Nobel in 1959 for his discovery of the DNA-making enzyme called DNA polymerase. Another acquaintance of Dr. Smith was the famous Dr. Paul Berg, who had studied aminoacyl-adenylates in Dr. Khorana's lab and who would later also earn a Nobel, in 1980, for his discoveries about gene splicing and recombinant DNA technology.

Another acquaintance at Vancouver involved Dr. Smith meeting his future wife, Helen Wood Christie, whom he married on the 6th of August, in 1960. They would later have three offspring and then separate in 1983. He and Elizabeth Raines would later live together for the remainder of his life, until his death on the 4th day of October, in 2000, at 68 years of age.

4. *Fast forward a few years– and Smith ended up at the University of Wisconsin–working on a synthesis of ribo-oligonucleotides. I remember oligonucleotides from college but not ribo- oligonucleotides. Help us out here.*

In 1961, Dr. Smith followed Dr. Khorana to the University of Wisconsin, where he took on a new academic post in Madison. Dr. Smith would spend only about one additional year as a postdoc under Dr. Khorana in Wisconsin. Then, the Smiths would move back to Vancouver, to the Fisheries Research Board of Canada, where Dr. Smith would take on a new position as leader of the Chemistry Division within the Vancouver Laboratory.

Oligonucleotides are short chains of DNA molecules. The ribo-oligonucleotides are short chains of RNA molecules. In Dr. Khorana's laboratory, Dr. Smith had learned how to synthesize these types of short-chain ribonucleotides.

Biological systems within living cells use these short RNA chains to prime the synthesis of DNA. Without these RNA primers, DNA synthesis, called replication, could not proceed. But the ribo-oligonucleotides could be used to feed bacteria in specific sequences to learn what amino acids they synthesized in response. These short RNA molecules were further useful for deciphering the genetic code.

In later years, these short stretches of RNA chains would be used as probes to target specific DNA sequences, making RNA-DNA hybrid molecules for detecting genes that underwent expression to make new proteins for specific functional purposes by cells. Other RNA chains could be used to bind the DNA encoding specified genes for the purpose of inhibiting their expression, perhaps even using them for therapeutic purposes.

5. *In the autumn of 1975– Smith began working with (ta-da!) Fred Sanger– assisting with the Escherichia coli phage ΦX174. We have previously written about Fred Sanger– but a bit of a summary about Sanger– and then please summarize the work the two of them did!*

Indeed we expressly addressed the famous Dr. Sanger in our first book *The Inventions and Discoveries of the World's Most Famous Scientists*, published in 2018.

Dr. Frederick (Fred) Sanger has the distinction of having earned two Nobel Prizes! For his first Nobel, granted in 1958, Sanger's work dealt with the sequence determination of amino acid chains along a protein molecule, namely that of insulin. Sanger's second Nobel was bestowed in 1980 for his discovery towards elucidating the sequences of nucleotides along a DNA molecule, a process also known as DNA sequencing.

In 1975 Dr. Smith went on a sabbatical leave from the University of British Columbia to spend approximately a year in Dr. Sanger's laboratory, which was located at the Medical Research Council Laboratory in Cambridge, England. The primary purpose of Dr. Smith's sabbatical to Cambridge was to learn the new so-called Sanger technique for sequencing DNA.

After he arrived at the Sanger laboratory in the fall semester of 1975, Dr. Smith was given a choice of projects to focus on, and he chose a topic that interested Dr. Sanger. At the time, Dr. Sanger and his colleagues were interested in determining the DNA genome sequence of the bacteriophage called ΦX174, pronounced phi-X-174, which is a virus that specifically targets the *Escherichia coli* bacterium. The ΦX174 phage DNA is single-stranded, rather than harboring the more traditional double-stranded DNA version like that of humans and many other organisms. Dr. Smith chose to help the Sanger lab by participating in the sequence determination of the phage's genomic DNA.

With Dr. Smith's extra pair of hands participating in the DNA sequencing work, the Sanger laboratory was able to finish the entire genome sequence of the ΦX174 phage. It had been an unprecedented and labor-intensive process.

The sequencing effort involved making use of ΦX174 phage's single-stranded genome as a template, a short DNA primer, also called an oligonucleotide, of which Dr. Smith had been an expert in producing, plus DNA polymerase enzyme, and, importantly, a number of so-called chain terminators, which were altered nucleotides that stopped the DNA elongation process, making shortened stretches of DNA products of varying lengths.

After the sequencing reactions were complete, the newly formed DNA chains of various lengths were run on an electrophoretic gel, to separate the DNA fragments based on their sizes and to be read along their overlapping chains. The order of the nucleotide bases could be determined along the DNA molecule by reading the gels.

This was the basis of the Sanger method for DNA sequencing. The new sequencing technique became also known as the chain-termination method.

The phage ΦX174 genome turned out to have 5,386 nucleotide bases along its single-stranded DNA genome molecule. The work was published, starting in February of 1977, with Dr. Smith included as a co-author along with Dr. Sanger and 7 additional co-authors. Later, in 1978, the group, with Dr. Smith still included, would publish a more finely-tuned phage sequence, plus the amino acid sequences of about 10 of the ΦX174 virally encoded proteins.

It had all been ground-breaking work at the time. It was, after all, the very first complete genome to be sequenced!

6. *Interestingly enough, some say Smith was the first B.C. (British Columbia) winner of the Nobel Prize – is this accurate?*

It is not *entirely* accurate. Though Dr. Smith was indeed a Canadian citizen living in British Columbia, having taken the oath in 1963, and a 1993 Nobel Laureate in Chemistry, it can be argued that Dr. Har Gobind Khorana, who had been an investigator at the University of British Columbia between the years 1952 and 1960, had already become a physiology or medicine Nobel Laureate in 1968; and U. British Columbia visiting investigator Dr. Han Dehmelt had become a physics Nobel Laureate in 1989.

In any case, garnering a Nobel, whether first, second, or last, regardless of geographical location, nevertheless signifies an outstanding achievement for anyone. Dr. Smith's invention of artificially altering the base sequences of DNA to just about any other desirable set of DNA sequences has forever revolutionized the field of molecular biology and many other areas of biological study. It is anticipated that Dr. Smith's site-directed mutagenesis technique will no doubt continue to be with us biomedical scientists for the duration of the unforeseeable future.

7. *As usual, there are some funny stories about Smith and how he came to his research – apparently he was chatting with some American scientist named Clyde Hutchison, having coffee in some British research institute – when – what happened?*

Indeed, the idea for a Nobel arrived upon Dr. Smith over a cup of coffee and a conversation with colleague Dr. Clyde A. Hutchison, III. Dr. Smith had met Dr. Hutchison in 1975 while on sabbatical in Dr. Sanger's lab at the MRC in Cambridge. Indeed, Dr. Hutchinson had been on the ΦX174 phage genome project with Sanger and a co-author of the seminal genome papers.

Dr. Hutchinson had been working on repairing mutations in DNA using very long stretches of DNA. During coffee at Cambridge, he explained to Dr. Smith how his DNA mutation-fixing procedure was rather inefficient. Dr. Smith then said to Dr. Hutchinson that he (Smith) was working with shorter DNA stretches in order to purify and separate longer strands of DNA.

According to legend, it is at this point that Dr. Smith realized his Nobel Prize-winning idea.

Dr. Smith reasoned that short DNA chains, his famous oligonucleotides, could be made, but with minor specific errors in the base sequences within them. They could probably also anneal to larger template DNA, molecules of which could serve as targets to be mutagenized, and the mutated oligonucleotides could still bind to the more extended templates, forming mismatches in the corresponding base-pairing between the large (DNA templates) and small (mutated oligonucleotides) hybrids of DNA. The annealed mutated oligonucleotides would harbor the desired mutations, and they could be synthesized in any mutated based sequences so desired.

They had a DNA template already in mind: the ΦX174 bacteriophage. You'll recall that it is already single-stranded. So Drs. Smith and Hutchinson wouldn't have to denature the DNA to separate any strands from each other. Their mutated oligonucleotides (known as DNA primers in today's parlance) would then anneal to the phage genomic DNA, complete with their mismatches!

Dr. Smith could then invoke the then well-known DNA polymerase I enzyme, extracted from *E. coli*, to work on the phage DNA template that was primed with a mutated oligonucleotide primer, and make new DNA out of it. The DNA polymerase I step makes double-stranded DNA, one strand unmutated, the original template, and the newly built strand, which harbors the desired mutated version. They added a virally T-4 encoded DNA ligase enzyme to connect the newly formed ends of the mutated DNA strands. The two strands are completed, and they somehow separated from each other and isolated. Continued replication would convert the one single mutated strand into the desired double-duplex stranded DNA. The mutation could then be found on both strands.

It took a while (several years) to iron out the rough edges and make the mutagenic invention more efficient, but they succeeded in mutagenizing the *E gene* codon named am3, which is an amber mutation that encodes a premature stop codon. They fixed the broken *gene E* to convert the aberrant stop codon into an amino acid coding codon, specifying a tryptophan residue. The wild-type *E gene* (or *gene E*) encodes a functional lysis protein E. The function of the repaired E gene product, lysin E, could readily be measured. If the lysin protein worked, then the oligonucleotide site-directed mutagenesis invention worked because the desired mutation, i.e., guanine changed to adenine in the codon number 587 of the *E gene*, consequently restored the codon to specify the tryptophan and make functional lysin E protein. The first Nobel Prize-winning site-specific (i.e., site-directed) mutagenesis had been successfully performed!

They confirmed the relevant DNA alterations using the Sanger Method to sequence both repaired and unrepaired DNA molecules. They then published the work in September of 1978 in *The Journal of Biological Chemistry*, after the manuscript had been already rejected by the prestigious *Proceedings of the National Academy of Science* and rejected later by the equally-prestigious journal called *Cell*.

8. *Scientists and geneticists can mutate a gene in three ways – and they are called substitution, deletion, and addition. I have heard and studied many deletions – but am not familiar with substitutions and additions – Can you clarify?*

A substitution mutation involves replacing a particular base with another (different) base. It's the same principle as a substitute teacher who fills in for a regular teacher. As shown in the figure, the A in codon GTA for valine has been replaced by T, to make GTT. In this case, the substitution point mutation does not change the amino acid—it remains still a valine. Thus, the substitution is referred to as silent.

In the second case, the substitution mutation involves changing the CCC codon for proline to ACC, which now codes for threonine. In this case, the C in CCC has been substituted with A to make the ACC. In effect, a proline has been substitute by threonine. The substitution mutation, at this point, is called missense.

In the non-sense point substitution mutation shown in the figure, the C in TAC codon for tyrosine is substituted by G to make the TAG codon, which now codes for a stop codon, meaning that the protein will be prematurely terminated or truncated. Thus, non-sense substitution mutations specify premature stop codon, quite often making shorter than usual versions of proteins, which are considered aberrant by a cell and consequently destroyed.

Likewise, in an addition (also called insertion) mutation, additional nucleotide bases are inserted into the DNA chain. On the other hand, a deletion mutation removes a nucleotide base (or perhaps several bases) from a DNA chain. In either case, whether addition or deletion mutations, often, the remaining sequences are offset by one or more of the added or deleted bases, resulting in a shifting of the codons downstream of the DNA modification. Such a situation is referred to as a reading-frame shift. The codons that are read by the ribosomes are shifted altogether, quite often making completely different codons. In many of these cases, the read-frame mutations introduce premature stop codons, making shorter aberrant polypeptides, which are also quite often destroyed.

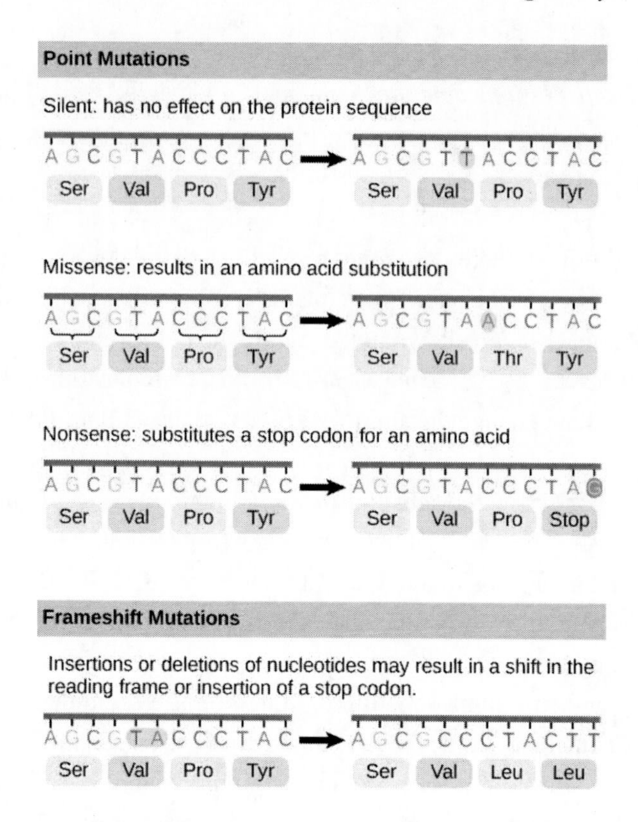

9. *Before his death, he predicted a change in the way we would do research. Tell us about this.*

In 1996, Dr. Smith gave an interview in which he made the prediction to which you are referring. He was speaking of the power of genomics. He said back then that once the genome sequences are known, the focus of research will primarily be devoted to examining the essential parts of the genomes and in identifying and understanding the functions of the various genetic elements of the locations along the genome.

During the time of Dr. Smith's interview, the race between two camps who were devoted to mapping and sequencing the entire human genome was in full swing. In 2003, when the human genome project was completed and, and the two groups had published together, a commentary had attributed Dr. Smith as having been accurate in his prediction.

Indeed, the field of genomics has led to a greater understanding of many elements of the genomes for a multitude of living organisms. Further, genomics has led to the development of bioinformatics, which is necessary for handling the immense quantities of sequence data and in making predictions of gene and protein structures and functions. The use of ever-faster computers and supercomputers will no doubt be of tremendous importance in making use of genomic data, meta-genomic data, and evolutionary relationships between genes, proteins, genomes, as living taxa, as well as in the various areas of biomedical sciences.

10. Michael Smith died around the turn of the century– the year 2000– leaving behind a tremendous legacy. What would you say are his main accomplishments?

The tremendous importance of Dr. Smith's site-specific mutagenesis for DNA is remarkable and cannot be overstated. The invention crosses many disparate fields of molecular-based studies. It speaks to molecular biology itself, genomics, cancer biology, proteomics, biochemistry, medicine, clinical therapy, gene therapy, genetic disease, biotechnology, cell biology, physiology, signal transduction, ecology, genetics, immunology, microbiology, gene editing, neuroscience, biomedical science, etc.

Another accomplishment includes Dr. Smith's involvement in the development of protein engineering. His invention had direct consequences in the establishment of the investigative study for molding proteins into desired structures and functions. Towards this, he devoted a great deal of time in his later years to the field of recombinant proteins. He worked on the useful application of recombinant DNA technology for advancing medicine, such as human and animal medicine, and in biological engineering.

For those who are more auditory or visual learners- or who enjoy YouTube Learning here are some sources:

https://www.youtube.com/watch?v=AznzHqwIa7U
https://www.youtube.com/watch?v=-CkUKLHj2a8

Some excellent mini-lectures and additional information and wonderful stories can be found at:

http://www.science.ca/scientists/scientistprofile.php?pID=18

Chapter 23

YOUYOU TU– ANTI-MALARIAL MEDICINES

1. *Youyou Tu is a Chinese Nobel Prize winner– where and when was she born and what led her into science?*

Youyou Tu was born on the 30th day of December, in the year 1930, in the city of Ningbo, China, located in the eastern province of Zhejiang. Incidentally, her first name is Youyou, and her family surname is Tu. In the Chinese tradition, however, the personal names are frequently written as in the opposite order, i.e., Tu Youyou.

Her early education was an excellent one, having had the opportunity to attend the best private educational institutions in the province. At the age of 6 years, she was enrolled in a private school called Ningbo Chongde Primary School, starting in 1936 until about 1941. At that time, she moved to a private middle school called Ningbo Qizheng, till about 1945, when she attended the private school called Ningbo Yougjiang Girl's School, for about a year.

Her interest in pursuing the study of science was brought about by a terrible illness that she had suffered as a teenager. Tu had contracted the Great Consumption, also known as tuberculosis or TB, an infectious ailment caused by a bacterium called *Mycobacterium tuberculosis*. The cough-laden illness has been called "consumption" because it consumes the patient.

Although she was home-schooled because of her illness, the episode, nevertheless, resulted in Tu having missed a great deal of private school, about two years' worth. After Tu's convalescence from TB, she resumed attendance at high school, enrolling in the private institution called Ningbo Xiaoshi High School, from 1948 to 1950, when she moved to Ningbo High School, till about 1951.

Having survived the terrible ordeal for years, Tu had made a life-changing decision to pursue the study of biomedical research for her lifelong career. The illness had convinced Tu that if she were to acquire biomedical science skills, then she could play an important positive role in the health of others, possibly by discovering new medicines.

2. *Now what led her to study malaria – and what parts of the world has it impacted. Plasmodium falciparum – how is this related to malaria – and where exactly does the word malaria come from?*

After her high school graduation and as a result of her decision to study biomedical research for her medical profession, Youyou Tu studied pharmaceutical sciences in the School of Pharmacy, at the Beijing (Peking) Medical University, taking her degree in 1955. In 1952, a year after she entered the Pharmacy Department at the medical school, the institution had been known as Peking University; and in 1955, when she graduated, it had been changed to Beijing Medical College. She then moved to the so-called China Academy of Traditional Chinese Medicine, focusing her studies on Chinese herbal medicines.

Malaria is a serious infectious disease caused by certain species of the protozoan genus called *Plasmodium*; the term malaria arises from Italian *mala aria*, meaning bad air. Medically speaking, the *Plasmodium falciparum* and *Plasmodium vivax* appear to be two of the most important infectious agents of malaria, being prevalent in tropical, sub-tropical (*P. falciparum*), and temperate regions of the world, especially in South America and Southeast Asia (*P. vivax*). Other important species include *Plasmodium ovale* (tropical Africa, plus Asia and South America), *Plasmodium malariae* (sub-tropical and temperate regions), *and Plasmodium knowlesi* (Southeast Asia, especially in Malaysia).

These *Plasmodium* blood parasites are transmitted to humans by the bites of mosquitoes, such as those from the genus *Anopheles*. When the human host is bitten by the *Anopheles,* it spits its saliva that's laden with the *Plasmodium* protozoan in the patient. The *Plasmodium* then moves via the blood to the liver where it multiplies inside the red blood cells of the patient. As the *Plasmodium* develops, it forms a so-called ring stage, which can form the basis of diagnosis using a microscope and examining a blood sample from the patient.

During the 1960s, the conventional treatment of malaria, chloroquine, had been compromised by the development of the chloroquine-resistant variants of the *Plasmodium falciparum,* leading to treatment failures and the resurgence of the malaria cases. After the implementation of new research programs in the mid-1960s by the U.S. and China, the programs of which were aimed at finding new anti-malarial medicines, thousands of candidate drugs were systematically tested, and no effective drugs were found.

It was at this point in the history of biomedical science, in 1969, that 39-year-old Tu, then still considered a young scientist, was appointed by the director of the China Academy of Traditional Chinese Medicine to run the program titled Project 523, an endeavor devoted to a systematic search of traditional Chinese medicines for potential antimalarial drugs. The new biomedical research effort ultimately led to her discovering the Nobel Prize-worthy anti-malaria medicine from sample number 191, containing artemisinin (or Qinghaosu, in Chinese), from an herb of the *Artemisia* family (or Qinghao, in Chinese).

3. *Apparently, ancient Chinese texts provided some background. What do we know about this?*

The field of traditional Chinese herbal medicine pertaining to malaria goes back thousands of years. Such ancient Chinese medicine involved carefully documented records, including published books and treatises.

The ancient literature on the topic of Chinese medicine is extensive.

One of the earliest known publications is the ancient classic book titled *Zhou Li* published sometime within the Zhou Dynasty of China, which lasted from 1046 to 256 B.C. Another set of classic works, such as the *Prescription for Universal Relief* and the famous *Malignant Malaria Guide,* go back to the Ming Dynasty, between 1368 and 1644 A.D., and the Qing Dynasty, between 1644 and 1911, respectively. Many of ancient Chinese works of literature included recipes for treatments, complete with testimonials by ancient Chinese physicians, personally attesting to the efficacies of their remedies.

In starting her research program in Project 523 on the systematic search for malaria treatments, Tu had evaluated the ancient Chinese texts and coalesced a list containing over 2,000 recipes for potential herbal-, animal-, and mineral-based remedies. The generation of the anti-malaria medicine list, consisting of candidates from the ancient Chinese medical literature, took three months.

Further concentrating the approximately 2,000 recipes into those primarily dealing with malaria, Tu then shortened the list to 640 anti-malaria candidates. As head of Project 523, she included the recipes for each of the candidates into a brochure titled *Antimalarial Collections of Recipes and Prescriptions*, sending copies, in mid-1969, of the brochure to the heads of scientific laboratories whose work focused on malaria research.

In one of the ancient texts called *A Handbook of Prescriptions for Emergencies*, written by Ge Hong, Tu had come across a passage praising the effectiveness of the so-called Qinghao, the sweet wormwood herbal plant, as a good fever reducer during bouts of malaria. The recipe called for placing a handful of the sweet wormwood, the Qinghao, within two liters of water, wringing out the resulting plant juice and consuming all of it.

4. *Sweet wormwood– how does this fit into the big picture?*

The term sweet wormwood is one of the common names given to the plant from which Tu's Nobel Prize-winning anti-malarial medicine, artemisinin, is extracted. The scientific name for the herbal plant is *Artemisia annua* L. (the "L." referring to the Carl Linnaeus system of classification). Other common names include sweet Annie, annual wormwood, and qing hao.

The sweet wormwood plant has been used by the Chinese, having brewed its leaves as a bitter tea for over 2 millennia. The plant has also been used since ancient times to reduce fevers, including those fevers brought about by malaria. Interestingly, the herbal sweet wormwood tea has been used historically for treating dizziness, chills, headaches, inflammation, nosebleeds, and gastrointestinal disorders. Externally, the sweet wormwood was used as an application on boils and abscesses. In recent times, the plant herb has been used as a flavor in European beverages.

The focus of the sweet wormwood plant changed to address its efficacy against malaria with the more modern biomedical studies of Tu, having published her findings in 1972.

5. *While early research was conducted on animals– apparently, she tested the drug on herself– what do we know about this?*

During her studies, Tu had recalled how the recipe from Ge Hong's ancient Chinese text had called for simply placing the plant leaves of

Artemisia annua L. into two liters of water, squeezing out the resulting juice and then drinking all of it. The preparation was to be used precisely for the purpose of treating malarial fevers, a common symptom of the disease. Furthermore, Tu ingeniously noticed that the preparation did not call for tea brewing. Thus, she astutely deduced that the heat from the boiling process might destroy the active principle contained in the *Artemisia annua* L. herb. Furthermore, Tu's genius lies in the fact that she noticed that the ancient text called for wringing the herbal leaves, predicting that the active anti-malarial principle must be contained with these leaves.

Therefore, Tu's experimental design involved the avoidance of heat in order to preserve the bioactivity harbored within the leaves of the *Artemisia annua* L. plant. Her design further focused on separating the leaves (predicted to contain the bioactive agent) from the plant stems (predicted to lack the bioactive agent). Using this protocol, Tu carefully prepared the plant extracts from various herbs, including the *Artemisia annua* L.

Next, Tu and her research team tested their various herbal plant extracts on rodents with malaria. They measured whether any of their samples would show any inhibition of the *Plasmodium* protozoa in the rodents. In the historical experiment of October 4, in 1971, Tu found that their sample number 191 completely inhibited the malaria parasites in the rodents!

Next, in late 1971 and early 1972, they tested an acidic and a neutral extract of the *Artemisia annua* L. herb on malaria-infected monkeys. The Tu research team found that the neutral version of the sweet wormwood extract maintained its effectiveness against malaria in the laboratory animals. Tu presented the results from these historic experiments at a conference in Nanjing, China, in March of 1972. The profound findings were widely disseminated.

Back in the laboratory after the successful conference presentation, Tu and her team conducted an equally startling experiment!

The shocking new experiment came about due to conflicting data regarding toxicity studies in test animals. Theoretically, it would have taken at least another year to resolve the conflicting issue on whether the herbal remedy was too toxic for humans. With the new malaria season looming near, potentially hundreds of thousands of new cases, if not millions, countless millions were on the verge of acquiring the infection.

In order to resolve the toxicity question in an expedited manner, Tu asked for permission to take the plant extracts herself, and she was granted that permission! She was wholeheartedly given the go-ahead to take the extracts!

In the month of July, in 1972, Tu and two of her laboratory personnel from her research team were voluntarily hospitalized, and the trio of humans took the extracts, on purpose! After close monitoring of the human volunteers for a week by the hospital staff, no side effects were noticed. Thus, the herbal extracts were next provided to an additional five human volunteers, and this time the dosages were enhanced!

The testing of the Qinghao herbal extract by Tu and her colleagues was not entirely without precedent. In traditional Chinese medical history, an ancient physician by the name of Dr. Shen Nong had recorded how he took many of the Chinese herbal medicines himself! He had claimed to have tasted hundreds of Chinese herbs on his own. The dosages of the Qinghao in the ancient Chinese texts, used for thousands of years, were much lower than those amounts contained within Tu's modern Qinghao preparations.

Such highly concentrated amounts of the bioactive principles inherent in her laboratory-based Qinghao extracts had not been tested before. One impetus in conducting the unprecedented experiment, however, was the fact that Dr. Shen Nong had tasted hundreds of herbs himself. Tu's feeling on the safety issue was: why couldn't they take more-concentrated Qinghao herbs, just as well?

6. Artemisinin and dihydroartemisinin– how are these two related?

In mid-1972, Tu and her research team began experiments that were devoted to the purification of the bioactive agent, the active ingredient of the Qinghao extract, which probably harbored many individual ingredients. First, the Tu team were successful in isolating crystals from a few of these ingredients, using a special biochemical tool called silica gel column chromatography. A single compound, called artemisinin, i.e., Qinghaosu, was isolated. See Figure 1.

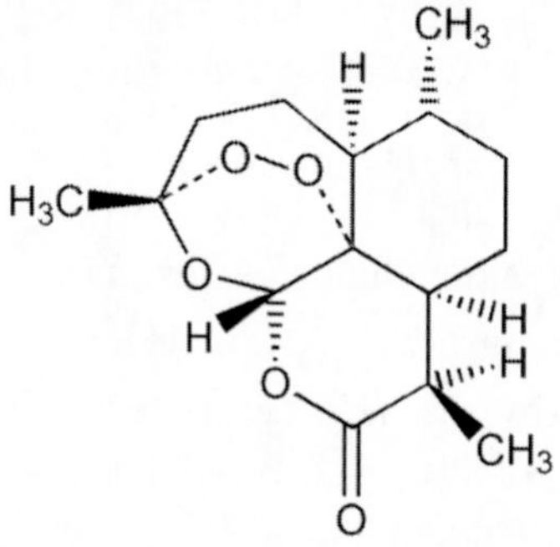

Figure 1. Artemisinin.

Clinical trials of the artemisinin in tablet form against the dreaded malaria were less than desirable. The tablets did not release the artemisinin in therapeutic amounts. New tablets were made, but the malaria season was already at an end, too late to make an effect dent against that year's malaria numbers, in 1973.

At about this same time, a new compound, called dihydroartemisinin, had been chemically derived from the original artemisinin by the Tu laboratory. The new compound differs from the old version in that the dihydroartemisinin harbors a hydroxyl group (–OH) where a carboxyl group (C═O) had been in the artemisinin. See Figure 2.

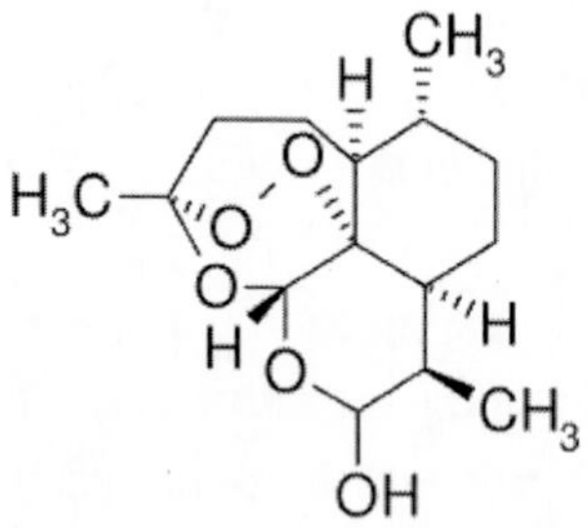

Figure 2. Dihydroartemisinin.

The dihydroartemisinin was actually demonstrated in the Tu laboratory to be more effective against the rodent form of malaria and in lower doses. In fact, dihydroartemisinin was shown to be ten times better than the artemisinin. To make matters better, the dihydroartemisinin structure, with its dedicated hydroxyl group, was less prone to the development of malarial resistance during medical treatments. Thus, both artemisinin and dihydroartemisinin have been used and studied over the many years since their discoveries by Tu.

7. What have I neglected to ask about this Nobel Prize winner?

Youyou Tu's published research findings had been given little attention in the Western world. In fact, for many years, up until the 2000s, traditional Chinese herbal medicine has been given a poor reputation by non-Chinese investigators. More recently, with many new modern studies of the Chinese remedies undergoing scientific scrutiny in peer-reviewed journals, their promise as medical treatments in Western biomedicine has been given scientific prominence. With the surprising bestowment of the Nobel to a key biomedical scientist who has been prominent in the Chinese herbal medicine field, perhaps this scientific and medical research area has officially been recognized as a *bona fide* field of modern biomedical science.

For future study:

https://www.youtube.com/watch?v=4Dh9lUbLTX0

Chapter 24

HAROLD VARMUS – VIRAL ONCOGENES AND CANCER

1. *Harold Varmus was born in New York City and seemed to have shifted from discipline to discipline. What can you tell us about his early academic endeavors?*

Dr. Harold Eliot Varmus would share the 1989 Nobel Prize in Medicine or Physiology with John Michael Bishop for their discovery pertaining to the oncogenesis in healthy cells by oncogenes from retroviruses. Varmus was born in Oceanside, New York, in the U.S. on the 18th day of the month of December in the year 1939, just prior to the entry of the U.S. into the Second World War. His parents were Beatrice and Frank Varmus, both of whom were believed to be of Jewish ancestry and second-generation immigrants. Beatrice Varmus was a social worker in the field of psychiatry, and Frank Varmus was a general physician and medical officer.

Harold Varmus graduated from Freeport High School in 1957. That same year Varmus enrolled in Amherst College, where he had initially taken pre-medicine courses, upon the advice of his father. Unfortunately, he had earned a low grade in a pre-medicine course, organic chemistry, taught by Professor Robert Whitney. The poor chemistry mark (he received a letter grade of C!) made Varmus feel as if medicine was not necessarily the right career choice for him. Instead, he chose to major in studies pertaining to literature, serving as editor-in-chief of the college newspaper and hoping to become an English Lit professor eventually. He, thus, took his undergraduate B.A. degree in English Literature in 1961, with high honors, *magna cum laude*. His senior undergraduate thesis had been based on the novels of Charles Dickens.

After college graduation, Varmus entered graduate school as a Wilson Fellow at Harvard University, concentrating his studies in English. His graduate thesis was geared towards poetry, and he took his M.A. degree in the field of English in 1962 from Harvard.

While in the midst of his first year of graduate school, however, Varmus had a dream that changed the direction of his career. He dreamt that he was already an English Lit professor who missed giving one of his lectures because of an illness. In the dream, his students had consequently rejoiced about his absence from the lecture hall. Because of his desire to feel needed in his career, he chose to go back to the study of medicine, as he had astutely deduced that as a physician if he were to become ill and miss work, his patients would have the opposite reaction of rejoicing—they would be upset about his absence, and this made Varmus feel as if he would be absolutely needed.

Another factor that influenced Varmus to reconsider medicine once again was the written works of one of his professors at Amherst, Dr. Douglas Bush, whose basic tenet was that fine literature had been written by individuals who were living in the world outside of academia and working in other professions. Thus, Varmus found another compelling motivation for his choice of becoming a physician—he could still enjoy literature!

After taking his M.A., Varmus applied to Harvard Medical School and was rejected by the prestigious medical institution. His interview with Harvard's dean of medical school admissions, Dr. Perry Culver, had been a sobering one. The characteristic "immature" had been bandied about during the meeting with dean Culver. Interestingly, four years earlier, his Nobel co-Laureate J. Michael Bishop had also sent his application to medical school at Harvard and had been accepted, graduating with his M.D. degree during the same year that Varmus had tried to gain acceptance in 1962.

In any case, Varmus had also applied to the famous College of Physicians and Surgeons (known as P&S), which was part of Columbia University, in New York. This interview had gone better at P&S than that at Harvard. Instead, Varmus related in later years that his interviewer Dr. David Seegal, had been more welcoming, and Varmus had been eagerly accepted. He recalled later that he took medical courses in hematology, microbiology, and immunology. He had been especially intrigued by certain aspects within molecular biology, such as the nature of the genetic code and genetic diseases. In 1966, Dr. Varmus took his M.D. degree from Columbia's P&S.

Dr. Varmus spent a short three months in Bareilly, India, initially desiring to gain experience abroad in the practice of medicine in the clinical arena, as a result of having been inspired by a course in parasitology. But the experience abroad was not to his liking, and he instead felt that conducting basic biomedical research was his biggest strength. Meanwhile, he served as a medical house officer during his residency program at Presbyterian Hospital at Columbia University, starting in 1966 until 1968. After the completion of this clinical-based work, Dr. Varmus would conduct biomedical research on a full-time basis. It began a scientific journey that would lead to the Nobel.

2. Donald Ganem and Varmus worked on Hepatitis B. What did they find?

Dr. Varmus had hired Dr. Don Ganem as a postdoctoral fellow in the 1970s, a few years after Varmus had started a faculty position at the University of California that was located in San Francisco (UCSF). After Dr. Ganem finished his postdoctoral training, he later returned to UCSF in the 1980s as a research faculty, and the two investigators continued to collaborate, working on the replication of hepatitis virus B.

Known also as HBV, hepatitis B virus infection has been associated with liver cancer. The mature HBV virion has a lipid-based envelope and had a genome consisting of a double-stranded form of DNA. Drs. Varmus and Ganem conducted a considerable amount of collaborative investigations, starting with their first paper published in 1982 and eventually publishing over 20 scientific papers together on the topic.

Initially, Drs. Ganem and Varmus focused on the hepatitis virus that affected ground squirrels. This virus also has a DNA-based genome, and the investigators examined various aspects of its virology. For instance, they studied the viral infection process in squirrels, the culturing of the virus in the lab, the viral genome sequence, the mode of its transmission, the immune response to the virus, the packing of the viral genome into its capsid, the assembly of the mature virion, the viral genomic recombination process that occurred during infection, and viral oncogenesis.

They also began studies of the human hepatitis B virus, starting in the mid-1980s. Along this vein, Drs. Varmus and Ganem worked with viral mutants, which altered the surfaces of the viruses, making them sort of resistant to the binding by human albumin in the serum and thus possibly avoiding some of the effects of the immune system.

Their next set of investigations on the human hepatitis B virus produced a startling result, and it changed the textbooks in microbiology and virology. Drs. Ganem and Varmus discovered that during the replication of the DNA genome in the HBV, it first went through the synthesis of a single-stranded RNA intermediate version of the viral genome. Next, they found that the viral RNA intermediate was then startlingly used as a template to synthesize double-stranded viral DNA! In essence, they discovered a reverse transcription mechanism for a non-retroviral virus.

The concept of reverse transcription had already been discovered by 1975 Nobel Laureates David Baltimore and Howard Temin, the former of whom has been discussed in another chapter in this book. The work of Varmus and Ganem was, nevertheless, a surprising discovery because it involved another virus that was ultimately unrelated to the so-called retroviruses, members of which included the notorious human immunodeficiency virus (HIV) and human T-cell leukemia viruses (HTLVs). Both HIV and HTLVs are dangerous pathogens, causing loss of the immune system and the so-called white blood cell cancer leukemia, respectively. Instead, Drs. Varmus and Ganem found a retroviral mechanism for genome replication for a member within a totally different family of viruses, the Hepadnaviridae family in which the human hepatitis B virus was the member.

3. *He worked with Y.W. Kan on hemoglobinopathies – I am familiar with hemoglobin, and obviously, pathology is involved – but why is this research relevant?*

Indeed, Dr. Varmus worked with Yuet Wai Kan, publishing several papers together, in the mid-1970s. As your question alludes, they studied a type of hemoglobinopathy, which refers to certain blood diseases in humans where the red blood cells are primarily affected. Such hemoglobinopathies may involve abnormal hemoglobin or a lack of it. If such conditions include a missing or low amount of hemoglobin, then such hemoglobinopathies are referred to as thalassemias.

In the case of their work together, they found that in an ailment known as beta- or β-thalassemia, the human RNA that encodes the β-chain of the blood hemoglobin was non-functional. In studying the alpha- or α-thalassemia, they found that DNA-based gene encoding the α-chain of hemoglobin was deleted, resulting in a missing α-chain protein of the hemoglobin. Thus, this result produced a lower than usual amount of intact hemoglobin molecules in the red blood cells of such human thalassemia patients.

This work was important because it provided two distinctive molecular explanations for these genetic diseases in humans. One such mechanism, in the β-thalassemia patients, pointed to a defect in the RNA that's typically translated into the β-chain of hemoglobin. The defective RNA could not serve as a template for protein synthesis, thus effectively reducing the blood concentrations of normal hemoglobin. The second faulty molecular mechanism, which was discovered in the α-thalassemia patients, involved a genetic mutation in the DNA of the human genome.

Both findings also provided a means for the diagnosis of these two types of hemoglobinopathies. In addition, the work was notable as it offered a new line of investigation for potential treatment, such as replacement therapy or even gene therapy. Lastly, on a fundamental level, the thalassemia work led the way to further protein structural analysis of hemoglobin itself.

4. *Again, collaborating with others seemed to be his forte– he was on a sabbatical and worked with Mike Fried in his laboratory at the Imperial Cancer Research Fund in London. What came out of THIS collaboration?*

Dr. Varmus had been an established research investigator at UCSF while on his 1-year sabbatical during the late 1970s in the London-based laboratory of Dr. Fried. In his Nobel Lecture, delivered on the 8th of December, in 1989, Dr. Varmus spoke of his work in Dr. Fried's laboratory. Drs. Varmus and Fried noticed three exciting facts regarding the retroviruses and transposons.

First, the investigators realized that the DNA structures of so-called proviral forms of the retroviruses and of certain unrelated mobile genetic elements had similar features in their nature. The term provirus refers to the fact that the genome of a virus has somehow inserted itself into the genome of the host that's infected by the virus. The expression mobile genetic element refers to the so-called transposon, which are pieces of DNA that move about, for example, between various locations within or between individual genomes.

Second, Drs. Fried and Varmus learned that in the course of transposition, i.e., during the movements of the transposons from one locus to another, the mobile process involved synthesis from an RNA template of a double-stranded DNA intermediate that was then used to insert into a new location elsewhere in a genome.

Third, they realized that in the host cells that had been infected with the retroviruses and conducted transposition themselves did not appear to make new viruses. This observation was apparently due to the cellular genomic integration of the retrovirus genome, a developmental stage of the infection called a provirus.

Taken together, based on these three observations, they formulated the hypothesis that, similar to the transposons, the retroviruses could also perform insertion mutations in the genomes of host cells that they infect and undergo the proviral stage. The provirus in which the retroviral genome had inserted or moved about could interrupt the genetic machinery in the genomic location that the virus entered itself into. The DNA of the genome had possibly been mutated by inserting a new piece of DNA, perhaps retroviral DNA, into the cell's genome! The process is known as insertional mutagenesis.

The experimental design that was used to test their hypothesis was rather ingenious. The experiments were conducted by Dr. Varmus in Dr. Fried's laboratory with the help of colleagues Dr. Suzanne Ortiz and Ms. Nancy Quintrell. They first employed host cells that had been grown in culture from rats and that had been infected with the Rous sarcoma virus (RSV), which had been discovered in 1910 by Dr. Peyton Rous as a virus that caused cancer. In the experiments of Dr. Varmus and co-workers, the RSV genome had integrated into the rat cell genome, forming a proviral integrated state of the RSV. Next, they infected these proviral-RSV rat cells with another integrating type of virus, called mouse leukemia virus (MLV). Then, the investigators searched the rat cells for MLV-infected clones by determining which of these rat cell clones had lost their RSV-associated characteristics, such as cellular transformation.

Surprisingly, they found two, out of many clones they had studied, that contained an insertion of the proviral MLV genome into the RSV proviral insertion site of the rat cell genome! The MLV insertion mutation was at a place where the *v-src* gene from RSV had been located within the rat genome, and the MLV-insert destroyed the gene expression feature of the *v-src* gene. The experimental results demonstrated, thus, that retroviruses such as MLV or RSV could be used to perform artificial insertion mutagenesis in the genomes of host cells and thus destroy target genes. The discovery had the potential for use as a way to inactivate desirable genes of interest in order to examine the functions of the products expressed by the mutagenized genes.

5. *Again, working with others, he investigated glucocorticoid action (with Gordon Tomkins and Keith Yamamoto). Now, what exactly was he looking at, and who were these collaborators? He must have loved to work with others!*

Indeed, Dr. Varmus was an astute investigative collaborator who worked with many biomedical scientists. According to PubMed, Dr. Varmus published one paper with Dr. Tomkins and eight articles with Dr. Yamamoto.

All three investigators co-authored one paper that was published in the prestigious journal plainly called *Cell*, in 1975. In that article, the trio and two other authors examined the effect of the glucocorticoid molecule called dexamethasone. This glucocorticoid is an artificially synthesized steroid that has been used to treat severe cases of inflammation. Dexamethasone also serves to block the pituitary-adrenal axis by preventing the action of corticotropin-releasing hormone, thus reducing the release of adrenocorticotropic hormone (ACTH) and β-endorphin from the pituitary gland, near the brain.

Dr. Varmus and his colleagues took cells from mice with mammary tumors and propagated the cancer cells artificially in laboratory cultures. The mice cancer cells had been induced with an oncogenic retrovirus called mouse mammary tumor virus (MMTV). To these virus-induced cancer cells, the dexamethasone was added. They observed an increase in the levels of viral RNA molecules inside the cancer cells. Apparently, the synthesis of the viral RNA occurred independently of the cellular machinery that makes either DNA or protein inside host cells. They speculated that the effects of the dexamethasone was at the level of regulation of the cellular membrane-bound receptor to which glucocorticoids bind. The dexamethasone could then be used to prepare large quantities of retroviral RNA for further study. It also provided a unique opportunity to study the relationship between virally-induced tumor growth and hormonal regulation.

Later work, in 1978, conducted together by Drs. Yamato and Varmus had been focused on examining the genomic structures of the MMTV, determining whether circular or linear genome structures had formed during infection. They also were able to map where specific deletion mutations had occurred when the genome assumed a circular formation. Another study had entailed using the glucocorticoids to conduct an evaluation of the RNA synthesis and genomic integration of the MMTV in the liver cells of rat hosts. They also examined how the regulation of the gene expression programs worked for the viral genes that were housed within the genome of the MMTV. Their prior hunch about the effects of the steroid hormone working at the level of the glucocorticoid receptor on the rat cell surfaces had gained a supporting boost by the new work.

6. *He studied bacterial gene regulation by cyclic AMP (again in collaboration with Bob Perlman and Benoit de Crombrugghe). What became of this research?*

The collaborative investigations of Drs. Varmus, Perlman, and de Crombrugghe had a circuitous route. The saga started first, in 1968, when Dr. Varmus had applied to a coveted post-graduate training program at the prestigious National Institutes of Health (NIH).

During his interview, however, with Dr. Jack Robbins, an endocrinologist, Varmus was steered toward working for a newly hired investigator, Dr. Ira Pastan, who was studying thyroid hormones at the time. This alternative direction had been recommended by Dr. Robbins because he had felt that because of Dr. Varmus's credentials, he had a slim chance of being accepted into the NIH program, especially risking rejection by many of the senior investigators. Thus, Dr. Varmus was slated to become Dr. Pastan's first clinical associate at the NIH.

It turned out to be a fortuitous collaborative research experience, not necessarily because of Drs. Varmus and Pastan shared similar expertise in thyroid hormones (although they indeed had this common interest) but because of a wholly new and startling discovery in Dr. Pastan's newfound NIH laboratory.

Sometime before Dr. Varmus's arrival to the NIH, Dr. Pastan abruptly changed research fields in order to study bacterial gene regulation. Working with Dr. Robert Perlman, the Pastan laboratory had discovered that cyclic AMP (cAMP) virtually abolished the catabolite repression phenomenon within the famous *lac* operon of *Escherichia coli*. It had been a significant finding towards regulating the expression of genes!

At first, Dr. Varmus had been unfamiliar with the new bacterial genetics field, and he dashed to the library to learn what the terms *lac* operon and catabolite repression meant! Dr. Varmus thus realized that the new research area involved the turning on and off of genes and that this earlier work was Nobel-worthy, having been performed by Drs. Francois Jacob and Jacques Monod at the Institute of Pasteur, in Paris, France.

In 1968, Dr. Varmus finally arrived at the NIH to study in Dr. Pastan's laboratory. It had been Varmus's first experience in the field of biomedical science. Drs. Perlman and Pastan recommended that Dr. Varmus make use of a newly discovered but cumbersome technique called nucleic acid hybridization to test the hypothesis that the observed effects of the cAMP on catabolite repression occurred at the level of RNA synthesis from the *E. coli* genes of the *lac* operon. Dr. Varmus was able to coax the *E. coli* bacteria to make messenger RNA from the genes of the *lac* operon. Next, they attached a radioactive isotope to the bacterial *lac* RNA. Then they hybridized the radiolabeled *lac* RNA from the *E. coli* with the DNA that had been purified from bacteriophage viruses, which also contained their versions of the *lac* operon. That is, they had formed bacteria-virus hybrids of RNA-DNA!

It was exciting work, and Dr. Varmus had become hooked on the idea of using molecular biological approaches in order to learn more about the biomedical sciences. Thus, the molecular biology that Dr. Varmus had learned in Dr. Pastan's lab would provide fortuitous research experience for working as a postdoctoral fellow in the laboratory of Dr. Mike Bishop at the University of California, at the city of San Francisco, in the U.S.

7. *Apparently, he was first interested in psychiatry and international health– but then we have to thank the lectures of the following for his transition to medical science– Elvin Kabat, Harry Rose, Herbert Rosenkrantz, Erwin Chargaff and Paul Marks. First, any thoughts on these scholars, and in a sense, why is it essential for budding scientists to be surrounded by real thinkers and scholars?*

Each of these individuals had made profoundly positive impressions upon Dr. Varmus and greatly influenced his interest in becoming a *bona fide* biomedical research scientist. Of these investigators whom you have mentioned, Drs. Kabat and Chargaff are likely the most well-known, especially amongst the biomedical scientists.

Dr. Elvin A. Kabat is probably most famous for having made the discovery in the late 1930s that he could separate the various types of antibodies of the immune system from serum samples of immunized animals by using the newly developed gel electrophoresis method. Dr. Kabat had further accurately predicted which distinctive domains of the antibodies were highly variable and able to bind diverse arrays of antigens. Additionally, in a classic immunology experiment, Dr. Kabat immunized animals with various sizes of sugar antigens, and in examining which of the sugars elicited the production of antibodies against the sugars, he had, in essence, discovered the minimal molecular size of an antigen that could generate a humoral immune response! Surprisingly, Dr. Kabat did not get a Nobel Prize.

Dr. Chargaff is quite famous amongst the molecular biologists for having deduced the relative ratios of the nitrogenous-based nucleotides in a variety of distinctive species of organisms. He discovered that the proportions of guanine to cytosine and of adenine to thymine were very close to 1.0 across many of the species he studied. These results were astutely exploited by Drs. James Watson and Francis Crick to make the deduction that in the double helix structure these nucleotide bases made chemical contacts with each other, with adenine binding thymine and cytosine binding guanine. Again, Dr. Chargaff did not receive a Nobel Prize, and he was apparently quite upset about the omission.

Dr. Harry M. Rose was a prominent virologist who studied the vaccinia virus, the causative agent of the cowpox disease. He also studied the structural features of the herpes simplex virus and then measured the virus's ability to bind and enter host cells. He had employed the electron microscope to study these and other viral microorganisms. Dr. Rose was apparently also well known for his blood agglutination studies pertaining to the immune response against blood injections into laboratory animals. He had found that when blood sera from rheumatoid arthritis (RA) patients were exposed to the sensitized versus non-sensitized erythrocytes, the agglutination response was higher in erythrocytes that were sensitized with human sera from the RA patients to a degree higher than those sera from healthy non-RA patients.

Dr. Paul Marks is quite well known among the cancer biologists. Dr. Marks had been one of Dr. Varmus's professors while he had been a medical student. The lectures given by professor Marks at the College of Physicians and Surgeons at Columbia University entailed the various mechanisms of disease generation from mutations in the genomic DNA of patients. Dr. Marks had correlated the effects of the mutations upon the physiological characteristics of the gene products. Dr. Marks became an influential pioneer in the field of cancer biomedical research. When Dr. Marks retired from his post as president of the Memorial Sloan Kettering Cancer Center in New York, it was Dr. Varmus himself who took over the vacant presidential position and eventually became its CEO.

8. *He earned the Nobel Prize with Mike Bishop– what exactly did they research together?*

In short, Drs. Varmus and Bishop discovered that certain genetic elements called proto-oncogenes were harbored by the genomes of normal living cells. They had further found that the cellular proto-oncogenes were evolutionarily related to the oncogenes from viral genomes. It was this work for which they would earn the coveted Nobel Prize in 1989 in the classification of medicine or physiology.

In 1970, Dr. Varmus had become a postdoctoral fellow in the laboratory of Dr. Bishop, who was then at the UCSF. Then, Dr. Varmus moved through the academic ranks at UCSF by becoming a lecturer and then ultimately becoming a full professor. It was during these years that Drs. Varmus and Bishop collaborated.

Before working together on their Nobel Prize-winning discovery, they had come across a radical new hypothesis that had been proposed by Drs. Robert Huebner and George Todaro. The novel postulate had been called the virogene-oncogene theory. In short, the original premise held that healthy cells harbored a sort of oncogene that could be activated somehow to initiate the transformation into tumor production. The rationale for the virogene-oncogene hypothesis was that certain RNA viruses were oncogenic, thus predicting that specific viral genes were responsible for inducing the tumorigenic potential in non-cancerous cells by transformation. Such viral genes, now known simply as viral oncogenes, could then mediate this cellular transformation into tumors and perhaps even to cancers. Evidence for the presence of the virally-encoded gene came from the laboratory of Howard Temin, then at the University of Wisconsin, who demonstrated that the genome of RSV had the *v-src* gene. At first, they called the genetic element "*x*" but later *sarc* or *src,* which were shortened versions of the term sarcoma, the cancer that was lethal in laboratory test chickens. Then they refined their terminology by referring to the viral oncogene as *v-src.* When mutated beyond repair, Dr. Temin found that the *v-src* gene lost its ability to transform healthy cells into cancerous ones. Next, Dr. Temin worked with Drs. David Baltimore and Satoshi Mizutani in which they discovered the reverse transcriptase enzyme, for which Temin and Baltimore would share the 1975 Nobel Prize in medicine or physiology with Dr. Renato Dulbecco, for his discovery that oncoviruses caused tumors.

The virogene-oncogene hypothesis also predicted that there must be a healthy version of virial oncogenes that do not realize tumors, and such genes were termed cellular or proto-oncogenes. Furthermore, the virogene-oncogene hypothesis predicted that dormant viral oncogenes or even cellular proto-oncogenes might somehow become activated to be oncogenic, that is, to generate cancer — the experimental work of Drs. Varmus and Bishop provided some of the first evidence in support of the virogene-oncogene hypothesis.

First, using Dr. Temin's *v-src* sequence data, Drs. Varmus and Bishop produced a genetic probe composed of DNA and labeled it with radioactivity. Then, they used the newly made labeled *v-src* DNA probe to detect the *v-src* gene in cultured cells that had been infected with RSV. When they examined controls cells that had not been infected with RSV, however, they discovered much to their surprise that the *v-src* DNA probe had detected the elements of a *v-src* gene within these uninfected cells! These cells had never been exposed to the RSV, and yet, these same uninfected control cells had the *v-src* gene!

Thus, Drs. Varmus and Bishop had discovered that a very similar piece of the RSV segment was harbored in the DNA of healthy uninfected host cells in culture. Because the RSV *v-src* gene was found in healthy cells, Varmus and Bishop coined the new term *c-src*, for the cellular origin of the gene. They deduced that the *c-src* gene must be some progenitor of the *v-src* gene and that *c-src* must encode an active product whereas the *v-src* encoded a newer variant that was inactive. Thus, they referred to their new progenitor *c-src* gene from healthy cells as a proto-oncogene. These findings were consistent with the virogene-oncogene hypothesis in that it provided evidence for the presence of a normal proto-oncogene in regular cells.

Sequence comparison of the *v-src* gene versus the *c-src* gene revealed that they differed from each other by only one or two nucleotide mutations! A minor mutational conversion of *c-src* to the *v-src* could then alter the normal proto-oncogene into an oncogene!

Today, many hundreds of oncogenes have been discovered. Their regular cellular versions often encode cell cycle control proteins or tumor suppressor functions, whereas their oncogenic counterparts lose cell growth and anti-tumor properties. The Src proteins are tyrosine kinase enzymes that have a plethora of cellular, molecular, and physiological functions throughout the body. The molecular fields of oncogenes and the biochemistry and cell biology of their protein products are significant areas of biomedical research.

9. *What have I neglected to ask about this influential scholar?*

Like his predecessor, Dr. Paul Marks, when Dr. Varmus took over in 2000 as president and CEO of the famous Memorial Sloan-Kettering Cancer Center, he likewise carried the baton towards becoming a major influential figure in the policies of biomedical sciences, especially towards research efforts in cancer biology.

Similarly, Dr. Varmus had become a significant player towards influencing many other aspects of basic and applied biomedical science research when he was appointed as the director of the NIH by President Bill Clinton in 1993 until 1999. During his tenure as NIH director, Dr. Varmus had to deal with many novel issues pertaining to biomedical research. Such items had included but were not limited to animal cloning, stem cells, gene therapy, biotechnology- and academic-based patents, research ethics, electronic-based journals, and scientific article publishing policies. Regarding the last item, Dr. Varmus helped to formulate a new plan that required all NIH award grantees to make their published data available to the outside public, forming a venue to do so, a database of the *National Center for Biotechnology Information* (NCBI) called PubMed Central. The new policy and its publishing database helped to circumvent the obstacles associated with the ever-rising and high costs of scientific journal subscriptions.

Furthermore, Dr. Varmus participated in and chaired the Science & Technology Committee that had been commissioned by then-presidential candidate Barack Obama in 2008. After President Obama took the White House, he appointed Dr. Varmus to co-chair his President's Council of Advisors on Science and Technology. Then, in 2010, Dr. Varmus took over as director of the National Cancer Institute (NCI) and served for five years. During his tenure at the NCI, Dr. Varmus helped to implement new directions in cancer research, such as the development of cancer genome projects and world-wide health programs.

In 2009, Dr. Varmus published an enlightening book titled *The Art and Politics of Science*. In the book, he included some of his biographical memoirs and the diverse array of his research interests. He also relates his experiences with public and scientific policies, paying particular attention to various controversial issues, such as human embryos, human cloning, global biomedicine and health, and scientific publishing in the age of electronic journals.

As of this writing, Dr. Varmus is 80 years old, and as long as he is alive, there is no doubt that he'll continue his positive influences in biomedical science and health. There is also no doubt that even if he stopped all activity, the legacy he has already left behind has had a profoundly positive influence on the lives and health of countless millions. His legacy will last for many generations to come.

For those interested in more information about this great scientist- go to:

https://m.youtube.com/watch?v=ct3bDM6YBEw
https://m.youtube.com/watch?v=MuNxHuvWP84

Chapter 25

NANCY WEXLER – HUNTINGTON DISEASE GENE

1. *Professor Varela, thanks for participating in this series of interviews about famous biomedical scientists. Let's first start with a female scientist – Nancy Wexler. Where was she born and educated?*

Dr. Nancy Sabin Wexler is a world-renowned American scientist, famous for her role with the discovery of the gene that was defective in the terribly debilitating genetic illness known as Huntington disease. Her groundbreaking population genetics-based work with Huntington disease led ultimately to the development of a useful diagnostic tool for the malady. Her public policy work has led to a potential treatment.

Prof. Wexler was born on the 19th day of July 1945, in Washington, D.C., and subsequently, her family moved to the state of Kansas, living in its capital, Topeka. Young Nancy was raised in an educated family environment.

Wexler's parents were Milton and Leonore Sabin Wexler. Her father Milton was first an attorney and later a clinical psychoanalyst and psychologist, trained in New York at Syracuse and at Columbia, and running a psychoanalytical practice in Los Angeles, and later near Washington, D.C. Wexler's mother Leonore Sabin had obtained an undergraduate degree, in 1934, from Hunter College, having majored in botany and zoology. Leonore was also educated at Columbia, earning her master's degree in zoology. The family had two siblings, Nancy and her older sister, Alice.

In 1967, at the age of 22 years, Wexler took her undergraduate A.B. degree in the fields of English and Social Relations, from Harvard-Radcliffe College, graduating with *cum laude* academic honors. As a Fulbright Scholar and psychology intern, Wexler was housed for two years at the University of West Indies in Jamaica. She also spent time in London getting trained there at the Hampstead Clinic Child Psychoanalytic Center. Wexler then enrolled in graduate school in 1968. In 1974, she earned her Ph.D. degree focusing on the discipline of clinical psychology from the University of Michigan, located in Ann Arbor. Dr. Wexler's Ph.D. thesis centered on the inherent psychological effects of dealing with family members who suffered from a genetic disease.

2. *Do you know how she first got involved in science and medical research?*

Dr. Wexler's interest in biomedical science and research undoubtedly began when she was 21 years old, in 1968. During one morning in August of that year, while Wexler's mother Leonore was on her way to jury duty, she had been admonished by a police officer informing her that she should have been ashamed to be so "inebriated" so early in the day. The fact is, however, that Wexler's mother had not actually been intoxicated; she was, instead, beginning to suffer from the debilitating effects of Huntington disease and was staggering about as she walked across a street. But no one had definitively known that at the time. Leonore Wexler had probably heard about certain relatives, such as her own father and three of her uncles, all of whom had succumbed to the effects of the sickness. The affliction had apparently been a closely guarded family secret.

Sometime shortly after this incident occurred with the police officer and her mother, Wexler's father gathered the two daughters together, Nancy and Alice, for a family meeting and announced to them that their mother had been diagnosed with the dreadful Huntington disease. Milton conveyed to his children that their mother's condition was irreversible, incurable, and that their mother would continue to degenerate, both mentally and physically. It was predicted at the time that Leonore would eventually die of the ailment within about 15 years.

Furthermore, Milton revealed, the two sisters each had a 50% chance of acquiring the terrible conditions themselves. Thus, Alice and Nancy Wexler would not actually know for sure whether they, too, would develop the same disease as their mother, until they each reached a certain age, possibly within the next 10 to 20 years.

The conversation that day was a permanent life-changing event for the entire family. The shocking news changed everything for everyone in the family, except for Leonore, who would have to continue living through the illness, eventually passing away from Huntington disease in 1978, on Mother's Day.

Wexler's father, Milton Wexler, in 1968, worked to establish a foundation dedicated to the study of hereditary diseases, hoping to find a cure to his wife's disease. As her mother continued to deteriorate, Nancy Wexler decided to do whatever she could to help circumvent the Huntington disease, if not for herself, then for the benefit of others who suffered as her mother had. Wexler's pursuit had developed into a lifetime of obsession and of achievement—all arising out of a history-changing afternoon that, in turn, eventually changed the course of biomedical research history.

3. Now, for the layperson, what exactly is Huntington Disease– and what are some of the signs and symptoms?

The Huntington disease, also known as Huntington's chorea, is a progressive neurodegenerative disorder that is characterized by the onset of abnormal physical and mental consequences.

The physical effects, known as the chorea, include involuntary, irregular, and spasmodic movements of the arms, legs, and face. Huntington patients experience an inability to coordinate their muscle movements, often walking with an irregular gait and experiencing other uncontrollable motor impairments. The mental effects include cognitive declines, such as memory and speech losses, plus psychiatric disorders, such as changes in mood, depression, and eventually declining towards dementia.

Another commonality is that the disease is inherited, affecting both males and females. The genetic defect is described as autosomal dominant, meaning that the gene is found not the sex chromosomes but in one of the somatic chromosomes and that patients with the disease need inherit the mutation in either copy of the two *huntingtin* genes, also called *HTT*, *HD* or *IT15*. Unfortunately, if an individual acquires only one mutated *huntingtin* gene, it is enough to cause the clinical disease, even if an affected person inherits a normal version of the gene from the other parent. This further means that children of a Huntington disease patient will have a 50-50 chance of inheriting the disorder themselves, as such progeny can inherit either a normal or a mutated version of the *huntingtin* gene from the parent patient.

While the symptoms of the Huntington ailment can vary in its severity and in the timing of its onset, ranging from childhood well into middle age, the patient almost invariably dies of it. In many cases of the affliction, the onset of the disease symptomology does not manifest itself until between 30 and 40 years of age.

Furthermore, because the nature of the mutation seems to accumulate with each succeeding generation, the Huntington disease onset may appear in correspondingly younger patients, who now have to live even longer with the disorders before these patients, too, then die from its effects.

Since the patients frequently are not aware that they are afflicted with the malady, they can unwittingly produce offspring in which each individual of the next generation has a 50-50 chance of inheriting a mutated version of the *huntingtin* gene. The end result of this type of affected gene frequency is that the Huntington disease manages to maintain itself in the human population for a seemingly never-ending series of generations to come. Dr. Wexler's work towards finding the gene may be the key to preventing this generational presence, with the consequent development of the molecular diagnosis at an earlier stage in the lives of at-risk individuals.

4. How was Nancy Wexler involved in locating the gene that seems to be the causal agent?

Dr. Wexler's work in this area of biomedical research was a key factor that ultimately led to the mapping of the defective genetic element to one of the human chromosomes and subsequent cloning of the causative *huntingtin* gene. Her efforts included taking family pedigrees and obtaining blood samples from Huntington disease patients who were living in an extremely remote location of Venezuela. Dr. Wexler's father, Milton, had heard about this region through his contacts with the various foundations. In particular, two closely located but remote villages, called Barranquitas and Lagunetas, both of which were adjacent to a large lake, called Lago de Maracaibo, in northwestern Venezuela. This region of the world had a large constellation of Huntington disease patients, forming an abnormally high disease prevalence. These victims of the malady constituted an enormous wealth of genetic samples for the genetic mapping of the causal agent.

A large number of DNA samples from the blood of Huntington disease patients, as well as of non-affected normal individuals, were needed in order to map the aberrant gene's chromosomal location on the human genome.

The invention of the so-called restriction fragment length polymorphism (RFLP) technology made it possible to start the gene-finding process. The RFLP method relied on the discovery of genetic markers consisting of minor variations in the DNA sequences involving so-called restriction endonuclease enzyme sites, places on the genomes where such restriction enzymes could bind to and cut into pieces of certain lengths, depending on the nature of the sequence variations, called polymorphisms. Such RFLP markers could possibly be used to link their locations to the Huntington disease gene.

This DNA technological approach was called genetic linkage mapping. The closer the RFLP markers were to the affected gene, the more reliable the linkage analysis data were. The main rub, however, was in obtaining enough blood samples from diseased and non-diseased individuals, all of which were required in order to establish the genetic link. At the time, many of these emerging methods had up till then been untested for gene searching. Thus, Dr. Wexler and her collaborating colleagues were wading in both unknown types of waters and in the biomedical sciences.

But first, the blood samples with their DNA elements embedded in them were needed. The logistics involved in getting to the Barranquitas and Lagunetas villages were nightmarish. The logistics involved *after* her arrival to Maracaibo, in July of the year 1979, were even worse. The heat and humidity were stifling. With such a remote research facility with which to conduct the sampling and the pedigree work, the laboratory was rudimentary by comparison to standards set forth in developed nations. Nevertheless, the facilities were demonstrated to be quite effective.

In Venezuela, Dr. Wexler and her assistants managed to locate many individuals who were afflicted with the Huntington malady and who were fraught with signs and symptoms reminiscent of her own late mother, a constant reminder of her of family's plight. It was the potent motivator in her pursuit of the genetic knowledge necessary to address the serious ailment from an unprecedented biomedical science perspective.

Dr. Wexler was quite fortunate to have located members of families who were seriously affected by the Huntington disease by having both parents also affected. Such a parental origin indicated that the offspring individuals were likely to homozygous for the affliction, meaning that both copies of the gene could be mutated. Such a finding would be considered genetic gold.

The Venezuelan excursions continued into the early 1980s, each taking months of labor-intensive work. All told, thousands of individual samples were collected, and several large pedigree trees were constructed. Dr. Wexler sent the blood samples to Dr. James Gusella, at the famed Massachusetts General Hospital, in Boston, MA, and to Dr. Michael Conneally, whose laboratory was housed at Indiana University, in Indianapolis, IN. Using a considerable number of RFLP markers, the two laboratories conducted a massive genetic linkage analysis. Using a DNA-DNA hybridization technique called a southern blot, a method first developed by Dr. Edwin Southern in 1975, the two laboratories of Drs. Gusella and Conneally were able to put Dr. Wexler's blood samples to good use by purifying the genomic DNA from the patients and from unaffected cohorts, then breaking the isolated DNA into smaller fragments using restriction enzymes, and then painstakingly hunting for any minute sequence RFLP marker variant that might be linked to the putative *huntingtin* gene.

This meticulous genetic search took almost 3 years, but eventually, the work paid off. The *huntingtin* gene was found to be linked to several RFLPs in chromosome 4 of the human genome!

To be more precise, the *huntingtin* gene seemed to be located somewhere near the so-called short arm of this fourth human chromosome, in a location referred to as the p arm, locus 16.3, that is, chromosome 4p.16.3. Their pioneering biomedical research finding was reported in the journal *Nature* in 1983 on the 17th day of November.

This genetic-based gene mapping result, to chromosome number 4, while a tremendous scientific achievement, nonetheless placed the *huntingtin* gene somewhere within a rather large stretch a previously unexplored region of DNA within the genome of humans. Thus, it took several additional years of detailed genetic refinement and of "chromosome-walking," i.e., using DNA primers to find their way to the target gene itself essentially. The gene search took a tremendous amount of effort in the research laboratories of many investigators and in terms of time. It was a monumental task. Eventually, the *huntingtin* gene was cloned in 1993. The sequencing of the mutated gene showed an abnormal repeat sequence, resulting in an aberrant protein.

5. Did she win any accolades or prizes for this discovery?

At this point, while it is clear that Dr. Wexler is most deserving of a Nobel, it is, nevertheless, not entirely as clear that she shall be ever bestowed the coveted honor for her contributions. It is perplexing. Perhaps the Nobel commission might eventually view her in a favorable light and grant her the award that she most definitively deserves.

As far as other accolades go, Dr. Wexler has been the recipient of several prestigious awards. In 2009, she earned the coveted Mary Woodard Lasker Award for public service, a precursor to the now known Lasker-Bloomberg award. In addition, she received the much-celebrated Benjamin Franklin medal in 2007, an award given to recipients for making substantial contributions to certain areas of science, Dr. Wexler being recognized for her great work in the life sciences.

Dr. Wexler has been appointed to several important committees pertaining to public policy and has been having a significant influence on each of these realms. Her positive influences have reached avenues affecting grant funding, bioethics, genome and biomedical research, scientific publishing, science policy, and women's health.

Dr. Wexler's personal and scientific stories are quite extraordinary, leading to tremendous advances in the nature of genetic diseases. While she is certainly famous on a world-wide scale not only amongst scientists, especially the biomedical scientists, in particular, she is quite famous amongst non-scientists, as well. I expect this universally positive recognition is due to her portrayal in a series of documentaries, interviews in print and video news media, and in popular books pertaining to advances in science, including books written by Dr. Wexler's sister, Dr. Alice Wexler, two books of which are titled "*Mapping Fate: a Family at Risk Confronts a Fatal Disease*" first published in 1995, and "*The Woman Who Walked into the*

Sea: Huntington's and the Making of a Genetic Disease," a best-seller, published in 2008.

6. What have I neglected to ask about this famous female scientist?

Dr. Wexler and her sister had been placed in an unprecedented circumstance of having to decide whether they, too, should be tested for the presence of the defective *huntingtin* gene. On the one hand, if they had chosen to get tested and found out that one or both had had the ailment, then perhaps arrangements could be made for dealing with the disease. On the other hand, if they were free of the genetic defect, then they had to consider whether to have children and so on. In the end, both siblings had decided not to undergo the testing for the gene's presence in their genomes. They had, however, also decided not to have children, presumably for fear of perpetuating the genetic defect to subsequent generations.

Dr. Wexler heads the Hereditary Disease Foundation, an important group initially founded by her father, Milton. This Foundation is devoted to the search for cures of genetic diseases by garnering financial support and granting of funding for relevant biomedical research studies. It is this Foundation that brought together many of the biomedical investigators who were to later search for the *huntingtin* gene, to map it to chromosome 4 of the genome, to clone the gene, to determine its DNA sequence, and to study the biochemistry of the affected protein. Such work may lead to eventual treatment by gene therapy or even gene-editing technology.

Folk singer Woody Guthrie also had Huntington disease. He died of it in 1967 at the age of 55 years. A committee devoted to combating the disease, initially called the Committee to Combat Huntington's Disease, now referred to as Huntington's disease Society of America. Consequently, Dr. Wexler's family knew the Guthrie family very well.

Although the normal function of the Huntingtin protein itself is largely unknown, it is thought to play a role in the development of embryos, and its presence in the neuronal cells of the brain indicates an important role in the central nervous system.

The molecular nature of the defective Huntingtin protein has been extensively studied. A widely studied mutation in the *huntingtin* gene, located on a clone initially called *it15* because it was an "interesting transcript" number 15, involves a so-called triplet repeat of nucleotides CAG. The CAG codon specifies the amino acid glutamate, which in the brain functions as a neurotransmitter by exciting neurons to fire up their electrical impulses.

While the normal *huntingtin* gene harbors about 10 to 35 of the CAG codon repeats, encoding a normal protein with a correspondingly similar number of resulting glutamates in a row, the mutated gene has a greater number of the CAG codon repeats, encoding anywhere between 40 and 80 repeated glutamates in the aberrant protein! These abnormal numbers of poly-glutamates on the disease-causing protein can prevent the initiation of RNA synthesis, a process called transcription. The mutated and dysfunctional Huntington protein prevents the start of transcription by somehow disrupting the binding between a protein called SP1 and another protein called TFIID. The SP1 protein is a transcription-initiation factor that binds regulatory elements on DNA, and the TFIID protein plays a role in forming the so-called transcriptional machinery.

The prevention of the start of transcription (i.e., mRNA synthesis) in nerve cells of the brain thus prevents the synthesis of a neurotransmitter receptor. How this, in turn, leads to neuron degeneracy and Huntington disease symptomology is currently a poorly understood but intensely active area of biomedical research.

Dr. Wexler was a key figure in the development of a potential treatment for Huntington disease. The prominent biomedical scientist made direct appeals to the U.S. Food and Drug Administration (FDA), providing personal testimony about her own experiences with the disease. Dr. Wexler has been credited with facilitating the eventual approval of a new chemotherapeutic agent, called tetrabenazine. The medicine is known to inhibit the activity of a certain class of proteins called transporters. The action of tetrabenazine is specific to a human-based transporter called VMAT2, a so-called presynaptic vesicular monoamine transporter type 2. The inhibition of the VMAT2 transporter by the tetrabenazine chemical results in a depletion of the neurotransmitter dopamine, which then apparently alleviates to a certain extent the involuntary movements that characterize the chorea aspect of the Huntington disease.

Another treatment avenue focuses on utilizing inhibitors of the dopamine receptor. Such receptor blockers are referred to as antipsychotic agents. Along these lines, certain anti-epileptic and anti-glutamatergic agents are also an intense area of research. Another experimental class of drugs called dopamine stabilizers is presently being studied in biomedical research laboratories for potential development.

For additional study:

https://www.youtube.com/watch?v=KpkkNd-lj5E
https://www.youtube.com/watch?v=OLNt85LEBsU
https://www.youtube.com/watch?v=_IWpzvpVsYk

SELECTED BIBLIOGRAPHY

Alberts, A. W. (1988). Discovery, biochemistry and biology of lovastatin. *Am J Cardiol*, *62*, 10J-15J.

Alberts, B., Johnson, A., Lewis, J., Morgan, D., Raff, M., Roberts, K. & Walter, P. (2015). *Molecular Biology of the Cell*. Garland Science.

Aloe, L. (2011). Rita Levi-Montalcini and the discovery of NGF, the first nerve cell growth factor. *Archives italiennes de biologie*, *149*, 175-181.

Andersen, J. L., He, G. X., Kakarla, P., Kumar, C. R. K. S., Lakra, W. S., Mukherjee, M. M., Ranaweera, I., Shrestha, U., Tran, T. & Varela, M. F. (2015). Multidrug efflux pumps from Enterobacteriaceae, *Vibrio cholerae* and *Staphylococcus aureus* bacterial food pathogens. *International journal of environmental research and public health*, *12*, 1487-1547.

Andrewes, C. H. (1971). Francis Peyton Rous 1879-1970. *Biogr Mem Fellows R Soc*, *17*, 643-662.

Atlas, R. M. (2000). Many Faces, Many Microbes. *American Society of Microbiology.*

Bauman, R. W., Primm, T. P. & Siegesmund, A. M. (2017). *Microbiology: With Diseases by Body System*. Pearson Education, Incorporated.

Beck, R. W. (2000). *A Chronology of Microbiology in Historical Context*. ASM Press.

Bliss, M. (1992). *Banting: A Biography*. University of Toronto Press.

Brock, T. D. (1999). *Milestones in microbiology 1546 to 1940*. ASM Press, Washington, DC.

Cajal, S. R., Craigie, E. H., Cano, J. & Cowan, W. M. (1989). *Recollections of My Life*. MIT Press.

Cajal, S. R., Swanson, N. & Swanson, L. W. (2004). *Advice for a Young Investigator*. MIT Press.

Chao, M. V. (2010). A Conversation with Rita Levi-Montalcini. *Annual Review of Physiology*, *72*, 1-13.

Crotty, S. (2001). *Ahead of the Curve: David Baltimore's Life in Science*. University of California Press.

Daintith, J. & Gjertsen, D. (1999). *A Dictionary of Scientists*. Oxford University Press, USA.

de Kruif, P. & Gonzalez-Crussi, F. (2002). *Microbe Hunters*. Houghton Mifflin Harcourt.

Debra, P. & Forster, E. (2000). *Louis Pasteur*. Johns Hopkins University Press.

Dulbecco, R. (1976). Francis Peyton Rous. *Biogr Mem Natl Acad Sci*, *48*, 275-306.

Diamond, J. (2017). *Guns, Germs, and Steel: The Fates of Human Societies*. W. W. Norton.

Edelman, G. M. & Gall, W. E. (1969). The antibody problem. *Annu Rev Biochem*, *38*, 415-466.

Elion, G. B. (1993). The Quest for a Cure. *Annual Review of Pharmacology and Toxicology 33*, 1-25. Garrett, L. 1994. *The Coming Plague: Newly Emerging Diseases in a World Out of Balance*. Farrar, Straus and Giroux.

Figl, M. & Pelinka, L. E. (2004). Karl Landsteiner, the discoverer of blood groups. *Resuscitation*, *63*, 251-254.

Gaynes, R. P. (2011). *Germ Theory: Medical Pioneers in Infectious Diseases*. ASM Press.

Geison, G. L. (2014). *The Private Science of Louis Pasteur*. Princeton University Press.

Gurdon, J. (2000). Not a total waste of time. An interview with John Gurdon. Interview by James C Smith. *The International Journal of Developmental Biology*, *44*, 93-99.

Hill, A. V. (1970). Autobiographical Sketch. *Perspectives in Biology and Medicine*, *14*, no. 1, 27-42.

Hunt, T. (2002). Nobel Lecture. Protein synthesis, proteolysis, and cell cycle transitions. *Biosci Rep*, *22*, 465-486.

Hutchison, C. A., 3rd. Phillips, S., Edgell, M. H., Gillam, S., Jahnke, P. & Smith, M. (1978). Mutagenesis at a specific position in a DNA sequence. *J Biol Chem*, *253*, 6551-6560.

Huxley, A. F. (1986). Discoveries on muscle: observation, theory, and experiment. *Br Med J* (*Clin Res Ed*), *293*, 115-117.

Joklik, W. K. (1999). *Microbiology: A Centenary Perspective*. ASM Press.

Just, E. E. (2018). *The Biology of the Cell Surface*. Franklin Classics Trade Press.

Katz, B. (1978). Archibald Vivian Hill, 26 September 1886--3 Jun 1977. *Biogr Mem Fellows R Soc*, *24*, 71-149.

Krasner, R. I. (2012). *20th Century Microbe Hunters*. Jones & Bartlett Learning.

Lekshmi, M., Ammini, P., Kumar, S. & Varela, M. F. (2017). *The Food Production Environment and the Development of Antimicrobial Resistance in Human Pathogens of Animal Origin. Microorganisms*, *5*.

Levy, S. B. (2002). *The antibiotic paradox: how the misuse of antibiotics destroys their curative power*, 2nd ed. Perseus Pub., Cambridge, MA.

Litwack, G. & Axelrod, J. (1986). *Biochemical Actions of Hormones*. Academic Press.

Liu, L. (2016). *Tu Youyou: China's First Female Nobel Prize Winner*. ACA Publishing Limited.

Maienschein, J. (1989). *100 Years Exploring Life, 1888-1988: The Marine Biological Laboratory at Woods Hole*. Jones and Bartlett Publishers.

Manning, K. R. (1983). *Black Apollo of Science: The Life of Ernest Everett Just*. Oxford University Press.

Milstein, C. & Munro, A. J. (1970). The genetic basis of antibody specificity. *Annu Rev Microbiol*, *24*, 335-358.

Mukherjee, S. (2016). *The Gene: An Intimate History*. Scribner.

Murray, P. R., Rosenthal, K. S. & Pfaller, M. A. (2015). *Medical Microbiology*. Elsevier Health Sciences.

Nelson, D. L. & Cox, M. M. (2017). *Lehninger Principles of Biochemistry*. WH Freeman.

Olby, R. (2013). *The Path to the Double Helix: The Discovery of DNA*. Dover Publications.

Parham, P. (2014). *The Immune System, Fourth Edition*. Taylor & Francis Group.

Pommerville, J. C. & Alcamo, I. E. (2013). *Alcamo's Fundamentals of Microbiology: Body systems edition.* Jones & Bartlett Learning.

Shaughnessy, M. F. & Varela, M. (2018). *The Inventions and Discoveries of the World's Most Famous Scientists*. Nova Science Publishers, Incorporated.

Sheetz, M. & Yu, H. (2018). *The Cell as a Machine*. Cambridge University Press.

Skloot, R. (2010). *The Immortal Life of Henrietta Lacks*. Crown/Archetype.

Stryer, L., Berg, J., Tymoczko, J. & Gatto, G. (2019). *Biochemistry*. Macmillan Learning.

Timmerman, L., Baltimore, D. & Cutchlow, T. (2016). *Hood: Trailblazer of the Genomics Age*. Bandera Press LLC.

Varela, M. & Shaughnessy, M. F. (2019). *Enter the World of Microbiology: Interviews about the World's Most Famous Microbiologists*. Nova Science Publishers, Incorporated.

Varela, M. F. & Wilson, T. H. (1996). Molecular biology of the lactose carrier of *Escherichia coli*. *Biochimica et Biophysica Acta*, *1276*, 21-34.

Walsh, C. & Wencewicz, T. A. (2016). *Antibiotics: Challenges, Mechanisms, Opportunities*. ASM Press.

Watson, J. D., Baker, T. A., Bell, S. P., Gann, A., Levine, M. & Losick, R. (2014*). Molecular Biology of the Gene*. Pearson.

Watson, J. D. & Stent, G. S. (1998). *Double Helix*. Scribner.

Wexler, A. (2008). *The Woman Who Walked Into the Sea: Huntington's and the Making of a Genetic Disease*. Yale University Press.

ABOUT THE AUTHORS

Manuel Varela, PhD
Professor
Eastern New Mexico University,
Portales, New Mexico, US
Email: Manuel.Varela@enmu.edu

Manuel F. Varela has a PhD in biomedical sciences emphasizing in biochemistry and molecular biology, from the University of New Mexico, Albuquerque, New Mexico. While in graduate school, he coined the term "Antiporter Motif" in 1995, an important and highly conserved amino acid sequence motif found in antiporters of a superfamily of transporters termed the major facilitator superfamily. Varela was a postdoc fellow studying microbial physiology under Prof. Thomas Hastings Wilson at Harvard Medical School, Boston, MA. Varela moved to ENMU and studied bacterial sugar transporters, drug resistance, and discovered the multi-drug efflux pumps LmrS from MRSA and EmrD-3 from *Vibrio cholerae*. He used comparative genomics to identify novel antimicrobial targets in cholera-causing bacteria. More recently, the Varela laboratory has been studying modulation of bacterial resistance to antimicrobial agents. Varela has published numerous primary papers, plus invited review articles and book chapters. In 2018, Prof. Michael F. Shaughnessy and Dr. Varela co-authored a book called "The Inventions and Discoveries of the World's Most Famous Scientists." Dr. Varela currently lives in Portales, New Mexico, with his wife and children.

Michael F. Shaughnessy
Professor
Eastern New Mexico University,
Portales, New Mexico, US
Email: Michael.Shaughnessy@enmu.edu

Michael F. Shaughnessy received his doctorate from the University of Nebraska- Lincoln under the tutelage of John A. Glover. He hold master's degrees in counseling and guidance and school psychology and his doctorate is in Educational Psychology. He has also done post-doctoral work in Brain Injury and Head Trauma at George Washington University and additional work in Special Education at Texas Tech University in Lubbock Texas in the field of Deaf/Blind. He has been a social studies teacher, coach, guidance counselor and school psychologist and has written, co-authored, edited or co-edited approximately 50 books. This is his third collaboration with Dr. Varela. He currently lives in Clovis, New Mexico with his wife and two dogs.

INDEX OF NAMES

A

B

G

H

J

K

L

M

N

O

P

Q

R

S

T

V

W

Y

INDEX OF TERMS

A

B

C

D

E

F

G

H

I

J

K

L

M

N

O

P

Q

R

S

T

U

V